THE
POWER
OF
MYTH

Also by Joseph Campbell

Where the Two Came to Their Father: A Navaho War Ceremonial
  (with Maud Oakes and Jeff King)

A Skeleton Key to Finnegans Wake
  (with Henry Morton Robinson)

The Hero with a Thousand Faces

The Masks of God: Primitive Mythology

The Masks of God: Oriental Mythology

The Masks of God: Occidental Mythology

The Masks of God: Creative Mythology

The Flight of the Wild Gander

The Mythic Image

Myths to Live By

Historical Atlas of World Mythology
   I. The Way of the Animal Powers
   II. The Way of the Seeded Earth (forthcoming)

The Inner Reaches of Outer Space

EDITED BY JOSEPH CAMPBELL

The Portable Arabian Nights

The Portable Jung

Myths, Dreams, and Religion

Papers from the Eranos Yearbooks (6 volumes)

EDITED AND COMPLETED FROM
  THE POSTHUMA OF HEINRICH ZIMMER

Myths and Symbols in Indian Art and Civilization

The King and the Corpse

Philosophies of India

The Art of Indian Asia (2 volumes)

Joseph Campbell

THE POWER OF MYTH

with Bill Moyers

BETTY SUE FLOWERS, Editor

ANCHOR BOOKS
DOUBLEDAY
NEW YORK LONDON TORONTO SYDNEY AUCKLAND

AN ANCHOR BOOK
PUBLISHED BY DOUBLEDAY
a division of Bantam Doubleday Dell Publishing Group, Inc.
1540 Broadway, New York, New York 10036

ANCHOR BOOKS, DOUBLEDAY, and the portrayal of an anchor
are trademarks of Doubleday, a division of Bantam Doubleday Dell
Publishing Group, Inc.

The fully illustrated edition of *The Power of Myth*
was originally published in both hardcover and
paperback by Doubleday in 1988. The Anchor Books
edition is published by arrangement with Doubleday.

Grateful acknowledgment is made to Barnes & Noble Books,
Totowa, New Jersey, for permission to quote from
"The Second Coming" by William Butler Yeats.

Campbell, Joseph, 1904–
    The power of myth / Joseph Campbell, with Bill Moyers;
    Betty Sue Flowers, editor.—1st Anchor Books ed.
        p.   cm.
    1. Myth.   2. Campbell, Joseph, 1904–   —Interviews.
3. Religion historians—United States—Interviews.
I. Moyers, Bill D.   II. Flowers, Betty S.   III. Title.
[BL304.C36   1990]   90-23860
291.1'3—dc20   CIP
ISBN 0-385-41886-8

Copyright © 1988 by Apostrophe S Productions, Inc., and
Alfred van der Marck Editions
ALL RIGHTS RESERVED
PRINTED IN THE UNITED STATES OF AMERICA
FIRST ANCHOR BOOKS EDITION: JULY 1991
10   9   8   7   6

To Judith, who has long heard the music

CONTENTS

EDITOR'S NOTE

This conversation between Bill Moyers and Joseph Campbell took place in 1985 and 1986 at George Lucas' Skywalker Ranch and later at the Museum of Natural History in New York. Many of us who read the original transcripts were struck by the rich abundance of material captured during the twenty-four hours of filming—much of which had to be cut in making the six-hour PBS series. The idea for a book arose from the desire to make this material available not only to viewers of the series but also to those who have long appreciated Campbell through reading his books.

In editing this book, I attempted to be faithful to the flow of the original conversation while at the same time taking advantage of the opportunity to weave in additional material on the topic from wherever it appeared in the transcripts. When I could, I followed the format of the TV series. But the book has its own shape and spirit and is designed to be a companion to the series, not a replica of it. The book exists, in part, because this is a conversation of ideas worth pondering as well as watching.

On a more profound level, of course, the book exists because

x EDITOR'S NOTE

Bill Moyers was willing to address the fundamental and difficult subject of myth—and because Joseph Campbell was willing to answer Moyers' penetrating questions with self-revealing honesty, based on a lifetime of living with myth. I am grateful to both of them for the opportunity to witness this encounter, and to Jacqueline Kennedy Onassis, the Doubleday editor, whose interest in the ideas of Joseph Campbell was the prime mover in the publication of this book. I am grateful, also, to Karen Bordelon, Alice Fisher, Lynn Cohea, Sonya Haddad, Joan Konner, and John Flowers for their support, and especially to Maggie Keeshen for her many retypings of the manuscript and for her keen editorial eye. For help with the manuscript, I am grateful to Judy Doctoroff, Andie Tucher, Becky Berman, and Judy Sandman. The major task of illustration research was done by Vera Aronow, Lynn Novick, Elizabeth Fischer, and Sabra Moore, with help from Annmari Ronnberg. Both Bill Moyers and Joseph Campbell read the manuscript and offered many helpful suggestions—but I am grateful that they resisted the temptation to rewrite their words into book talk. Instead, they let the conversation itself live on the page.

—BETTY SUE FLOWERS
University of Texas at Austin

INTRODUCTION

For weeks after Joseph Campbell died, I was reminded of him just about everywhere I turned.

Coming up from the subway at Times Square and feeling the energy of the pressing crowd, I smiled to myself upon remembering the image that once had appeared to Campbell there: "The latest incarnation of Oedipus, the continued romance of Beauty and the Beast, stands this afternoon on the corner of Forty-second Street and Fifth Avenue, waiting for the traffic light to change."

At a preview of John Huston's last film, *The Dead,* based on a story by James Joyce, I thought again of Campbell. One of his first important works was a key to *Finnegans Wake.* What Joyce called "the grave and constant" in human sufferings Campbell knew to be a principal theme of classic mythology. "The secret cause of all suffering," he said, "is mortality itself, which is the prime condition of life. It cannot be denied if life is to be affirmed."

Once, as we were discussing the subject of suffering, he mentioned in tandem Joyce and Igjugarjuk. "Who is Igjugarjuk?" I said, barely able to imitate the pronunciation. "Oh," replied Campbell, "he was the shaman of a Caribou Eskimo tribe in northern Canada, the one who told European visitors that the only true wisdom 'lives far from mankind, out in the great loneliness, and can be reached only through suffering. Privation and suffering alone open the mind to all that is hidden to others.' "

"Of course," I said, "Igjugarjuk."

Joe let pass my cultural ignorance. We had stopped walking. His eyes were alight as he said, "Can you imagine a long evening around the fire with Joyce and Igjugarjuk? Boy, I'd like to sit in on *that*."

Campbell died just before the twenty-fourth anniversary of John F. Kennedy's assassination, a tragedy he had discussed in mythological terms during our first meeting years earlier. Now, as that melancholy remembrance came around again, I sat talking with my grown children about Campbell's reflections. The solemn state funeral he had described as "an illustration of the high service of ritual to a society," evoking mythological themes rooted in human need. "This was a ritualized occasion of the greatest social necessity," Campbell had written. The public murder of a president, "representing our whole society, the living social organism of which ourselves were the members, taken away at a moment of exuberant life, required a compensatory rite to reestablish the sense of solidarity. Here was an enormous nation, made those four days into a unanimous community, all of us participating in the same way, simultaneously, in a single symbolic event." He said it was "the first and only thing of its kind in peacetime that has ever given me the sense of being a member of this whole national community, engaged as a unit in the observance of a deeply significant rite."

That description I recalled also when one of my colleagues had been asked by a friend about our collaboration with Campbell: "Why do you need the mythology?" She held the familiar, modern opinion that "all these Greek gods and stuff" are irrelevant to the human condition today. What she did not know —what most do not know—is that the remnants of all that "stuff" line the walls of our interior system of belief, like shards of broken pottery in an archaeological site. But as we are organic beings, there is energy in all that "stuff." Rituals evoke it. Consider the position of judges in our society, which Campbell saw in mythological, not sociological, terms. If this position were just a role, the judge could wear a gray suit to court instead of the magisterial black robe. For the law to hold authority beyond mere coercion, the power of the judge must be ritualized, mythologized. So must much of life today, Campbell said, from religion and war to love and death.

Walking to work one morning after Campbell's death, I stopped before a neighborhood video store that was showing scenes from George Lucas' *Star Wars* on a monitor in the window. I stood there thinking of the time Campbell and I had watched the movie together at Lucas' Skywalker Ranch in California. Lucas and Campbell had become good friends after the filmmaker, acknowledging a debt to Campbell's work, invited the scholar to view the *Star Wars* trilogy. Campbell reveled in the ancient themes and motifs of mythology unfolding on the wide screen in powerful contemporary images. On this particular visit, having again exulted over the perils and heroics of Luke Skywalker, Joe grew animated as he talked about how Lucas "has put the newest and most powerful spin" to the classic story of the hero.

"And what is that?" I asked.

"It's what Goethe said in Faust but which Lucas has dressed in modern idiom—the message that technology is not going to save us. Our computers, our tools, our machines are not enough. We have to rely on our intuition, our true being."

"Isn't that an affront to reason?" I said. "And aren't we already beating a hasty retreat from reason, as it is?"

"That's not what the hero's journey is about. It's not to deny reason. To the contrary, by overcoming the dark passions, the hero symbolizes our ability to control the irrational savage within us." Campbell had lamented on other occasions our failure "to admit within ourselves the carnivorous, lecherous fever" that is endemic to human nature. Now he was describing the hero's journey not as a courageous act but as a life lived in self-discovery, "and Luke Skywalker was never more rational than when he found within himself the resources of character to meet his destiny."

Ironically, to Campbell the end of the hero's journey is not the aggrandizement of the hero. "It is," he said in one of his lectures, "not to identify oneself with any of the figures or powers experienced. The Indian yogi, striving for release, identifies himself with the Light and never returns. But no one with a will to the service of others would permit himself such an escape. The ultimate aim of the quest must be neither release nor ecstasy for oneself, but the wisdom and the power to serve others." One of the many distinctions between the celebrity and the hero, he said, is that one lives only for self while the other acts to redeem society.

Joseph Campbell affirmed life as adventure. "To hell with it," he said, after his university adviser tried to hold him to a narrow academic curriculum. He gave up on the pursuit of a doctorate and went instead into the woods to read. He continued all his life to read books about the world: anthropology, biology, philosophy, art, history, religion. And he continued to remind others that one sure path into the world runs along the printed page. A few days after his death, I received a letter from one of his former students who now helps to edit a major magazine. Hearing of the series on which I had been working with Campbell, she wrote to share how this man's "cyclone of energy blew across all the intellectual possibilities" of the students who sat "breathless in his classroom" at Sarah Lawrence College. "While all of us listened spellbound," she wrote, "we did stagger under the weight of his weekly reading assignments. Finally, one of our number stood up and confronted him (Sarah Lawrence style), saying: 'I *am* taking three other courses, you know. All of them assigned reading, you know. How do you expect me to complete all this in a week?' Campbell just laughed and said, 'I'm astonished you tried. You have the rest of your life to do the reading.' "

She concluded, "And I still haven't finished—the never ending example of his life and work."

One could get a sense of that impact at the memorial service held for him at the Museum of Natural History in New York. Brought there as a boy, he had been transfixed by the totem poles and masks. Who made them? he wondered. What did they mean? He began to read everything he could about Indians, their myths and legends. By ten he was into the pursuit that made him one of the world's leading scholars of mythology and one of the most exciting teachers of our time; it was said that "he could make the bones of folklore and anthropology live." Now, at the memorial service in the museum where three quarters of a century earlier his imagination had first been excited, people gathered to pay honor to his memory. There was a performance by Mickey Hart, the drummer for the Grateful Dead, the rock group with whom Campbell shared a fascination with percussion. Robert Bly played a dulcimer and read poetry dedicated to Campbell. Former students spoke, as did friends whom he had made after he retired and moved with his wife, the dancer Jean Erdman, to Hawaii. The great publishing houses of New York were represented. So were writers and scholars, young and old, who had found their pathbreaker in Joseph Campbell.

And journalists. I had been drawn to him eight years earlier when, self-appointed, I was attempting to bring to television the lively minds of our time. We had taped two programs at the museum, and so compellingly had his presence permeated the screen that more than fourteen thousand people wrote asking for transcripts of the conversations. I vowed then that I would come after him again, this time for a more systematic and thorough exploration of his ideas. He wrote or edited some twenty books, but it was as a teacher that I had experienced him, one rich in the lore of the world and the imagery of language, and I wanted others to experience him as teacher, too. So the desire to share the treasure of the man inspired my PBS series and this book.

A journalist, it is said, enjoys a license to be educated in public; we are the lucky ones, allowed to spend our days in a continuing course of adult education. No one has taught me more of late than Campbell, and when I told him he would have to bear the responsibility for whatever comes of having me as a pupil, he laughed and quoted an old Roman: "The fates lead him who will; him who won't they drag."

He taught, as great teachers teach, by example. It was not his manner to try to talk anyone into anything (except once, when he persuaded Jean to marry him). Preachers err, he told me, by trying "to talk people into belief; better they reveal the radiance of their own discovery." How he did reveal a joy for learning and living! Matthew Arnold believed the highest criticism is "to know the best that is known and thought in the world, and by in its turn making this known, to create a current of true and fresh ideas." This is what Campbell did. It was impossible to listen to him—truly to hear him—without realizing in one's own consciousness a stirring of fresh life, the rising of one's own imagination.

He agreed that the "guiding idea" of his work was to find "the commonality of themes in world myths, pointing to a constant requirement in the human psyche for a centering in terms of deep principles."

"You're talking about a search for the meaning of life?" I asked.

"No, no, no," he said. "For the *experience* of being alive."

I have said that mythology is an interior road map of experience, drawn by people who have traveled it. He would, I suspect, not settle for the journalist's prosaic definition. To him mythology was "the song of the universe," "the music of the spheres"—music we dance to even when we cannot name the tune. We are hearing its refrains "whether we listen with aloof amusement to the mumbo jumbo of some witch doctor of the Congo, or read with cultivated rapture translations from sonnets of Lao-tsu, or now and again crack the hard nutshell of an argument of Aquinas, or catch suddenly the shining meaning of a bizarre Eskimoan fairy tale."

He imagined that this grand and cacophonous chorus began when our primal ancestors told stories to themselves about the animals that they killed for food and about the supernatural world to which the animals seemed to go when they died. "Out there somewhere," beyond the visible plain of existence, was the "animal master," who held over human beings the power of life and death: if he failed to send the beasts back to be sacrificed again, the hunters and their kin would starve. Thus early societies learned that "the essence of life is that it lives by killing and eating; that's the great mystery that the myths have to deal with." The hunt became a ritual of sacrifice, and the hunters in turn performed acts of atonement to the departed spirits of the animals, hoping to coax them into returning to be sacrificed again. The beasts were seen as envoys from that other world, and Campbell surmised "a magical, wonderful accord" growing between the hunter and the hunted, as if they were locked in a "mystical, timeless" cycle of death, burial, and resurrection. Their art—the paintings on cave walls—and oral literature gave form to the impulse we now call religion.

As these primal folk turned from hunting to planting, the stories they told to interpret the mysteries of life changed, too. Now the seed became the magic symbol of the endless cycle. The plant died, and was buried, and its seed was born again. Campbell was fascinated by how this symbol was seized upon by the world's great religions as the revelation of eternal truth—that from death comes life, or as he put it: "From sacrifice, bliss."

"Jesus had the eye," he said. "What a magnificent reality he saw in the mustard seed." He would quote the words of Jesus from the gospel of John—"Truly, truly, I say unto you, unless a grain of wheat falls into the earth and dies, it remains alone; but if it dies, it bears much fruit"—and in the next breath, the Koran: "Do you think that you shall enter the Garden of Bliss without such trials as came to those who passed away before you?" He roamed this vast literature of the spirit, even translating the Hindu scriptures from Sanskrit, and continued to collect more recent stories which he added to the wisdom of the ancients. One story he especially liked told of the trouble woman who came to the Indian saint and sage Ramakrishna, saying, "O Master, I do not find that I love God." And he asked, "Is there nothing, then, that you love?" To this she answered, "My little nephew." And he said to her, "There is your love and service to God, in your love and service to that child."

"And there," said Campbell, "is the high message of religion: 'Inasmuch as ye have done it unto one of the least of these . . .' "

A spiritual man, he found in the literature of faith those principles common to the human spirit. But they had to be liberated from tribal lien, or the religions of the world would remain—as in the Middle East and Northern Ireland today—the source of disdain and aggression. The images of God are many, he said, calling them "the masks of eternity" that both cover and reveal "the Face of Glory." He wanted to know what it means that God assumes such different masks in different cultures, yet how it is that comparable stories can be found in these divergent traditions—stories of creation, of virgin births, incarnations, death and resurrection, second comings, and judgment days. He liked the insight of the Hindu scripture: "Truth is one; the sages call it by many names." All our names and images for God are masks, he said, signifying the ultimate reality that by definition transcends language and art. A myth is a mask of God, too—a metaphor for what lies behind the visible world. However the mystic traditions differ, he said, they are in accord in calling us to a deeper awareness of the very act of living itself. The unpardonable sin, in Campbell's book, was the sin of inadvertence, of not being alert, not quite awake.

I never met anyone who could better tell a story. Listening to him talk of primal societies, I was transported to the wide plains under the great dome of the open sky, or to the forest dense, beneath a canopy of trees, and I began to understand how the voices of the gods spoke from the wind and thunder, and the spirit of God flowed in every mountain stream, and the whole earth bloomed as a sacred place—the realm of mythic imagination. And I asked: Now that we moderns have stripped the earth of its mystery—have made, in Saul Bellow's description, "a housecleaning of belief"—how are our imaginations to be nourished? By Hollywood and made-for-TV movies?

Campbell was no pessimist. He believed there is a "point of

wisdom beyond the conflicts of illusion and truth by which lives can be put back together again." Finding it is the "prime question of the time." In his final years he was striving for a new synthesis of science and spirit. "The shift from a geocentric to a heliocentric world view," he wrote after the astronauts touched the moon, "seemed to have removed man from the center—and the center seemed so important. Spiritually, however, the center is where sight is. Stand on a height and view the horizon. Stand on the moon and view the whole earth rising—even, by way of television, in your parlor." The result is an unprecedented expansion of horizon, one that could well serve in our age, as the ancient mythologies did in theirs, to cleanse the doors of perception "to the wonder, at once terrible and fascinating, of ourselves and of the universe." He argued that it is not science that has diminished human beings or divorced us from divinity. On the contrary, the new discoveries of science "rejoin us to the ancients" by enabling us to recognize in this whole universe "a reflection magnified of our own most inward nature; so that we are indeed its ears, its eyes, its thinking, and its speech—or, in theological terms, God's ears, God's eyes, God's thinking, and God's Word." The last time I saw him I asked him if he still believed—as he once had written—"that we are at this moment participating in one of the very greatest leaps of the human spirit to a knowledge not only of outside nature but also of our own deep inward mystery."

He thought a minute and answered, "The greatest ever."

When I heard the news of his death, I tarried awhile in the copy he had given me of *The Hero with a Thousand Faces*. And I thought of the time I first discovered the world of the mythic hero. I had wandered into the little public library of the town where I grew up and, casually exploring the stacks, pulled down a book that opened wonders to me: Prometheus, stealing fire from the gods for the sake of the human race; Jason, braving the dragon to seize the Golden Fleece; the Knights of the Round Table, pursuing the Holy Grail. But not until I met Joseph Campbell did I understand that the Westerns I saw at the Saturday matinees had borrowed freely from those ancient tales. And that the stories we learned in Sunday school corresponded with those of other cultures that recognized the soul's high adventure, the quest of mortals to grasp the reality of God. He helped me to see the connections, to understand how the pieces fit, and not merely to fear less but to welcome what he described as "a mighty multicultural future."

He was, of course, criticized for dwelling on the psychological interpretation of myth, for seeming to confine the contemporary role of myth to either an ideological or a therapeutic function. I am not competent to enter that debate, and leave it for others to wage. He never seemed bothered by the controversy. He just kept on teaching, opening others to a new way of seeing.

It was, above all, the authentic life he lived that instructs us. When he said that myths are clues to our deepest spiritual potential, able to lead us to delight, illumination, and even rapture, he spoke as one who had been to the places he was inviting others to visit.

What did draw me to him?

Wisdom, yes; he was very wise.

And learning; he did indeed "know the vast sweep of our panoramic past as few men have ever known it."

But there was more.

A story's the way to tell it. He was a man with a thousand stories. This was one of his favorites. In Japan for an international conference on religion, Campbell overheard another American delegate, a social philosopher from New York, say to a Shinto priest, "We've been now to a good many ceremonies and have seen quite a few of your shrines. But I don't get your ideology. I don't get your theology." The Japanese paused as though in deep thought and then slowly shook his head. "I think we don't have ideology," he said. "We don't have theology. We dance."

And so did Joseph Campbell—to the music of the spheres.

—BILL MOYERS

THE
POWER
OF
MYTH

I
MYTH AND
THE MODERN WORLD

*People say that what we're all seeking is a meaning for life. I
don't think that's what we're really seeking. I think that what
we're seeking is an experience of being alive, so that our life
experiences on the purely physical plane will have resonances
within our own innermost being and reality, so that we actually
feel the rapture of being alive.*

MOYERS: Why myths? Why should we care about myths?
What do they have to do with my life?

CAMPBELL: My first response would be, "Go on, live your life,
it's a good life—you don't need mythology." I don't believe in
being interested in a subject just because it's said to be important.
I believe in being caught by it somehow or other. But you may
find that, with a proper introduction, mythology will catch you.
And so, what can it do for you if it does catch you?

One of our problems today is that we are not well acquainted
with the literature of the spirit. We're interested in the news of
the day and the problems of the hour. It used to be that the
university campus was a kind of hermetically sealed-off area where

the news of the day did not impinge upon your attention to the inner life and to the magnificent human heritage we have in our great tradition—Plato, Confucius, the Buddha, Goethe, and others who speak of the eternal values that have to do with the centering of our lives. When you get to be older, and the concerns of the day have all been attended to, and you turn to the inner life—well, if you don't know where it is or what it is, you'll be sorry.

Greek and Latin and biblical literature used to be part of everyone's education. Now, when these were dropped, a whole tradition of Occidental mythological information was lost. It used to be that these stories were in the minds of people. When the story is in your mind, then you see its relevance to something happening in your own life. It gives you perspective on what's happening to you. With the loss of that, we've really lost something because we don't have a comparable literature to take its place. These bits of information from ancient times, which have to do with the themes that have supported human life, built civilizations, and informed religions over the millennia, have to do with deep inner problems, inner mysteries, inner thresholds of passage, and if you don't know what the guide-signs are along the way, you have to work it out yourself. But once this subject catches you, there is such a feeling, from one or another of these traditions, of information of a deep, rich, life-vivifying sort that you don't want to give it up.

MOYERS: So we tell stories to try to come to terms with the world, to harmonize our lives with reality?

CAMPBELL: I think so, yes. Novels—great novels—can be wonderfully instructive. In my twenties and thirties and even on into my forties, James Joyce and Thomas Mann were my teachers. I read everything they wrote. Both were writing in terms of what might be called the mythological traditions. Take, for example, the story of Tonio, in Thomas Mann's *Tonio Kröger*. Tonio's father was a substantial businessman, a major citizen in his hometown. Little Tonio, however, had an artistic temperament, so he moved to Munich and joined a group of literary people who felt themselves above the mere money earners and family men.

So here is Tonio between two poles: his father, who was a good father, responsible and all of that, but who never did the thing he wanted to in all his life—and, on the other hand, the one who leaves his hometown and becomes a critic of that kind of life. But Tonio found that he really loved these hometown people. And although he thought himself a little superior in an intellectual way to them and could describe them with cutting words, his heart was nevertheless with them.

But when he left to live with the bohemians, he found that they were so disdainful of life that he couldn't stay with them, either. So he left them, and wrote a letter back to someone in the group, saying, "I admire those cold, proud beings who adventure upon the paths of great and daemonic beauty and despise 'mankind'; but I do not envy them. For if anything is capable of making a poet of a literary man, it is my hometown love of the human, the living and ordinary. All warmth derives from this love, all kindness and all humor. Indeed, to me it even seems that this must be that love of which it is written that one may 'speak with the tongues of men and of angels,' and yet, lacking love, be 'as sounding brass or a tinkling cymbal.' "

And then he says, "The writer must be true to truth." And that's a killer, because the only way you can describe a human being truly is by describing his imperfections. The perfect human being is uninteresting—the Buddha who leaves the world, you know. It is the imperfections of life that are lovable. And when the writer sends a dart of the true word, it hurts. But it goes with love. This is what Mann called "erotic irony," the love for that which you are killing with your cruel, analytical word.

MOYERS: I cherish that image: my hometown love, the feeling you get for that place, no matter how long you've been away or even if you never return. That was where you first discovered people. But why do you say you love people for their imperfections?

4 THE POWER OF MYTH

CAMPBELL: Aren't children lovable because they're falling down all the time and have little bodies with the heads too big? Didn't Walt Disney know all about this when he did the seven dwarfs? And these funny little dogs that people have—they're lovable because they're so imperfect.

MOYERS: Perfection *would* be a bore, wouldn't it?

CAMPBELL: It would have to be. It would be inhuman. The umbilical point, the humanity, the thing that makes you human and not supernatural and immortal—that's what's lovable. That is why some people have a very hard time loving God, because there's no imperfection there. You can be in awe, but that would not be real love. It's Christ on the cross that becomes lovable.

MOYERS: What do you mean?

CAMPBELL: Suffering. Suffering is imperfection, is it not?

MOYERS: The story of human suffering, striving, living—

CAMPBELL: —and youth coming to knowledge of itself, what it has to go through.

MOYERS: I came to understand from reading your books—*The Masks of God* or *The Hero with a Thousand Faces*, for example—that what human beings have in common is revealed in myths. Myths are stories of our search through the ages for truth, for meaning, for significance. We all need to tell our story and to understand our story. We all need to understand death and to cope with death, and we all need help in our passages from birth to life and then to death. We need for life to signify, to touch the eternal, to understand the mysterious, to find out who we are.

CAMPBELL: People say that what we're all seeking is a meaning for life. I don't think that's what we're really seeking. I think that what we're seeking is an experience of being alive, so that our life experiences on the purely physical plane will have res-onances within our own innermost being and reality, so that we actually feel the rapture of being alive. That's what it's all finally about, and that's what these clues help us to find within ourselves.

MOYERS: Myths are clues?

CAMPBELL: Myths are clues to the spiritual potentialities of the human life.

MOYERS: What we're capable of knowing and experiencing within?

CAMPBELL: Yes.

MOYERS: You changed the definition of a myth from the *search* for meaning to the *experience* of meaning.

CAMPBELL: Experience of *life*. The mind has to do with meaning. What's the meaning of a flower? There's a Zen story about a sermon of the Buddha in which he simply lifted a flower. There was only one man who gave him a sign with his eyes that he understood what was said. Now, the Buddha himself is called "the one thus come." There's no meaning. What's the meaning of the universe? What's the meaning of a flea? It's just there. That's it. And your own meaning is that you're there. We're so engaged in doing things to achieve purposes of outer value that we forget that the inner value, the rapture that is associated with being alive, is what it's all about.

MOYERS: How do you get that experience?

CAMPBELL: Read myths. They teach you that you can turn inward, and you begin to get the message of the symbols. Read other people's myths, not those of your own religion, because you tend to interpret your own religion in terms of facts—but if you read the other ones, you begin to get the message. Myth helps you to put your mind in touch with this experience of being alive. It tells you what the experience is. Marriage, for example. What is marriage? The myth tells you what it is. It's the reunion of the separated duad. Originally you were one. You are now two in the world, but the recognition of the spiritual identity is what marriage is. It's different from a love affair. It has nothing to do with that. It's another mythological plane of experience. When people get married because they think it's a long-time love affair, they'll be divorced very soon, because all love affairs end in disappointment. But marriage is recognition of a spiritual identity. If we live a proper life, if our minds are on the right qualities in regarding the person of the opposite sex, we will find our proper male or female counterpart. But if we are distracted by certain sensuous interests, we'll marry the wrong person. By marrying the right person, we reconstruct the image of the incarnate God, and that's what marriage is.

MOYERS: The right person? How does one choose the right person?

CAMPBELL: Your heart tells you. It ought to.

MOYERS: Your inner being.

CAMPBELL: That's the mystery.

MOYERS: You recognize your other self.

CAMPBELL: Well, I don't know, but there's a flash that comes, and something in you knows that this is the one.

MOYERS: If marriage is this reunion of the self with the self, with the male or female grounding of ourselves, why is it that marriage is so precarious in our modern society?

CAMPBELL: Because it's not regarded as a marriage. I would say that if the marriage isn't a first priority in your life, you're not married. The marriage means the two that are one, the two become one flesh. If the marriage lasts long enough, and if you are acquiescing constantly to it instead of to individual personal whim, you come to realize that that is true—the two really are one.

MOYERS: One not only biologically but spiritually.

CAMPBELL: *Primarily* spiritually. The biological is the distraction which may lead you to the wrong identification.

MOYERS: Then the necessary function of marriage, perpetuating ourselves in children, is not the primary one.

CAMPBELL: No, that's really just the elementary aspect of marriage. There are two completely different stages of marriage. First is the youthful marriage following the wonderful impulse that nature has given us in the interplay of the sexes biologically in order to produce children. But there comes a time when the child graduates from the family and the couple is left. I've been amazed at the number of my friends who in their forties or fifties go apart. They have had a perfectly decent life together with the child, but they interpreted their union in terms of their relationship through the child. They did not interpret it in terms of their own personal relationship to each other.

Marriage is a relationship. When you make the sacrifice in marriage, you're sacrificing not to each other but to unity in a relationship. The Chinese image of the Tao, with the dark and light interacting—that's the relationship of yang and yin, male and female, which is what a marriage is. And that's what you have become when you have married. You're no longer this one alone; your identity is in a relationship. Marriage is not a simple love affair, it's an ordeal, and the ordeal is the sacrifice of ego to a relationship in which two have become one.

MOYERS: So marriage is utterly incompatible with the idea of doing one's own thing.

CAMPBELL: It's not simply one's own thing, you see. It is, in a sense, doing one's own thing, but the one isn't just you, it's the two together as one. And that's a purely mythological image signifying the sacrifice of the visible entity for a transcendent good. This is something that becomes beautifully realized in the second stage of marriage, what I call the alchemical stage, of the two experiencing that they are one. If they are still living as they were in the primary stage of marriage, they will go apart when their children leave. Daddy will fall in love with some little nubile girl and run off, and Mother will be left with an empty house and heart, and will have to work it out on her own, in her own way.

MOYERS: That's because we don't understand the two levels of marriage.

CAMPBELL: You don't make a commitment.

MOYERS: We presume to—we make a commitment for better or for worse.

CAMPBELL: That's the remnant of a ritual.

MOYERS: And the ritual has lost its force. The ritual that once conveyed an inner reality is now merely form. And that's true in the rituals of society and in the personal rituals of marriage and religion.

CAMPBELL: How many people before marriage receive spiritual instruction as to what the marriage means? You can stand up in front of a judge and in ten minutes get married. The marriage ceremony in India lasts three days. That couple is glued.

MOYERS: You're saying that marriage is not just a social arrangement, it's a spiritual exercise.

CAMPBELL: It's primarily a spiritual exercise, and the society is supposed to help us have the realization. Man should not be in the service of society, society should be in the service of man. When man is in the service of society, you have a monster state, and that's what is threatening the world at this minute.

MOYERS: What happens when a society no longer embraces a powerful mythology?

CAMPBELL: What we've got on our hands. If you want to find out what it means to have a society without any rituals, read the New York *Times*.

MOYERS: And you'd find?

CAMPBELL: The news of the day, including destructive and violent acts by young people who don't know how to behave in a civilized society.

MOYERS: Society has provided them no rituals by which they become members of the tribe, of the community. All children need to be twice born, to learn to function rationally in the present world, leaving childhood behind. I think of that passage in the first book of Corinthians: "When I was a child, I spake as a child, I understood as a child, I thought as a child: but when I became a man, I put away childish things."

CAMPBELL: That's exactly it. That's the significance of the puberty rites. In primal societies, there are teeth knocked out, there are scarifications, there are circumcisions, there are all kinds of things done. So you don't have your little baby body anymore, you're something else entirely.

When I was a kid, we wore short trousers, you know, knee pants. And then there was a great moment when you put on long pants. Boys now don't get that. I see even five-year-olds walking around with long trousers. When are they going to know that they're now men and must put aside childish things?

MOYERS: Where do the kids growing up in the city—on 125th and Broadway, for example—where do these kids get their myths today?

CAMPBELL: They make them up themselves. This is why we have graffiti all over the city. These kids have their own gangs and their own initiations and their own morality, and they're doing the best they can. But they're dangerous because their own laws are not those of the city. They have not been initiated into our society.

MOYERS: Rollo May says there is so much violence in American society today because there are no more great myths to help young men and women relate to the world or to understand that world beyond what is seen.

CAMPBELL: Yes, but another reason for the high level of violence here is that America has no ethos.

MOYERS: Explain.

CAMPBELL: In American football, for example, the rules are very strict and complex. If you were to go to England, however, you would find that the rugby rules are not that strict. When I was a student back in the twenties, there were a couple of young men who constituted a marvelous forward-passing pair. They went to Oxford on scholarship and joined the rugby team and one day they introduced the forward pass. And the English players said, "Well, we have no rules for this, so please don't. We don't play that way."

Now, in a culture that has been homogeneous for some time, there are a number of understood, unwritten rules by which people live. There is an ethos there, there is a mode, an understanding that, "we don't do it that way."

MOYERS: A mythology.

CAMPBELL: An unstated mythology, you might say. This is the way we use a fork and knife, this is the way we deal with people, and so forth. It's not all written down in books. But in America we have people from all kinds of backgrounds, all in a cluster, together, and consequently law has become very important in this country. Lawyers and law are what hold us together. There is no ethos. Do you see what I mean?

MOYERS: Yes. It's what De Tocqueville described when he first arrived here a hundred and sixty years ago to discover "a tumult of anarchy."

CAMPBELL: What we have today is a demythologized world. And, as a result, the students I meet are very much interested in mythology because myths bring them messages. Now, I can't tell you what the messages are that the study of mythology is bringing to young people today. I know what it did for me. But it is doing something for them. When I go to lecture at any college, the room is bursting with students who have come to hear what I have to say. The faculty very often assigns me to a room that's a little small—smaller than it should have been because they didn't know how much excitement there was going to be in the student body.

MOYERS: Take a guess. What do you think the mythology, the stories they're going to hear from you, do for them?

CAMPBELL: They're stories about the wisdom of life, they really are. What we're learning in our schools is not the wisdom of life. We're learning technologies, we're getting information. There's a curious reluctance on the part of faculties to indicate the life values of their subjects. In our sciences today—and this includes anthropology, linguistics, the study of religions, and so forth—there is a tendency to specialization. And when you know how much a specialist scholar has to know in order to be a competent specialist, you can understand this tendency. To study Buddhism, for instance, you have to be able to handle not only all the European languages in which the discussions of the Oriental come, particularly French, German, English, and Italian, but also Sanskrit, Chinese, Japanese, Tibetan, and several other languages. Now, this is a tremendous task. Such a specialist can't also be wondering about the difference between the Iroquois and Algonquin.

Specialization tends to limit the field of problems that the specialist is concerned with. Now, the person who isn't a specialist, but a generalist like myself, sees something over here that he has learned from one specialist, something over there that he has learned from another specialist—and neither of them has considered the problem of why this occurs here and also there. So the generalist—and that's a derogatory term, by the way, for academics—gets into a range of other problems that are more genuinely human, you might say, than specifically cultural.

MOYERS: Then along comes the journalist who has a license to explain things he doesn't understand.

CAMPBELL: That is not only a license but something that is put upon him—he has an obligation to educate himself in public. Now, I remember when I was a young man going to hear Heinrich Zimmer lecture. He was the first man I know of to speak about myths as though they had messages that were valid for life, not just interesting things for scholars to fool around with. And that confirmed me in a feeling I had had ever since boyhood.

MOYERS: Do you remember the first time you discovered myth? The first time the story came alive in you?

CAMPBELL: I was brought up as a Roman Catholic. Now, one of the great advantages of being brought up a Roman Catholic is that you're taught to take myth seriously and to let it operate on your life and to live in terms of these mythic motifs. I was brought up in terms of the seasonal relationships to the cycle of Christ's coming into the world, teaching in the world, dying, resurrecting, and returning to heaven. The ceremonies all through the year keep you in mind of the eternal core of all that changes in time. Sin is simply getting out of touch with that harmony.

And then I fell in love with American Indians because Buffalo Bill used to come to Madison Square Garden every year with his marvelous Wild West Show. And I wanted to know more about Indians. My father and mother were very generous parents and found what books were being written for boys about Indians at that time. So I began to read American Indian myths, and it wasn't long before I found the same motifs in the American Indian stories that I was being taught by the nuns at school.

MOYERS: Creation—

CAMPBELL: —creation, death and resurrection, ascension to heaven, virgin births—I didn't know what it was, but I recognized the vocabulary. One after another.

MOYERS: And what happened?

CAMPBELL: I was excited. That was the beginning of my interest in comparative mythology.

MOYERS: Did you begin by asking, "Why does it say it this way while the Bible says it that way?"

CAMPBELL: No, I didn't start the comparative analysis until many years later.

MOYERS: What appealed to you about the Indian stories?

CAMPBELL: In those days there was still American Indian lore in the air. Indians were still around. Even now, when I deal with myths from all parts of the world, I find the American Indian tales and narratives to be very rich, very well developed.

And then my parents had a place out in the woods where the Delaware Indians had lived, and the Iroquois had come down and fought them. There was a big ledge where we could dig for Indian arrowheads and things like that. And the very animals that play the role in the Indian stories were there in the woods around me. It was a grand introduction to this material.

MOYERS: Did these stories begin to collide with your Catholic faith?

CAMPBELL: No, there was no collision. The collision with my religion came much later in relation to scientific studies and things of that kind. Later I became interested in Hinduism, and there were the same stories again. And in my graduate work I was dealing with the Arthurian medieval material, and there were the same stories again. So you can't tell me that they're not the same stories. I've been with them all my life.

MOYERS: They come from every culture but with timeless themes.

CAMPBELL: The themes are timeless, and the inflection is to the culture.

MOYERS: So the stories may take the same universal theme but apply it slightly differently, depending upon the accent of the people who are speaking?

CAMPBELL: Oh, yes. If you were not alert to the parallel themes, you perhaps would think they were quite different stories, but they're not.

MOYERS: You taught mythology for thirty-eight years at Sarah Lawrence. How did you get these young women, coming to college from their middle-class backgrounds, from their orthodox religions—how did you get them interested in myths?

CAMPBELL: Young people just grab this stuff. Mythology teaches you what's behind literature and the arts, it teaches you about your own life. It's a great, exciting, life-nourishing subject. Mythology has a great deal to do with the stages of life, the initiation ceremonies as you move from childhood to adult responsibilities, from the unmarried state into the married state. All of those rituals are mythological rites. They have to do with your recognition of the new role that you're in, the process of throwing off the old one and coming out in the new, and entering into a responsible profession.

When a judge walks into the room, and everybody stands up, you're not standing up to that guy, you're standing up to the robe that he's wearing and the role that he's going to play. What makes him worthy of that role is his integrity, as a representative of the principles of that role, and not some group of prejudices of his own. So what you're standing up to is a mythological character. I imagine some kings and queens are the most stupid, absurd, banal people you could run into, probably interested only in horses and women, you know. But you're not responding to them as personalities, you're responding to them in their mythological roles. When someone becomes a judge, or President of the United States, the man is no longer that man, he's the representative of an eternal office; he has to sacrifice his personal desires and even life possibilities to the role that he now signifies.

MOYERS: So there are mythological rituals at work in our society. The ceremony of marriage is one. The ceremony of the inauguration of a President or judge is another. What are some of the other rituals that are important to society today?

CAMPBELL: Joining the army, putting on a uniform, is another. You're giving up your personal life and accepting a socially determined manner of life in the service of the society of which you are a member. This is why I think it is obscene to judge people in terms of civil law for performances that they rendered in time of war. They were acting not as individuals, they were acting as agents of something above them and to which they had by dedication given themselves. To judge them as though they were individual human beings is totally improper.

MOYERS: You've seen what happens when primitive societies are unsettled by white man's civilization. They go to pieces, they disintegrate, they become diseased. Hasn't the same thing been happening to us since our myths began to disappear?

CAMPBELL: Absolutely, it has.

MOYERS: Isn't that why conservative religions today are calling for the old-time religion?

CAMPBELL: Yes, and they're making a terrible mistake. They are going back to something that is vestigial, that doesn't serve life.

MOYERS: But didn't it serve us?

CAMPBELL: Sure it did.

MOYERS: I understand the yearning. In my youth I had fixed stars. They comforted me with their permanence. They gave me a known horizon. And they told me there was a loving, kind, and just father out there looking down on me, ready to receive me, thinking of my concerns all the time. Now, Saul Bellow says that science has made a housecleaning of beliefs. But there was value in these things for me. I am today what I am because of those beliefs. I wonder what happens to children who don't have those fixed stars, that known horizon—those myths?

CAMPBELL: Well, as I said, all you have to do is read the newspaper. It's a mess. On this immediate level of life and structure, myths offer life models. But the models have to be appropriate to the time in which you are living, and our time has changed so fast that what was proper fifty years ago is not proper today. The virtues of the past are the vices of today. And many of what were thought to be the vices of the past are the necessities of today. The moral order has to catch up with the moral necessities of actual life in time, here and now. And that is what we are not doing. The old-time religion belongs to another age, another people, another set of human values, another universe. By going back you throw yourself out of sync with history. Our kids lose their faith in the religions that were taught to them, and they go inside.

MOYERS: Often with the help of a drug.

CAMPBELL: Yes. The mechanically induced mystical experience is what you have there. I have attended a number of psychological conferences dealing with this whole problem of the difference between the mystical experience and the psychological crack-up. The difference is that the one who cracks up is drowning in the water in which the mystic swims. You have to be prepared for this experience.

MOYERS: You talk about this peyote culture emerging and becoming dominant among Indians as a consequence of the loss of the buffalo and their earlier way of life.

CAMPBELL: Yes. Ours is one of the worst histories in relation to the native peoples of any civilized nation. They are nonpersons. They are not even reckoned in the statistics of the voting population of the United States. There was a moment shortly after the American Revolution when there were a number of distinguished Indians who actually participated in American government and life. George Washington said that Indians should be incorporated as members of our culture. But instead, they were turned into vestiges of the past. In the nineteenth century, all the Indians of the southeast were put into wagons and shipped under military guard out to what was then called Indian Territory, which was given to the Indians in perpetuity as their own world—then a couple of years later was taken away from them.

Recently, anthropologists studied a group of Indians in north-western Mexico who live within a few miles of a major area for the natural growth of peyote. Peyote is their animal—that is to say, they associate it with the deer. And they have very special missions to go collect peyote and bring it back.

These missions are mystical journeys with all of the details of the typical mystical journey. First, there is disengagement from secular life. Everybody who is going to go on this expedition has to make a complete confession of all the faults of his or her recent living. And if they don't, the magic is not going to work. Then they start on the journey. They even speak a special language, a negative language. Instead of saying yes, for example, they say no, or instead of saying, "We are going," they say, "We are coming." They are in another world.

Then they come to the threshold of the adventure. There are special shrines that represent stages of mental transformation on the way. And then comes the great business of collecting the peyote. The peyote is killed as though it were a deer. They sneak up on it, shoot a little arrow at it, and then perform the ritual of collecting the peyote.

The whole thing is a complete duplication of the kind of experience that is associated with the inward journey, when you leave the outer world and come into the realm of spiritual beings. They identify each little stage as a spiritual transformation. They are in a sacred place all the way.

MOYERS: Why do they make such an intricate process out of it?

CAMPBELL: Well, it has to do with the peyote being not simply a biological, mechanical, chemical effect but one of spiritual transformation. If you undergo a spiritual transformation and have not had preparation for it, you do not know how to evaluate what has happened to you, and you get the terrible experiences of a bad trip, as they used to call it with LSD. If you know where you are going, you won't have a bad trip.

MOYERS: So this is why it is a psychological crisis if you are drowning in the water where—

CAMPBELL: —where you ought to be able to swim, but you weren't prepared. That is true of the spiritual life, anyhow. It is a terrifying experience to have your consciousness transformed.

MOYERS: You talk a lot about consciousness.

CAMPBELL: Yes.

MOYERS: What do you mean by it?

CAMPBELL: It is a part of the Cartesian mode to think of consciousness as being something peculiar to the head, that the head is the organ originating consciousness. It isn't. The head is an organ that inflects consciousness in a certain direction, or to a certain set of purposes. But there is a consciousness here in the body. The whole living world is informed by consciousness.

I have a feeling that consciousness and energy are the same thing somehow. Where you really see life energy, there's consciousness. Certainly the vegetable world is conscious. And when you live in the woods, as I did as a kid, you can see all these different consciousnesses relating to themselves. There is a plant consciousness and there is an animal consciousness, and we share both these things. You eat certain foods, and the bile knows whether there's something there for it to go to work on. The whole process is consciousness. Trying to interpret it in simply mechanistic terms won't work.

MOYERS: How do we transform our consciousness?

CAMPBELL: That's a matter of what you are disposed to think

about. And that's what meditation is for. All of life is a meditation, most of it unintentional. A lot of people spend most of life in meditating on where their money is coming from and where it's going to go. If you have a family to bring up, you're concerned for the family. These are all very important concerns, but they have to do with physical conditions, mostly. But how are you going to communicate spiritual consciousness to the children if you don't have it yourself? How do you get that? What the myths are for is to bring us into a level of consciousness that is spiritual.

Just for example: I walk off Fifty-first Street and Fifth Avenue into St. Patrick's Cathedral. I've left a very busy city and one of the most economically inspired cities on the planet. I walk into that cathedral, and everything around me speaks of spiritual mysteries. The mystery of the cross, what's that all about there? The stained glass windows, which bring another atmosphere in. My consciousness has been brought up onto another level altogether, and I am on a different platform. And then I walk out, and I'm back on the level of the street again. Now, can I hold something from the cathedral consciousness? Certain prayers or meditations are designed to hold your consciousness on that level instead of letting it drop down here all the way. And then what you can finally do is to recognize that this is simply a lower level of that higher consciousness. The mystery that is expressed there is operating in the field of your money, for example. All money is congealed energy. I think that that's the clue to how to transform your consciousness.

MOYERS: Don't you sometimes think, as you consider these stories, that you are drowning in other people's dreams?

CAMPBELL: I don't listen to other people's dreams.

MOYERS: But all of these myths are other people's dreams.

CAMPBELL: Oh, no, they're not. They are the world's dreams. They are archetypal dreams and deal with great human problems. I know when I come to one of these thresholds now. The myth tells me about it, how to respond to certain crises of disappointment or delight or failure or success. The myths tell me where I am.

MOYERS: What happens when people become legends? Can you say, for example, that John Wayne has become a myth?

CAMPBELL: When a person becomes a model for other people's lives, he has moved into the sphere of being mythologized.

MOYERS: This happens so often to actors in films, where we get so many of our models.

CAMPBELL: I remember, when I was a boy, Douglas Fairbanks was the model for me. Adolphe Menjou was the model for my brother. Of course those men were playing the roles of mythic figures. They were educators toward life.

MOYERS: No figure in movie history is more engaging to me than Shane. Did you see the movie *Shane*?

CAMPBELL: No, I didn't.

MOYERS: It is the classic story of the stranger who rides in from outside and does good for others and rides away, not waiting for his reward. Why is it that films affect us this way?

CAMPBELL: There is something magical about films. The person you are looking at is also somewhere else at the same time. That is a condition of the god. If a movie actor comes into the theater, everybody turns and looks at the movie actor. He is the real hero of the occasion. He is on another plane. He is a multiple presence.

What you are seeing on the screen really isn't he, and yet the "he" comes. Through the multiple forms, the form of forms out of which all of this comes is right there.

MOYERS: Movies seem to create these large figures, while television merely creates celebrities. They don't become models as much as they do objects of gossip.

CAMPBELL: Perhaps that's because we see TV personalities in the home instead of in a special temple like the movie theater.

MOYERS: I saw a photograph yesterday of this latest cult figure from Hollywood, Rambo, the Vietnam veteran who returns to rescue prisoners of war, and through violent swaths of death and destruction he brings them back. I understand it is the most popular movie in Beirut. The photograph showed the new Rambo doll that has been created and is being sold by the same company that produces the Cabbage Patch dolls. In the foreground is the image of a sweet, lovable Cabbage Patch doll, and behind it, the brute force, Rambo.

CAMPBELL: Those are two mythic figures. The image that comes to my mind now is of Picasso's *Minotauromachy*, an engraving that shows a great monster bull approaching. The philosopher is climbing up a ladder in terror to get away. In the bullring there is a horse, which has been killed, and on the sacrificed horse lies a female matador who has also been killed. The only creature facing this terrific monster is a little girl with a flower. Those are the two figures you have just spoken of— the simple, innocent, childlike one, and the terrific threat. You see the problems of the modern day.

MOYERS: The poet Yeats felt we were living in the last of a great Christian cycle. His poem "The Second Coming" says, "Turning and turning in the widening gyre/The falcon cannot hear the falconer;/Things fall apart; the centre cannot hold;/Mere anarchy is loosed upon the world,/The blood-dimmed tide is loosed, and everywhere/The ceremony of innocence is drowned." What do you see slouching "towards Bethlehem to be born"?

CAMPBELL: I don't know what's coming, any more than Yeats knew, but when you come to the end of one time and the beginning of a new one, it's a period of tremendous pain and turmoil. The threat we feel, and everybody feels—well, there is this notion of Armageddon coming, you know.

MOYERS: "I have become Death, the Destroyer of worlds," Oppenheimer said when he saw the first atomic bomb explode. But you don't think that will be our end, do you?

CAMPBELL: It won't be the end. Maybe it will be the end of life on this planet, but that is not the end of the universe. It is just a bungled explosion in terms of all the explosions that are going on in all the suns of the universe. The universe is a bunch of exploding atomic furnaces like our sun. So this is just a little imitation of the whole big job.

MOYERS: Can you imagine that somewhere else other creatures can be sitting, investing their transient journey with the kind of significance that our myths and great stories do?

CAMPBELL: No. When you realize that if the temperature goes up fifty degrees and stays there, life will not exist on this earth, and that if it drops, let's say, another hundred degrees and stays there, life will not be on this earth; when you realize how very delicate this balance is, how the quantity of water is so important—well, when you think of all the accidents of the environment that have fostered life, how can you think that the life we know would exist on any other particle of the universe, no matter how many of these satellites around stars there may be?

MOYERS: This fragile life always exists in the crucible of terror and possible extinction. And the image of the Cabbage Patch doll juxtaposed with the vicious Rambo is not at odds with what we know of life through mythology?

CAMPBELL: No, it isn't.

MOYERS: Do you see some new metaphors emerging in a modern medium for the old universal truths?

CAMPBELL: I see the possibility of new metaphors, but I don't see that they have become mythological yet.

MOYERS: What do you think will be the myths that will incorporate the machine into the new world?

CAMPBELL: Well, automobiles have gotten into mythology. They have gotten into dreams. And airplanes are very much in the service of the imagination. The flight of the airplane, for example, is in the imagination as the release from earth. This is the same thing that birds symbolize, in a certain way. The bird is symbolic of the release of the spirit from bondage to the earth, just as the serpent is symbolic of the bondage to the earth. The airplane plays that role now.

MOYERS: Any others?

CAMPBELL: Weapons, of course. Every movie that I have seen on the airplane as I traveled back and forth between California and Hawaii shows people with revolvers. There is the Lord Death, carrying his weapon. Different instruments take over the roles that earlier instruments now no longer serve. But I don't see any more than that.

MOYERS: So the new myths will serve the old stories. When I saw Star Wars, I remembered the phrase from the apostle Paul, "I wrestle against principalities and powers." That was two thousand years ago. And in the caves of the early Stone Age hunter, there are scenes of wrestling against principalities and powers. Here in our modern technological myths we are still wrestling.

CAMPBELL: Man should not submit to the powers from outside but command them. How to do it is the problem.

MOYERS: After our youngest son had seen Star Wars for the twelfth or thirteenth time, I said, "Why do you go so often?" He said, "For the same reason you have been reading the Old Testament all of your life." He was in a new world of myth.

CAMPBELL: Certainly Star Wars has a valid mythological perspective. It shows the state as a machine and asks, "Is the machine going to crush humanity or serve humanity? Humanity comes not from the machine but from the heart. What I see in *Star Wars* is the same problem that *Faust* gives us: Mephistopheles, the machine man, can provide us with all the means, and is thus likely to determine the aims of life as well. But of course the characteristic of Faust, which makes him eligible to be saved, is that he seeks aims that are not those of the machine.

Now, when Luke Skywalker unmasks his father, he is taking off the machine role that the father has played. The father was the uniform. That is power, the state role.

MOYERS: Machines help us to fulfill the idea that we want the world to be made in our image, and we want it to be what we think it ought to be.

CAMPBELL: Yes. But then there comes a time when the machine begins to dictate to you. For example, I have bought this wonderful machine—a computer. Now I am rather an authority on gods, so I identified the machine—it seems to me to be an Old Testament god with a lot of rules and no mercy.

MOYERS: There is a fetching story about President Eisenhower and the first computers—

CAMPBELL: —Eisenhower went into a room full of computers. And he put the question to these machines, "Is there a God?" And they all start up, and the lights flash, and the wheels turn, and after a while a voice says, "*Now* there is."

MOYERS: But isn't it possible to develop toward your computer the same attitude of the chieftain who said that all things speak of God? If it isn't a special, privileged revelation, God is everywhere in his work, including the computer.

CAMPBELL: Indeed so. It's a miracle, what happens on that screen. Have you ever looked inside one of those things?

MOYERS: No, and I don't intend to.

CAMPBELL: You can't believe it. It's a whole hierarchy of angels—all on slats. And those little tubes—those are miracles.

I have had a revelation from my computer about mythology. You buy a certain software, and there is a whole set of signals that lead to the achievement of your aim. If you begin fooling around with signals that belong to another system of software, they just won't work.

Similarly, in mythology—if you have a mythology in which the metaphor for the mystery is the father, you are going to have a different set of signals from what you would have if the metaphor for the wisdom and mystery of the world were the mother. And they are two perfectly good metaphors. Neither one is a fact. These are metaphors. It is as though the universe were my father. It is as though the universe were my mother. Jesus says, "No one gets to the father but by me." The father that he was talking about was the biblical father. It might be that you can get to the father only by way of Jesus. On the other hand, suppose you are going by way of the mother. There you might prefer Kali, and the hymns to the goddess, and so forth. That is simply another way to get to the mystery of your life. You must understand that each religion is a kind of software that has its own set of signals and will work.

If a person is really involved in a religion and really building his life on it, he better stay with the software that he has got. But a chap like myself, who likes to play with the software— well, I can run around, but I probably will never have an experience comparable to that of a saint.

MOYERS: But haven't some of the greatest saints borrowed from anywhere they could? They have taken from this and from that, and constructed a new software.

CAMPBELL: That is what is called the development of a religion. You can see it in the Bible. In the beginning, God was simply the most powerful god among many. He is just a local tribal god. And then in the sixth century, when the Jews were in Babylon, the notion of a world savior came in, and the biblical divinity moved into a new dimension.

You can keep an old tradition going only by renewing it in

terms of current circumstances. In the period of the Old Testament, the world was a little three-layer cake, consisting of a few hundred miles around the Near Eastern centers. No one had ever heard of the Aztecs, or even of the Chinese. When the world changes, then the religion has to be transformed.

MOYERS: But it seems to me that is in fact what we are doing.

CAMPBELL: That is in fact what we had better do. But my notion of the real horror today is what you see in Beirut. There you have the three great Western religions, Judaism, Christianity, and Islam—and because the three of them have three different names for the same biblical god, they can't get on together. They are stuck with their metaphor and don't realize its reference. They haven't allowed the circle that surrounds them to open. It is a closed circle. Each group says, "We are the chosen group, and we have God."

Look at Ireland. A group of Protestants was moved to Ireland in the seventeenth century by Cromwell, and it never has opened up to the Catholic majority there. The Catholics and Protestants represent two totally different social systems, two different ideals.

MOYERS: Each needs a new myth.

CAMPBELL: Each needs its own myth, all the way. Love thine enemy. Open up. Don't judge. All things are Buddha things. It is there in the myth. It is already there.

MOYERS: You tell a story about a local jungle native who once said to a missionary, "Your god keeps himself shut up in a house as if he were old and infirm. Ours is in the forest and in the fields and on the mountains when the rain comes." And I think that is probably true.

CAMPBELL: Yes. You see, this is a problem you get in the book of Kings and in Samuel. The various Hebrew kings were sacrificing on the mountaintops. And they did wrong in the sight of Yahweh. The Yahweh cult was a specific movement in the Hebrew community, which finally won. This was a pushing through of a certain temple-bound god against the nature cult, which was celebrated all over the place.

And this imperialistic thrust of a certain in-group culture is continued in the West. But it has got to open to the nature of things now. If it can open, all the possibilities are there.

MOYERS: Of course, we moderns are stripping the world of its natural revelations, of nature itself. I think of that pygmy legend of the little boy who finds the bird with the beautiful song in the forest and brings it home.

CAMPBELL: He asks his father to bring food for the bird, and the father doesn't want to feed a mere bird, so he kills it. And the legend says the man killed the bird, and with the bird he killed the song, and with the song, himself. He dropped dead, completely dead, and was dead forever.

MOYERS: Isn't that a story about what happens when human beings destroy their environment? Destroy their world? Destroy nature and the revelations of nature?

CAMPBELL: They destroy their own nature, too. They kill the song.

MOYERS: And isn't mythology the story of the song?

CAMPBELL: Mythology *is* the song. It is the song of the imagination, inspired by the energies of the body. Once a Zen master stood up before his students and was about to deliver a sermon. And just as he was about to open his mouth, a bird sang. And he said, "The sermon has been delivered."

MOYERS: I was about to say that we are creating new myths, but you say no, every myth we tell today has some point of origin in our past experience.

CAMPBELL: The main motifs of the myths are the same, and they have always been the same. If you want to find your own mythology, the key is with what society do you associate? Every mythology has grown up in a certain society in a bounded field.

Then they come into collision and relationship, and they amalgamate, and you get a more complex mythology.

But today there are no boundaries. The only mythology that
is valid today is the mythology of the planet—and we don't have
such a mythology. The closest thing I know to a planetary mythology is Buddhism, which sees all beings as Buddha beings.
The only problem is to come to the recognition of that. There
is nothing to do. The task is only to know what is, and then to
act in relation to the brotherhood of all of these beings.

MOYERS: Brotherhood?

CAMPBELL: Yes. Now brotherhood in most of the myths I
know of is confined to a bounded community. In bounded com-
munities, aggression is projected outward.

For example, the ten commandments say, "Thou shalt not
kill." Then the next chapter says, "Go into Canaan and kill
everybody in it." That is a bounded field. The myths of participation and love pertain only to the in-group, and the out-group
is totally other. This is the sense of the word "gentile"—the
person is not of the same order.

MOYERS: And unless you wear my costume, we are not kin.

CAMPBELL: Yes. Now, what is a myth? The dictionary definition of a myth would be stories about gods. So then you have
to ask the next question: What is a god? A god is a personification
of a motivating power or a value system that functions in human
life and in the universe—the powers of your own body and of
nature. The myths are metaphorical of spiritual potentiality in
the human being, and the same powers that animate our life
animate the life of the world. But also there are myths and gods
that have to do with specific societies or the patron deities of
the society. In other words, there are two totally different orders
of mythology. There is the mythology that relates you to your
nature and to the natural world, of which you're a part. And
there is the mythology that is strictly sociological, linking you
to a particular society. You are not simply a natural man, you

are a member of a particular group. In the history of European mythology, you can see the interaction of these two systems. Usually the socially oriented system is of a nomadic people who are moving around, so you learn that's where your center is, in that group. The nature-oriented mythology would be of an earth-cultivating people.

Now, the biblical tradition is a socially oriented mythology. Nature is condemned. In the nineteenth century, scholars thought of mythology and ritual as an attempt to control nature. But that is magic, not mythology or religion. Nature religions are not attempts to control nature but to help you put yourself in accord with it. But when nature is thought of as evil, you don't put yourself in accord with it, you control it, or try to, and hence the tension, the anxiety, the cutting down of forests, the annihilation of native people. And the accent here separates us from nature.

MOYERS: Is this why we so easily dominate or subjugate nature—because we have contempt for it, because we see it only as something to serve us?

CAMPBELL: Yes. I will never forget the experience I had when I was in Japan, a place that never heard of the Fall and the Garden of Eden. One of the Shinto texts says that the processes of nature cannot be evil. Every natural impulse is not to be corrected but to be sublimated, to be beautified. There is a glorious interest in the beauty of nature and cooperation with nature, so that in some of those gardens you don't know where nature begins and art ends—this was a tremendous experience.

MOYERS: But, Joe, Tokyo today refutes that ideal in such flagrant ways. Tokyo is a city where nature has virtually disappeared, except as contained in small gardens that are still cherished by some of the people.

CAMPBELL: There is a saying in Japan, Rock with the waves. Or, as we say in boxing, Roll with the punches. It is only about a hundred and twenty-five years ago that Perry broke Japan open.

And in that time they have assimilated a terrific load of me-chanical material. But what I found in Japan was that they were holding their own head against this, and assimilating this machine world to themselves. When you go inside the buildings, then you are back in Japan. It is the outside that looks like New York.

MOYERS: "Holding their own head." That is an interesting idea because, even though the cities emerge around them, within the soul, the place where the inner person dwells, they are still, as you say, in accord with nature.

CAMPBELL: But in the Bible, eternity withdraws, and nature is corrupt, nature has fallen. In biblical thinking, we live in exile.

MOYERS: As we sit here and talk, there is one story after another of car bombings in Beirut—by the Muslims of the Christians, by the Christians of the Muslims, and by the Christians of the Christians. It strikes me that Marshall McLuhan was right when he said that television has made a global village of the world—but he didn't know the global village would be Beirut. What does that say to you?

CAMPBELL: It says to me that they don't know how to apply their religious ideas to contemporary life, and to human beings rather than just to their own community. It's a terrible example of the failure of religion to meet the modern world. These three mythologies are fighting it out. They have disqualified themselves for the future.

MOYERS: What kind of new myth do we need?

CAMPBELL: We need myths that will identify the individual not with his local group but with the planet. A model for that is the United States. Here were thirteen different little colony nations that decided to act in the mutual interest, without disregarding the individual interests of any one of them.

MOYERS: There is something about that on the Great Seal of the United States.

CAMPBELL: That's what the Great Seal is all about. I carry a copy of the Great Seal in my pocket in the form of a dollar bill. Here is the statement of the ideals that brought about the formation of the United States. Look at this dollar bill. Now here is the Great Seal of the United States. Look at the pyramid on the left. A pyramid has four sides. These are the four points of the compass. There is somebody at this point, there's somebody at that point, and there's somebody at this point. When you're down on the lower levels of this pyramid, you will be either on one side or on the other. But when you get up to the top, the points all come together, and there the eye of God opens.

MOYERS: And to them it was the god of reason.

CAMPBELL: Yes. This is the first nation in the world that was ever established on the basis of reason instead of simply warfare. These were eighteenth-century deists, these gentlemen. Over here we read, "In God We Trust." But that is not the god of the Bible. These men did not believe in a Fall. They did not think the mind of man was cut off from God. The mind of man, cleansed of secondary and merely temporal concerns, beholds with the radiance of a cleansed mirror a reflection of the rational mind of God. Reason puts you in touch with God. Consequently, for these men, there is no special revelation anywhere, and none is needed, because the mind of man cleared of its fallibilities is sufficiently capable of the knowledge of God. All people in the world are thus capable because all people in the world are capable of reason.

All men are capable of reason. That is the fundamental principle of democracy. Because everybody's mind is capable of true knowledge, you don't have to have a special authority, or a special revelation telling you that this is the way things should be.

MOYERS: And yet these symbols come from mythology.

CAMPBELL: Yes, but they come from a certain quality of mythology. It's not the mythology of a special revelation. The Hindus, for example, don't believe in special revelation. They speak of a state in which the ears have opened to the song of the universe. Here the eye has opened to the radiance of the mind of God. And that's a fundamental deist idea. Once you reject the idea of the Fall in the Garden, man is not cut off from his source.

Now back to the Great Seal. When you count the number of ranges on this pyramid, you find there are thirteen. And when you come to the bottom, there is an inscription in Roman numerals. It is, of course, 1776. Then, when you add one and seven and seven and six, you get twenty-one, which is the age of reason, is it not? It was in 1776 that the thirteen states declared independence. The number thirteen is the number of transformation and rebirth. At the Last Supper there were twelve apostles and one Christ, who was going to die and be reborn. Thirteen is the number of getting out of the field of the bounds of twelve into the transcendent. You have the twelve signs of the zodiac and the sun. These men were very conscious of the number thirteen as the number of resurrection and rebirth and new life, and they played it up here all the way through.

MOYERS: But, as a practical matter, there were thirteen states.

CAMPBELL: Yes, but wasn't that symbolic? This is not simply coincidental. This is the thirteen states as themselves symbolic of what they were.

MOYERS: That would explain the other inscription down there, "Novus Ordo Seclorum."

CAMPBELL: "A new order of the world." This is a new order of the world. And the saying above, "Annuit Coeptis," means "He has smiled on our accomplishments" or "our activities."

MOYERS: He—

CAMPBELL: He, the eye, what is represented by the eye. Reason. In Latin you wouldn't have to say "he," it could be "it" or "she" or "he." But the divine power has smiled on our doings. And so this new world has been built in the sense of God's original creation, and the reflection of God's original creation, through reason, has brought this about.

If you look behind that pyramid, you see a desert. If you look before it, you see plants growing. The desert, the tumult in Europe, wars and wars and wars—we have pulled ourselves out of it and created a state in the name of reason, not in the name of power, and out of that will come the flowerings of the new life. That's the sense of that part of the pyramid.

Now look at the right side of the dollar bill. Here's the eagle, the bird of Zeus. The eagle is the downcoming of the god into the field of time. The bird is the incarnation principle of the deity. This is the bald eagle, the American eagle. This is the American counterpart of the eagle of the highest god, Zeus.

He comes down, descending into the world of the pairs of opposites, the field of action. One mode of action is war and the other is peace. So in one of his feet the eagle holds thirteen arrows—that's the principle of war. In the other he holds a laurel leaf with thirteen leaves—that is the principle of peaceful conversation. The eagle is looking in the direction of the laurel. That is the way these idealists who founded our country would wish us to be looking—diplomatic relationships and so forth. But thank God he's got the arrows in the other foot, in case this doesn't work.

Now, what does the eagle represent? He represents what is indicated in this radiant sign above his head. I was lecturing once at the Foreign Service Institute in Washington on Hindu mythology, sociology, and politics. There's a saying in the Hindu book of politics that the ruler must hold in one hand the weapon of war, the big stick, and in the other the peaceful sound of the song of cooperative action. And there I was, standing with my two hands like this, and everybody in the room laughed. I couldn't understand. And then they began pointing. I looked back, and here was this picture of the eagle hanging on the wall behind my head in just the same posture that I was in. But when I looked, I also noticed this sign above his head, and that there were nine feathers in his tail. Nine is the number of the descent of the divine power into the world. When the Angelus rings, it rings nine times.

Now, over on the eagle's head are thirteen stars arranged in the form of a Star of David.

MOYERS: This used to be Solomon's Seal.

CAMPBELL: Yes. Do you know why it's called Solomon's Seal?

MOYERS: No.

CAMPBELL: Solomon used to seal monsters and giants and things into jars. You remember in the *Arabian Nights* when they'd open the jar and out would come the genie? I noticed the Solomon's Seal here, composed of thirteen stars, and then I saw that each of the triangles was a Pythagorean tetrakys.

MOYERS: The tetrakys being?

CAMPBELL: This is a triangle composed of ten points, one point in the middle and four points to each side, adding up to nine: one, two, three, four/five, six, seven/eight, nine. This is the primary symbol of Pythagorean philosophy, susceptible of a number of interrelated mythological, cosmological, psychological, and sociological interpretations, one of which is the dot at the apex as representing the creative center out of which the universe and all things have come.

MOYERS: The center of energy, then?

CAMPBELL: Yes. The initial sound (a Christian might say, the creative Word), out of which the whole world was precipitated, the big bang, the pouring of the transcendent energy into and expanding through the field of time. As soon as it enters the field of time, it breaks into pairs of opposites, the one becomes two. Now, when you have two, there are just three ways in which they can relate to one another: one way is of this one dominant over that; another way is of that one dominant over this; and a third way is of the two in balanced accord. It is then, finally, out of these three manners of relationship that all things within the four quarters of space derive.

There is a verse in Lao-tzu's *Tao-te Ching* which states that out of the Tao, out of the transcendent, comes the One. Out of the One come Two; out of the Two come Three; and out of the Three come all things.

So what I suddenly realized when I recognized that in the Great Seal of the United States there were two of these symbolic triangles interlocked was that we now had thirteen points, for our thirteen original states, and that there were now, furthermore, no less than six apexes, one above, one below, and four (so to say) to the four quarters. The sense of this, it seemed to me, might be that from above or below, or from any point of the compass, the creative Word might be heard, which is the great thesis of democracy. Democracy assumes that anybody from any quarter can speak, and speak truth, because his mind is not cut off from the truth. All he has to do is clear out his passions and then speak.

So what you have here on the dollar bill is the eagle representing this wonderful image of the way in which the transcendent manifests itself in the world. That's what the United States is founded on. If you're going to govern properly, you've got to govern from the apex of the triangle, in the sense of the world eye at the top.

Now, when I was a boy, we were given George Washington's farewell address and told to outline the whole thing, every single statement in relation to every other one. So I remember it absolutely. Washington said, "As a result of our revolution, we have disengaged ourselves from involvement in the chaos of Europe." His last word was that we not engage in foreign alliances. Well, we held on to his words until the First World War. And then we canceled the Declaration of Independence and rejoined the British conquest of the planet. And so we are now on one side of the pyramid. We've moved from one to two. We are politically, historically, now a member of one side of an argument. We do not represent that principle of the eye up there. And all of our concerns have to do with economics and politics and not with the voice and sound of reason.

MOYERS: The voice of reason—is that the philosophical way suggested by these mythological symbols?

CAMPBELL: That's right. Here you have the important transition that took place about 500 B.C. This is the date of the Buddha and of Pythagoras and Confucius and Lao-tzu, if there was a Lao-tzu. This is the awakening of man's reason. No longer is he informed and governed by the animal powers. No longer is he guided by the analogy of the planted earth, no longer by the courses of the planets—but by reason.

MOYERS: The way of—

CAMPBELL: —the way of man. And of course what destroys reason is passion. The principal passion in politics is greed. That is what pulls you down. And that's why we're on this side instead of the top of the pyramid.

MOYERS: That's why our founders opposed religious intolerance—

CAMPBELL: That was out entirely. And that's why they rejected the idea of the Fall, too. All men are competent to know the mind of God. There is no revelation special to any people.

MOYERS: I can see how, from your years of scholarship and deep immersion in these mythological symbols, you would read the Great Seal that way. But wouldn't it have been surprising to most of those men who were deists, as you say, to discover these mythological connotations about their effort to build a new country?

CAMPBELL: Well, why did they use them?

MOYERS: Aren't a lot of these Masonic symbols?

CAMPBELL: They are Masonic signs, and the meaning of the Pythagorean tetrakys has been known for centuries. The information would have been found in Thomas Jefferson's library. These were, after all, learned men. The eighteenth-century Enlightenment was a world of learned gentlemen. We haven't had men of that quality in politics very much. It's an enormous good fortune for our nation that that cluster of gentlemen had the power and were in a position to influence events at that time.

MOYERS: What explains the relationship between these symbols and the Masons, and the fact that so many of these founding fathers belonged to the Masonic order? Is the Masonic order an expression somehow of mythological thinking?

CAMPBELL: Yes, I think it is. This is a scholarly attempt to reconstruct an order of initiation that would result in spiritual revelation. These founding fathers who were Masons actually studied what they could of Egyptian lore. In Egypt, the pyramid represents the primordial hillock. After the annual flood of the Nile begins to sink down, the first hillock is symbolic of the reborn world. That's what this seal represents.

MOYERS: You sometimes confound me with the seeming contradiction at the heart of your own belief system. On the one hand, you praise these men who were inspirers and creatures of the Age of Reason, and on the other hand, you salute Luke Skywalker in *Star Wars* for that moment when he says, "Turn off the computer and trust your feelings." How do you reconcile the role of science, which is reason, with the role of faith, which is religion?

CAMPBELL: No, no, you have to distinguish between reason and thinking.

MOYERS: Distinguish between reason and thinking? If I think, am I not reasoning things out?

CAMPBELL: Yes, your reason is one kind of thinking. But thinking things out isn't necessarily reason in this sense. Figuring out how you can break through a wall is not reason. The mouse who figures out, after it bumps its nose here, that perhaps he can get around there, is figuring something out the way we figure things out. But that's not reason. Reason has to do with finding the ground of being and the fundamental structuring of order of the universe.

MOYERS: So when these men talked about the eye of God being reason, they were saying that the ground of our being as a society, as a culture, as a people, derives from the fundamental character of the universe?

CAMPBELL: That's what this first pyramid says. This is the pyramid of the world, and this is the pyramid of our society, and they are of the same order. This is God's creation, and this is our society.

MOYERS: We have a mythology for the way of the animal powers. We have a mythology for the way of the seeded earth —fertility, creation, the mother goddess. And we have a mythology for the celestial lights, for the heavens. But in modern times we have moved beyond the animal powers, beyond nature and the seeded earth, and the stars no longer interest us except as exotic curiosities and the terrain of space travel. Where are we now in our mythology for the way of man?

CAMPBELL: We can't have a mythology for a long, long time to come. Things are changing too fast to become mythologized.

MOYERS: How do we live without myths then?

CAMPBELL: The individual has to find an aspect of myth that relates to his own life. Myth basically serves four functions. The first is the mystical function—that is the one I've been speaking about, realizing what a wonder the universe is, and what a wonder you are, and experiencing awe before this mystery. Myth opens the world to the dimension of mystery, to the realization of the mystery that underlies all forms. If you lose that, you don't have

MYTH AND THE MODERN WORLD 39

a mythology. If mystery is manifest through all things, the universe becomes, as it were, a holy picture. You are always addressing the transcendent mystery through the conditions of your actual world.

The second is a cosmological dimension, the dimension with which science is concerned—showing you what the shape of the universe is, but showing it in such a way that the mystery again comes through. Today we tend to think that scientists have all the answers. But the great ones tell us, "No, we haven't got all the answers. We're telling you how it works—but what is it?" You strike a match, what's fire? You can tell me about oxidation, but that doesn't tell me a thing.

The third function is the sociological one—supporting and validating a certain social order. And here's where the myths vary enormously from place to place. You can have a whole mythology for polygamy, a whole mythology for monogamy. Either one's okay. It depends on where you are. It is this sociological function of myth that has taken over in our world—and it is out of date.

MOYERS: What do you mean?

CAMPBELL: Ethical laws. The laws of life as it should be in the good society. All of Yahweh's pages and pages and pages of what kind of clothes to wear, how to behave to each other, and so forth, in the first millennium B.C.

But there is a fourth function of myth, and this is the one that I think everyone must try today to relate to—and that is the pedagogical function, of how to live a human lifetime under any circumstances. Myths can teach you that.

MOYERS: So the old story, so long known and transmitted through the generations, isn't functioning, and we have not yet learned a new one?

CAMPBELL: The story that we have in the West, so far as it is based on the Bible, is based on a view of the universe that belongs to the first millennium B.C. It does not accord with our concept either of the universe or of the dignity of man. It belongs entirely somewhere else.

We have today to learn to get back into accord with the wisdom of nature and realize again our brotherhood with the animals and with the water and the sea. To say that the divinity informs the world and all things is condemned as pantheism. But pan*theism* is a misleading word. It suggests that a personal god is supposed to inhabit the world, but that is not the idea at all. The idea is trans-theological. It is of an undefinable, inconceivable mystery, thought of as a power, that is the source and end and supporting ground of all life and being.

MOYERS: Don't you think modern Americans have rejected the ancient idea of nature as a divinity because it would have kept us from achieving dominance over nature? How can you cut down trees and uproot the land and turn the rivers into real estate without killing God?

CAMPBELL: Yes, but that's not simply a characteristic of modern Americans, that is the biblical condemnation of nature which they inherited from their own religion and brought with them, mainly from England. God is separate from nature, and nature is condemned of God. It's right there in Genesis: we are to be the masters of the world.

But if you will think of ourselves as coming out of the earth, rather than having been thrown in here from somewhere else, you see that we are the earth, we are the consciousness of the earth. These are the eyes of the earth. And this is the voice of the earth.

MOYERS: Scientists are beginning to talk quite openly about the Gaia principle.

CAMPBELL: There you are, the whole planet as an organism.

MOYERS: Mother Earth. Will new myths come from this image?

CAMPBELL: Well, something might. You can't predict what a myth is going to be any more than you can predict what you're going to dream tonight. Myths and dreams come from the same place. They come from realizations of some kind that have then to find expression in symbolic form. And the only myth that is going to be worth thinking about in the immediate future is one that is talking about the planet, not the city, not these people, but the planet, and everybody on it. That's my main thought for what the future myth is going to be.

And what it will have to deal with will be exactly what all myths have dealt with—the maturation of the individual, from dependency through adulthood, through maturity, and then to the exit; and then how to relate to this society and how to relate this society to the world of nature and the cosmos. That's what the myths have all talked about, and what this one's got to talk about. But the society that it's got to talk about is the society of the planet. And until that gets going, you don't have anything.

MOYERS: So you suggest that from this begins the new myth of our time?

CAMPBELL: Yes, this is the ground of what the myth is to be. It's already here: the eye of reason, not of my nationality; the eye of reason, not of my religious community; the eye of reason, not of my linguistic community. Do you see? And this would be the philosophy for the planet, not for this group, that group, or the other group.

When you see the earth from the moon, you don't see any divisions there of nations or states. This might be the symbol, really, for the new mythology to come. That is the country that we are going to be celebrating. And those are the people that we are one with.

MOYERS: No one embodies that ethic to me more clearly in the works you have collected than Chief Seattle.

CAMPBELL: Chief Seattle was one of the last spokesmen of the Paleolithic moral order. In about 1852, the United States

Government inquired about buying the tribal lands for the ar-
riving people of the United States, and Chief Seattle wrote a
marvelous letter in reply. His letter expresses the moral, really,
of our whole discussion.

"The President in Washington sends word that he wishes to
buy our land. But how can you buy or sell the sky? The land?
The idea is strange to us. If we do not own the freshness of the
air and the sparkle of the water, how can you buy them?

"Every part of this earth is sacred to my people. Every shining
pine needle, every sandy shore, every mist in the dark woods,
every meadow, every humming insect. All are holy in the memory and experience of my people.

"We know the sap which courses through the trees as we know
the blood that courses through our veins. We are part of the
earth and it is part of us. The perfumed flowers are our sisters.
The bear, the deer, the great eagle, these are our brothers. The
rocky crests, the juices in the meadow, the body heat of the
pony, and man, all belong to the same family.

"The shining water that moves in the streams and rivers is
not just water, but the blood of our ancestors. If we sell you our
land, you must remember that it is sacred. Each ghostly reflection
in the clear waters of the lakes tells of events and memories in
the life of my people. The water's murmur is the voice of my
father's father.

"The rivers are our brothers. They quench our thirst. They
carry our canoes and feed our children. So you must give to the
rivers the kindness you would give any brother.

"If we sell you our land, remember that the air is precious to
us, that the air shares its spirit with all the life it supports. The
wind that gave our grandfather his first breath also receives his
last sigh. The wind also gives our children the spirit of life. So
if we sell you our land, you must keep it apart and sacred, as a
place where man can go to taste the wind that is sweetened by
the meadow flowers.

"Will you teach your children what we have taught our children? That the earth is our mother? What befalls the earth befalls all the sons of the earth.

"This we know: the earth does not belong to man, man belongs to the earth. All things are connected like the blood that unites us all. Man did not weave the web of life, he is merely a strand in it. Whatever he does to the web, he does to himself.

"One thing we know: our god is also your god. The earth is precious to him and to harm the earth is to heap contempt on its creator.

"Your destiny is a mystery to us. What will happen when the buffalo are all slaughtered? The wild horses tamed? What will happen when the secret corners of the forest are heavy with the scent of many men and the view of the ripe hills is blotted by talking wires? Where will the thicket be? Gone! Where will the eagle be? Gone! And what is it to say goodbye to the swift pony and the hunt? The end of living and the beginning of survival.

"When the last Red Man has vanished with his wilderness and his memory is only the shadow of a cloud moving across the prairie, will these shores and forests still be here? Will there be any of the spirit of my people left?

"We love this earth as a newborn loves its mother's heartbeat. So, if we sell you our land, love it as we have loved it. Care for it as we have cared for it. Hold in your mind the memory of the land as it is when you receive it. Preserve the land for all children and love it, as God loves us all.

"As we are part of the land, you too are part of the land. This earth is precious to us. It is also precious to you. One thing we know: there is only one God. No man, be he Red Man or White Man, can be apart. We *are* brothers after all."

II

THE JOURNEY INWARD

One thing that comes out in myths is that at the bottom of the abyss comes the voice of salvation. The black moment is the moment when the real message of transformation is going to come. At the darkest moment comes the light.

MOYERS: Someone asked me, "Why are you drawn to these myths? What do you see in what Joseph Campbell is saying?" And I answered, "These myths speak to me because they express what I know inside is true." Why is this so? Why does it seem that these stories tell me what I know inside is true? Does that come from the ground of my being, the unconscious that I have inherited from all that has come before me?

CAMPBELL: That's right. You've got the same body, with the same organs and energies, that Cro-Magnon man had thirty thousand years ago. Living a human life in New York City or living a human life in the caves, you go through the same stages of childhood, coming to sexual maturity, transformation of the dependency of childhood into the responsibility of manhood or womanhood, marriage, then failure of the body, gradual loss of its powers, and death. You have the same body, the same bodily experiences, and so you respond to the same images. For example, a constant image is that of the conflict of the eagle and the serpent. The serpent bound to the earth, the eagle in spiritual flight—isn't that conflict something we all experience? And then, when the two amalgamate, we get a wonderful dragon, a serpent with wings. All over the earth people recognize these images. Whether I'm reading Polynesian or Iroquois or Egyptian myths, the images are the same, and they are talking about the same problems.

MOYERS: They just wear different costumes when they appear at different times?

CAMPBELL: Yes. It's as though the same play were taken from one place to another, and at each place the local players put on local costumes and enact the same old play.

MOYERS: And these mythic images are carried forward from generation to generation, almost unconsciously.

CAMPBELL: That's utterly fascinating, because they are speaking about the deep mystery of yourself and everything else. It is a *mysterium*, a mystery, *tremendum et fascinans*—tremendous, horrific, because it smashes all of your fixed notions of things, and at the same time utterly fascinating, because it's of your own nature and being. When you start thinking about these things, about the inner mystery, inner life, the eternal life, there aren't too many images for you to use. You begin, on your own, to have the images that are already present in some other system of thought.

MOYERS: There was a sense during medieval times of reading the world as if the world had messages for you.

CAMPBELL: Oh, it certainly does. The myths help you read the messages. They tell you the typical probabilities.

MOYERS: Give me an example.

CAMPBELL: One thing that comes out in myths, for example,

is that at the bottom of the abyss comes the voice of salvation. The black moment is the moment when the real message of transformation is going to come. At the darkest moment comes the light.

MOYERS: Like Roethke's poem, "In a Dark Time, the Eye Begins to See." You're saying that myths have brought this consciousness to you.

CAMPBELL: I live with these myths, and they tell me this all the time. This is the problem that can be metaphorically understood as identifying with the Christ in you. The Christ in you doesn't die. The Christ in you survives death and resurrects. Or you can identify that with Shiva. I am Shiva—this is the great meditation of the yogis in the Himalayas.

MOYERS: And heaven, that desired goal of most people, is within us.

CAMPBELL: Heaven and hell are within us, and all the gods are within us. This is the great realization of the Upanishads of India in the ninth century B.C. All the gods, all the heavens, all the worlds, are within us. They are magnified dreams, and dreams are manifestations in image form of the energies of the body in conflict with each other. That is what myth is. Myth is a manifestation in symbolic images, in metaphorical images, of the energies of the organs of the body in conflict with each other. This organ wants this, that organ wants that. The brain is one of the organs.

MOYERS: So when we dream, we are fishing in some vast ocean of mythology that—

CAMPBELL: —that goes down and down and down. You can get all mixed up with complexes, you know, things like that, but really, as the Polynesian saying goes, you are then "standing on a whale fishing for minnows." We are standing on a whale. The ground of being is the ground of our being, and when we simply turn outward, we see all of these little problems here and there. But, if we look inward, we see that we are the source of them all.

MOYERS: You talk about mythology existing here and now in dreamtime. What is dreamtime?

CAMPBELL: This is the time you get into when you go to sleep and have a dream that talks about permanent conditions within your own psyche as they relate to the temporal conditions of your life right now.

MOYERS: Explain that.

CAMPBELL: For example, you may be worried about whether you are going to pass an exam. Then you have a dream of some kind of failure, and you find that failure will be associated with many other failures in your life. They are all piled up together there. Freud says even the most fully expounded dream is not really fully expounded. The dream is an inexhaustible source of spiritual information about yourself.

Now the level of dream of "Will I pass the exam?" or "Should I marry this girl?"—that is purely personal. But, on another level, the problem of passing an exam is not simply a personal problem. Everyone has to pass a threshold of some kind. That is an archetypal thing. So there is a basic mythological theme there even though it is a personal dream. These two levels—the personal aspect and then the big general problem of which the person's problem is a local example—are found in all cultures. For example, everyone has the problem of facing death. This is a standard mystery.

MOYERS: What do we learn from our dreams?

CAMPBELL: You learn about yourself.

MOYERS: How do we pay attention to our dreams?

CAMPBELL: All you have to do is remember your dream in

the first place, and write it down. Then take one little fraction of the dream, one or two images or ideas, and associate with them. Write down what comes to your mind, and again what comes to your mind, and again. You'll find that the dream is based on a body of experiences that have some kind of significance in your life and that you didn't know were influencing you. Soon the next dream will come along, and your interpretation will go further.

MOYERS: A man once told me that he didn't remember dreaming until he retired. Suddenly, having no place to focus his energy, he began to dream and dream and dream. Do you think that we tend to overlook the significance of dreaming in our modern society?

CAMPBELL: Ever since Freud's *Interpretation of Dreams* was published, there has been a recognition of the importance of dreams. But even before that there were dream interpretations. People had superstitious notions about dreams—for example, "Something is going to happen because I dreamed it is going to happen."

MOYERS: Why is a myth different from a dream?

CAMPBELL: Oh, because a dream is a personal experience of that deep, dark ground that is the support of our conscious lives, and a myth is the society's dream. The myth is the public dream and the dream is the private myth. If your private myth, your dream, happens to coincide with that of the society, you are in good accord with your group. If it isn't, you've got an adventure in the dark forest ahead of you.

MOYERS: So if my private dreams are in accord with the public mythology, I'm more likely to live healthily in that society. But if my private dreams are out of step with the public—

CAMPBELL: —you'll be in trouble. If you're forced to live in that system, you'll be a neurotic.

MOYERS: But aren't many visionaries and even leaders and heroes close to the edge of neuroticism?

CAMPBELL: Yes, they are.

MOYERS: How do you explain that?

CAMPBELL: They've moved out of the society that would have protected them, and into the dark forest, into the world of fire, of original experience. Original experience has not been interpreted for you, and so you've got to work out your life for yourself. Either you can take it or you can't. You don't have to go far off the interpreted path to find yourself in very difficult situations. The courage to face the trials and to bring a whole new body of possibilities into the field of interpreted experience for other people to experience—that is the hero's deed.

MOYERS: You say dreams come up from the psyche.

CAMPBELL: I don't know where else they come from. They come from the imagination, don't they? The imagination is grounded in the energy of the organs of the body, and these are the same in all human beings. Since imagination comes out of one biological ground, it is bound to produce certain themes. Dreams are dreams. There are certain characteristics of dreams that can be enumerated, no matter who is dreaming them.

MOYERS: I think of a dream as something very private, while a myth is something very public.

CAMPBELL: On some levels a private dream runs into truly mythic themes and can't be interpreted except by an analogy with a myth. Jung speaks of two orders of dream, the personal dream and the archetypal dream, or the dream of mythic dimension. You can interpret a personal dream by association, figuring out what it is talking about in your own life, or in relation to your own personal problem. But every now and then a dream comes up that is pure myth, that carries a mythic theme, or that is said, for example, to come from the Christ within.

MOYERS: From the archetypal person within us, the archetypal self we are.

CAMPBELL: That's right. Now there is another, deeper meaning of dreamtime—which is of a time that is no time, just an enduring state of being. There is an important myth from Indonesia that tells of this mythological age and its termination. In the beginning, according to this story, the ancestors were not distinguished as to sex. There were no births, there were no deaths. Then a great public dance was celebrated, and in the course of the dance one of the participants was trampled to death and torn to pieces, and the pieces were buried. At the moment of that killing the sexes became separated, so that death was now balanced by begetting, begetting by death, while from the buried parts of the dismembered body food plants grew. Time had come into being, death, birth, and the killing and eating of other living beings, for the preservation of life. The timeless time of the beginning had been terminated by a communal crime, a deliberate murder or sacrifice.

Now, one of the main problems of mythology is reconciling the mind to this brutal precondition of all life, which lives by the killing and eating of lives. You don't kid yourself by eating only vegetables, either, for they, too, are alive. So the essence of life is this eating of itself! Life lives on lives, and the reconciliation of the human mind and sensibilities to that fundamental fact is one of the functions of some of those very brutal rites in which the ritual consists chiefly of killing—in imitation, as it were, of that first, primordial crime, out of which arose this temporal world, in which we all participate. The reconciliation of mind to the conditions of life is fundamental to all creation stories. They're very like each other in this respect.

MOYERS: Take the creation story in Genesis, for example. How is it like other stories?

CAMPBELL: Well, you read from Genesis, and I'll read from creation stories in other cultures, and we'll see.

MOYERS: Genesis 1: "In the beginning God created the heavens and the earth. The earth was without form and void, and darkness was upon the face of the deep."

CAMPBELL: This is from "The Song of the World," a legend of the Pima Indians of Arizona: "In the beginning there was only darkness everywhere—darkness and water. And the darkness gathered thick in places, crowding together and then separating, crowding and separating. . . ."

MOYERS: Genesis 1: "And the Spirit of God was moving over the face of the waters. And God said, 'Let there be light'; and there was light."

CAMPBELL: And this is from the Hindu Upanishads, from about the eighth century B.C.: "In the beginning, there was only the great self reflected in the form of a person. Reflecting, it found nothing but itself. Then its first word was, 'This am I.' "

MOYERS: Genesis 1: "So God created man in his own image, in the image of God he created him; male and female he created them. And God blessed them, and God said to them, 'Be fruitful and multiply.' "

CAMPBELL: Now, this is from a legend of the Bassari people of West Africa: "Unumbotte made a human being. Its name was Man. Unumbotte next made an antelope, named Antelope. Unumbotte made a snake, named Snake. . . . And Unumbotte said to them, 'The earth has not yet been pounded. You must pound the ground smooth where you are sitting.' Unumbotte gave them seeds of all kinds, and said: 'Go plant these.' "

MOYERS: Genesis 2: "Thus the heavens and the earth were finished, and all the host of them. And on the seventh day God finished his work which he had done. . . ."

CAMPBELL: And now again from the Pima Indians: "I make the world and lo, the world is finished. Thus I make the world, and lo! The world is finished."

MOYERS: And Genesis 1: "And God saw everything that he had made, and behold, it was very good."

CAMPBELL: And from the Upanishads: "Then he realized, I indeed, I am this creation, for I have poured it forth from myself. In that way he became this creation. Verily, he who knows this becomes in this creation a creator."

That is the clincher there. When you know this, then you have identified with the creative principle, which is the God power in the world, which means in you. It is beautiful.

MOYERS: But Genesis continues: " 'Have you eaten of the tree of which I commanded you not to eat?' The man said, 'The woman whom thou gavest to be with me, she gave me fruit of the tree, and I ate.' Then the Lord God said to the woman, 'What is this that you have done?' The woman said, 'The serpent beguiled me, and I ate.' "

You talk about buck passing, it starts very early.

CAMPBELL: Yes, it has been tough on serpents. The Bassari legend continues in the same way. "One day Snake said, 'We too should eat these fruits. Why must we go hungry?' Antelope said, 'But we don't know anything about this fruit.' Then Man and his wife took some of the fruit and ate it. Unumbotte came down from the sky and asked, 'Who ate the fruit?' They answered, 'We did.' Unumbotte asked, 'Who told you that you could eat that fruit?' They replied, 'Snake did.' " It is very much the same story.

MOYERS: What do you make of it—that in these two stories the principal actors point to someone else as the initiator of the Fall?

CAMPBELL: Yes, but it turns out to be the snake. In both of these stories the snake is the symbol of life throwing off the past and continuing to live.

MOYERS: Why?

CAMPBELL: The power of life causes the snake to shed its skin, just as the moon sheds its shadow. The serpent sheds its skin to be born again, as the moon its shadow to be born again. They are equivalent symbols. Sometimes the serpent is represented as a circle eating its own tail. That's an image of life. Life sheds one generation after another, to be born again. The serpent represents immortal energy and consciousness engaged in the field of time, constantly throwing off death and being born again. There is something tremendously terrifying about life when you look at it that way. And so the serpent carries in itself the sense of both the fascination and the terror of life.

Furthermore, the serpent represents the primary function of life, mainly eating. Life consists in eating other creatures. You don't think about that very much when you make a nice-looking meal. But what you're doing is eating something that was recently alive. And when you look at the beauty of nature, and you see the birds picking around—they're eating things. You see the cows grazing, they're eating things. The serpent is a traveling alimentary canal, that's about all it is. And it gives you that primary sense of shock, of life in its most primal quality. There is no arguing with that animal at all. Life lives by killing and eating itself, casting off death and being reborn, like the moon. This is one of the mysteries that these symbolic, paradoxical forms try to represent.

Now the snake in most cultures is given a positive interpretation. In India, even the most poisonous snake, the cobra, is a sacred animal, and the mythological Serpent King is the next thing to the Buddha. The serpent represents the power of life engaged in the field of time, and of death, yet eternally alive. The world is but its shadow—the falling skin.

The serpent was revered in the American Indian traditions, too. The serpent was thought of as a very important power to be made friends with. Go down to the pueblos, for example, and watch the snake dance of the Hopi, where they take the snakes in their mouths and make friends with them and then send them back to the hills. The snakes are sent back to carry the human message to the hills, just as they have brought the message of the hills to the humans. The interplay of man and nature is illustrated in this relationship with the serpent. A serpent flows like water and so is watery, but its tongue continually flashes fire. So you have the pair of opposites together in the serpent.

MOYERS: In the Christian story the serpent is the seducer.

CAMPBELL: That amounts to a refusal to affirm life. In the biblical tradition we have inherited, life is corrupt, and every natural impulse is sinful unless it has been circumcised or baptized. The serpent was the one who brought sin into the world. And the woman was the one who handed the apple to man. This identification of the woman with sin, of the serpent with sin, and thus of life with sin, is the twist that has been given to the whole story in the biblical myth and doctrine of the Fall.

MOYERS: Does the idea of woman as sinner appear in other mythologies?

CAMPBELL: No, I don't know of it elsewhere. The closest thing to it would be perhaps Pandora with Pandora's box, but that's not sin, that's just trouble. The idea in the biblical tradition of the Fall is that nature as we know it is corrupt, sex in itself is corrupt, and the female as the epitome of sex is a corrupter. Why was the knowledge of good and evil forbidden to Adam and Eve? Without that knowledge, we'd all be a bunch of babies still in Eden, without any participation in life. Woman brings life into the world. Eve is the mother of this temporal world. Formerly you had a dreamtime paradise there in the Garden of Eden—no time, no birth, no death—no life. The serpent, who dies and is resurrected, shedding its skin and renewing its life, is the lord of the central tree, where time and eternity come together. He is the primary god, actually, in the Garden of Eden. Yahweh, the one who walks there in the cool of the evening, is just a visitor. The Garden is the serpent's place. It is an old, old story. We have Sumerian seals from as early as 3500 B.C. showing the serpent and the tree and the goddess, with the

goddess giving the fruit of life to a visiting male. The old mythology of the goddess is right there.

Now, I saw a fantastic thing in a movie, years and years ago,
of a Burmese snake priestess, who had to bring rain to her people
by climbing up a mountain path, calling a king cobra from his
den, and actually kissing him three times on the nose. There
was the cobra, the giver of life, the giver of rain, as a divine
positive figure, not a negative one.

MOYERS: But how do you explain the difference between that
image and the image of the snake in Genesis?

CAMPBELL: There is actually a historical explanation based
on the coming of the Hebrews into Canaan and their subjugation
of the people of Canaan. The principal divinity of the people of
Canaan was the Goddess, and associated with the Goddess is
the serpent. This is the symbol of the mystery of life. The male-
god-oriented group rejected it. In other words, there is a historical
rejection of the Mother Goddess implied in the story of the
Garden of Eden.

MOYERS: It does seem that this story has done women a great
disservice by casting Eve as responsible for the Fall. Why are
women the ones held responsible for the downfall?

CAMPBELL: They represent life. Man doesn't enter life except
by woman, and so it is woman who brings us into this world of
pairs of opposites and suffering.

MOYERS: What is the myth of Adam and Eve trying to tell us
about the pairs of opposites? What is the meaning?

CAMPBELL: It started with the sin, you see—in other words,
moving out of the mythological dreamtime zone of the Garden
of Paradise, where there is no time, and where men and women
don't even know that they are different from each other. The
two are just creatures. God and man are practically the same.
God walks in the cool of the evening in the garden where they
are. And then they eat the apple, the knowledge of the opposites.

And when they discover they are different, the man and woman cover their shame. You see, they had not thought of themselves as opposites. Male and female is one opposition. Another opposition is the human and God. Good and evil is a third opposition. The primary oppositions are the sexual and that between human beings and God. Then comes the idea of good and evil in the world. And so Adam and Eve have thrown themselves out of the Garden of Timeless Unity, you might say, just by that act of recognizing duality. To move out into the world, you have to act in terms of pairs of opposites.

There's a Hindu image that shows a triangle, which is the Mother Goddess, and a dot in the center of the triangle, which is the energy of the transcendent entering the field of time. And then from this triangle there come pairs of triangles in all directions. Out of one comes two. All things in the field of time are pairs of opposites. So this is the shift of consciousness from the consciousness of identity to the consciousness of participation in duality. And then you are into the field of time.

MOYERS: Is the story trying to tell us that, prior to what happened in this Garden to destroy us, there was a unity of life?

CAMPBELL: It's a matter of planes of consciousness. It doesn't have to do with anything that happened. There is the plane of consciousness where you can identify yourself with that which transcends pairs of opposites.

MOYERS: Which is?

CAMPBELL: Unnameable. Unnameable. It is transcendent of all names.

MOYERS: God?

CAMPBELL: "God" is an ambiguous word in our language because it appears to refer to something that is known. But the transcendent is unknowable and unknown. God is transcendent, finally, of anything like the name "God." God is beyond names and forms. Meister Eckhart said that the ultimate and highest leave-taking is leaving God for God, leaving your notion of God for an experience of that which transcends all notions.

The mystery of life is beyond all human conception. Everything we know is within the terminology of the concepts of being and not being, many and single, true and untrue. We always think in terms of opposites. But God, the ultimate, is beyond the pairs of opposites, that is all there is to it.

MOYERS: Why do we think in terms of opposites?

CAMPBELL: Because we can't think otherwise.

MOYERS: That's the nature of reality in our time.

CAMPBELL: That's the nature of our *experience* of reality.

MOYERS: Man-woman, life-death, good-evil—

CAMPBELL: —I and you, this and that, true and untrue— every one of them has its opposite. But mythology suggests that behind that duality there is a singularity over which this plays like a shadow game. "Eternity is in love with the productions of time," says the poet Blake.

MOYERS: What does that mean, "Eternity is in love with the productions of time"?

CAMPBELL: The source of temporal life is eternity. Eternity pours itself into the world. It is a basic mythic idea of the god who becomes many in us. In India, the god who lies in me is called the "inhabitant" of the body. To identify with that divine, immortal aspect of yourself is to identify yourself with divinity.

Now, eternity is beyond all categories of thought. This is an important point in all of the great Oriental religions. We want to think about God. God is a thought. God is a name. God is an idea. But its reference is to something that transcends all thinking. The ultimate mystery of being is beyond all categories of thought. As Kant said, the thing in itself is no thing. It transcends thingness, it goes past anything that could be thought. The best things can't be told because they transcend thought.

The second best are misunderstood, because those are the thoughts that are supposed to refer to that which can't be thought about. The third best are what we talk about. And myth is that field of reference to what is absolutely transcendent.

MOYERS: What can't be known or named except in our feeble attempt to clothe it in language.

CAMPBELL: The ultimate word in our English language for that which is transcendent is God. But then you have a concept, don't you see? You think of God as the father. Now, in religions where the god or creator is the mother, the whole world is her body. There is nowhere else. The male god is usually somewhere else. But male and female are two aspects of one principle. The division of life into sexes was a late division. Biologically, the amoeba isn't male and female. The early cells are just cells. They divide and become two by asexual reproduction. I don't know at what levels sexuality comes in, but it's late. That's why it's absurd to speak of God as of either this sex or that sex. The divine power is antecedent to sexual separation.

MOYERS: But isn't the only way a human being can try to grope with this immense idea to assign it a language that he or she understands? God, he, God, she—

CAMPBELL: Yes, but you don't understand it if you think it is a he or a she. The he or a she is a springboard to spring you into the transcendent, and transcendent means to "transcend," to go past duality. Everything in the field of time and space is *dual*. The incarnation appears either as male or as female, and each of us is the incarnation of God. You're born in only one aspect of your actual metaphysical duality, you might say. This is represented in the mystery religions, where an individual goes through a series of initiations opening him out inside into a deeper and deeper depth of himself, and there comes a moment when he realizes that he is both mortal and immortal, both male and female.

MOYERS: Do you think there was such a place as the Garden of Eden?

CAMPBELL: Of course not. The Garden of Eden is a metaphor for that innocence that is innocent of time, innocent of opposites, and that is the prime center out of which consciousness then becomes aware of the changes.

MOYERS: But if there is in the idea of Eden this innocence, what happens to it? Isn't it shaken, dominated, and corrupted by fear?

CAMPBELL: That's it. There is a wonderful story of the deity, of the Self that said, "I am." As soon as it said "I am," it was afraid.

MOYERS: Why?

CAMPBELL: It was an entity now, in time. Then it thought, "What should I be afraid of, I'm the only thing that is." And as soon as it said that, it felt lonesome, and wished that there were another, and so it felt desire. It swelled, split in two, became male and female, and begot the world.

Fear is the first experience of the fetus in the womb. There's a Czechoslovakian psychiatrist, Stanislav Grof, now living in California, who for years treated people with LSD. And he found that some of them re-experienced birth and, in the re-experiencing of birth, the first stage is that of the fetus in the womb, without any sense of "I" or of being. Then shortly before birth the rhythm of the uterus begins, and there's terror! Fear is the first thing, the thing that says "I." Then comes the horrific stage of getting born, the difficult passage through the birth canal, and then—my God, light! Can you imagine! Isn't it amazing that this repeats just what the myth says—that Self said, "I am," and immediately felt fear? And then when it realized it was alone, it felt desire for another and became two. That is the breaking into the world of light and the pairs of opposites.

MOYERS: What does it say about what all of us have in com-

mon that so many of these stories contain similar elements—
the forbidden fruit, the woman? For example, these myths, these
creation stories, contain a "thou shalt not." Man and woman
rebel against that prohibition and move out on their own. After
years and years of reading these things, I am still overwhelmed
at the similarities in cultures that are far, far apart.

CAMPBELL: There is a standard folk tale motif called The One
Forbidden Thing. Remember Bluebeard, who says to his wife,
"Don't open that closet"? And then one always disobeys. In the
Old Testament story God points out the one forbidden thing.
Now, God must have known very well that man was going to
eat the forbidden fruit. But it was by doing that that man became
the initiator of his own life. Life really began with that act of
disobedience.

MOYERS: How do you explain these similarities?

CAMPBELL: There are two explanations. One explanation is
that the human psyche is essentially the same all over the world.
The psyche is the inward experience of the human body, which
is essentially the same in all human beings, with the same organs,
the same instincts, the same impulses, the same conflicts, the
same fears. Out of this common ground have come what Jung
has called the archetypes, which are the common ideas of myths.

MOYERS: What are archetypes?

CAMPBELL: They are elementary ideas, what could be called
"ground" ideas. These ideas Jung spoke of as archetypes of the
unconscious. "Archetype" is the better term because "elementary
idea" suggests headwork. Archetype of the unconscious means
it comes from below. The difference between the Jungian archetypes of the unconscious and Freud's complexes is that the
archetypes of the unconscious are manifestations of the organs
of the body and their powers. Archetypes are biologically
grounded, whereas the Freudian unconscious is a collection of
repressed traumatic experiences from the individual's lifetime.

The Freudian unconscious is a personal unconscious, it is biographical. The Jungian archetypes of the unconscious are biological. The biographical is secondary to that.

All over the world and at different times of human history, these archetypes, or elementary ideas, have appeared in different costumes. The differences in the costumes are the results of environment and historical conditions. It is these differences that the anthropologist is most concerned to identify and compare.

Now, there is also a countertheory of diffusion to account for the similarity of myths. For instance, the art of tilling the soil goes forth from the area in which it was first developed, and along with it goes a mythology that has to do with fertilizing the earth, with planting and bringing up the food plants—some such myth as that just described, of killing a deity, cutting it up, burying its members, and having the food plants grow. Such a myth will accompany an agricultural or planting tradition. But you won't find it in a hunting culture. So there are historical as well as psychological aspects of this problem of the similarity of myths.

MOYERS: Human beings subscribe to one or more of these stories of creation. What do you think we are looking for when we subscribe to one of these myths?

CAMPBELL: I think what we are looking for is a way of experiencing the world that will open to us the transcendent that informs it, and at the same time forms ourselves within it. That is what people want. That is what the soul asks for.

MOYERS: You mean we are looking for some accord with the mystery that informs all things, what you call that vast ground of silence which we all share?

CAMPBELL: Yes, but not only to find it but to find it actually in our environment, in our world—to recognize it. To have some kind of instruction that will enable us to experience the divine presence.

MOYERS: In the world and in us.

CAMPBELL: In India there is a beautiful greeting, in which the palms are placed together, and you bow to the other person. Do you know what that means?

MOYERS: No.

CAMPBELL: The position of the palms together—this we use when we pray, do we not? That is a greeting which says that the god that is in you recognizes the god in the other. These people are aware of the divine presence in all things. When you enter an Indian home as a guest, you are greeted as a visiting deity.

MOYERS: But weren't the people who told these stories, who believed them and acted on them, asking simpler questions? Weren't they asking, for example, who made the world? How was the world made? Why was the world made? Aren't these the questions that these creation stories are trying to address?

CAMPBELL: No. It's through that answer that they see that the creator is present in the whole world. You see what I mean? This story from the Upanishads that we have just read—"I see that I am this creation," says the god. When you see that God is the creation, and that you are a creature, you realize that God is within you, and in the man or woman with whom you are talking, as well. So there is the realization of two aspects of the one divinity. There is a basic mythological motif that originally all was one, and then there was separation—heaven and earth, male and female, and so forth. How did we lose touch with the unity? One thing you can say is that the separation was somebody's fault—they ate the wrong fruit or said the wrong words to God so that he got angry and then went away. So now the eternal is somehow away from us, and we have to find some way to get back in touch with it.

There is another theme, in which man is thought of as having come not from above but from the womb of Mother Earth. Often, in these stories, there is a great ladder or rope up which people climb. The last people to want to get out are two great big fat heavy people. They grab the rope, and snap!—it breaks. So we are separated from our source. In a sense, because of our minds, we actually are separated, and the problem is to reunite that broken cord.

MOYERS: There are times when I think maybe primitive men and women were just telling these stories to entertain themselves.

CAMPBELL: No, they are not entertainment stories. We know they are not entertainment stories because they can be told only at certain times of the year and under certain conditions.

There are two orders of myths. The great myths, like the myth of the Bible, for example, are the myths of the temple, of the great sacred rituals. They explain the rites by which the people are living in harmony with themselves and each other and with the universe. The understanding of these stories as allegorical is normal.

MOYERS: You think that the first humans who told the story of the creation had some intuitive awareness of the allegorical nature of these stories?

CAMPBELL: Yes. They were saying it is *as if* it were thus. The notion that somebody literally made the world—that is what is known as artificialism. It is the child's way of thinking: the table is made, so somebody made the table. The world is here, so somebody must have made it. There is another point of view involving emanation and precipitation without personification. A sound precipitates air, then fire, then water and earth—and that's how the world becomes. The whole universe is included in this first sound, this vibration, which then commits all things to fragmentation in the field of time. In this view, there is not someone outside who said, "Let it happen."

In most cultures there are two or three creation stories, not just one. There are two in the Bible, even though people treat them as one story. You remember in the Garden of Eden story of Chapter 2: God is trying to think of ways to entertain Adam, whom he has created to be his gardener, to take care of his garden. That is an old, old story that was borrowed from ancient Sumer. The gods wanted somebody to take care of their garden and cultivate the food that they needed, so they created man. That's the background of the myth of Chapters 2 and 3 in Genesis.

But Yahweh's gardener is bored. So God tries to invent toys for him. He creates the animals, but all the man can do is name them. Then God thinks of this grand idea of drawing the soul of woman out of Adam's own body—which is a very different creation story from Chapter 1 of Genesis, where God created Adam and Eve together in the image of himself as male and female. There God is himself the primordial androgyne. Chapter 2 is by far the earlier story, coming from perhaps the eighth century or so B.C., whereas Chapter 1 is of a so-called priestly text, of about the fourth century B.C., or later. In the Hindu story of the Self that felt fear, then desire, then split in two, we have a counterpart of Genesis 2. In Genesis, it is man, not the god, who splits in two.

The Greek legend that Aristophanes tells in Plato's *Symposium* is another of this kind. Aristophanes says that in the beginning there were creatures composed of what are now two human beings. And those were of three sorts: male/female, male/male, and female/female. The gods then split them all in two. But after they had been split apart, all they could think of to do was to embrace each other again in order to reconstitute the original units. So we all now spend our lives trying to find and re-embrace our other halves.

MOYERS: You say that mythology is the study of mankind's one great story. What is that one great story?

CAMPBELL: That we have come forth from the one ground of being as manifestations in the field of time. The field of time is a kind of shadow play over a timeless ground. And you play the game in the shadow field, you enact your side of the polarity with all your might. But you know that your enemy, for example, is simply the other side of what you would see as yourself if you could see from the position of the middle.

MOYERS: So the one great story is our search to find our place in the drama?

CAMPBELL: To be in accord with the grand symphony that this world is, to put the harmony of our own body in accord with that harmony.

MOYERS: When I read these stories, no matter the culture or origin, I feel a sense of wonder at the spectacle of the human imagination groping to try to understand this existence, to invest in their small journey these transcendent possibilities. Has that ever happened to you?

CAMPBELL: I think of mythology as the homeland of the muses, the inspirers of art, the inspirers of poetry. To see life as a poem and yourself participating in a poem is what the myth does for you.

MOYERS: A poem?

CAMPBELL: I mean a vocabulary in the form not of words but of acts and adventures, which connotes something transcendent of the action here, so that you always feel in accord with the universal being.

MOYERS: When I read these myths, I am simply in awe of the mystery of it all. We can presume, but we cannot penetrate.

CAMPBELL: That is the point. The person who thinks he has found the ultimate truth is wrong. There is an often-quoted verse in Sanskrit, which appears in the Chinese *Tao-te Ching* as well: "He who thinks he knows, doesn't know. He who knows that he doesn't know, knows. For in this context, to know is not to know. And not to know is to know."

MOYERS: Far from undermining my faith, your work in mythology has liberated my faith from the cultural prisons to which it had been sentenced.

CAMPBELL: It liberated my own, and I know it is going to do that with anyone who gets the message.

MOYERS: Are some myths more or less true than others?

CAMPBELL: They are true in different senses. Every mythology has to do with the wisdom of life as related to a specific culture at a specific time. It integrates the individual into his society and the society into the field of nature. It unites the field of nature with my nature. It's a harmonizing force. Our own mythology, for example, is based on the idea of duality: good and evil, heaven and hell. And so our religions tend to be ethical in their accent. Sin and atonement. Right and wrong.

MOYERS: The tension of opposites: love-hate, death-life.

CAMPBELL: Ramakrishna once said that if all you think of are your sins, then you are a sinner. And when I read that, I thought of my boyhood, going to confession on Saturdays, meditating on all the little sins that I had committed during the week. Now I think one should go and say, "Bless me, Father, for I have been great, these are the good things I have done this week." Identify your notion of yourself with the positive, rather than with the negative.

You see, religion is really a kind of second womb. It's designed to bring this extremely complicated thing, which is a human being, to maturity, which means to be self-motivating, self-acting. But the idea of sin puts you in a servile condition throughout your life.

MOYERS: But that's not the Christian idea of creation and the Fall.

CAMPBELL: I once heard a lecture by a wonderful old Zen philosopher, Dr. D. T. Suzuki. He stood up with his hands slowly rubbing his sides and said, "God against man. Man against God. Man against nature. Nature against man. Nature against God. God against nature—very funny religion!"

MOYERS: Well, I have often wondered, what would a member of a hunting tribe on the North American plains think, gazing up on Michelangelo's creation?

CAMPBELL: That is certainly not the god of other traditions. In the other mythologies, one puts oneself in accord with the world, with the mixture of good and evil. But in the religious system of the Near East, you identify with the good and fight against the evil. The biblical traditions of Judaism, Christianity, and Islam all speak with derogation of the so-called nature religions.

The shift from a nature religion to a sociological religion makes it difficult for us to link back to nature. But actually all of those cultural symbols are perfectly susceptible to interpretation in terms of the psychological and cosmological systems, if you choose to look at them that way.

Every religion is true one way or another. It is true when understood metaphorically. But when it gets stuck to its own metaphors, interpreting them as facts, then you are in trouble.

MOYERS: What is the metaphor?

CAMPBELL: A metaphor is an image that suggests something else. For instance, if I say to a person, "You are a nut," I'm not suggesting that I think the person is literally a nut. "Nut" is a metaphor. The reference of the metaphor in religious traditions is to something transcendent that is not literally any thing. If you think that the metaphor is itself the reference, it would be like going to a restaurant, asking for the menu, seeing beefsteak written there, and starting to eat the menu.

For example, Jesus ascended to heaven. The denotation would seem to be that somebody ascended to the sky. That's literally what is being said. But if that were really the meaning of the message, then we have to throw it away, because there would have been no such place for Jesus literally to go. We know that Jesus could not have ascended to heaven because there is no physical heaven anywhere in the universe. Even ascending at the speed of light, Jesus would still be in the galaxy. Astronomy and physics have simply eliminated that as a literal, physical possibility. But if you read "Jesus ascended to heaven" in terms of its metaphoric connotation, you see that he has gone inward—not into outer space but into inward space, to the place from which all being comes, into the consciousness that is the source of all things, the kingdom of heaven within. The images are outward, but their reflection is inward. The point is that we should ascend with him by going inward. It is a metaphor of returning to the source, alpha and omega, of leaving the fixation on the body behind and going to the body's dynamic source.

MOYERS: Aren't you undermining one of the great traditional doctrines of the classic Christian faith—that the burial and the resurrection of Jesus prefigures our own?

CAMPBELL: That would be a mistake in the reading of the symbol. That is reading the words in terms of prose instead of in terms of poetry, reading the metaphor in terms of the denotation instead of the connotation.

MOYERS: And poetry gets to the unseen reality.

CAMPBELL: That which is beyond even the concept of reality, that which transcends all thought. The myth puts you there all the time, gives you a line to connect with that mystery which you are.

Shakespeare said that art is a mirror held up to nature. And that's what it is. The nature is your nature, and all of these wonderful poetic images of mythology are referring to something in you. When your mind is simply trapped by the image out there so that you never make the reference to yourself, you have misread the image.

The inner world is the world of your requirements and your energies and your structure and your possibilities that meets the outer world. And the outer world is the field of your incarnation. That's where you are. You've got to keep both going. As Novalis said, "The seat of the soul is there where the inner and outer worlds meet."

MOYERS: So the story of Jesus ascending to heaven is a message in a bottle from a shore someone has visited before.

CAMPBELL: That's right—Jesus did. Now, according to the normal way of thinking about the Christian religion, we cannot identify with Jesus, we have to imitate Jesus. To say, "I and the Father are one," as Jesus said, is blasphemy for us. However, in the Thomas gospel that was dug up in Egypt some forty years ago, Jesus says, "He who drinks from my mouth will become as I am, and I shall be he." Now, that is exactly Buddhism. We are all manifestations of Buddha consciousness, or Christ consciousness, only we don't know it. The word "Buddha" means "the one who waked up." We are all to do that—to wake up to the Christ or Buddha consciousness within us. This is blasphemy in the normal way of Christian thinking, but it is the very essence of Christian Gnosticism and of the Thomas gospel.

MOYERS: Is reincarnation also a metaphor?

CAMPBELL: Certainly it is. When people ask, "Do you believe in reincarnation," I just have to say, "Reincarnation, like heaven, is a metaphor."

The metaphor in Christianity that corresponds to reincarnation is purgatory. If one dies with such a fixation on the things of this world that one's spirit is not ready to behold the beatific vision, then one has to undergo a purgation, one has to be purged clean of one's limitations. The limitations are what are called sins. Sin is simply a limiting factor that limits your consciousness and fixes it in an inappropriate condition.

In the Oriental metaphor, if you die in that condition, you come back again to have more experiences that will clarify, clarify, clarify, until you are released from these fixations. The reincarnating monad is the principal hero of Oriental myth. The monad puts on various personalities, life after life. Now the reincarnation idea is not that you and I as the personalities that we are will be reincarnated. The personality is what the monad throws off. Then the monad puts on another body, male or female, depending on what experiences are necessary for it to clear itself of this attachment to the field of time.

MOYERS: And what does the idea of reincarnation suggest?

CAMPBELL: It suggests that you are more than you think you are. There are dimensions of your being and a potential for realization and consciousness that are not included in your concept of yourself. Your life is much deeper and broader than you conceive it to be here. What you are living is but a fractional inkling of what is really within you, what gives you life, breadth, and depth. But you can live in terms of that depth. And when you can experience it, you suddenly see that all the religions are talking of that.

MOYERS: Is this a chief motif of mythological stories through time?

CAMPBELL: No, the idea of life as an ordeal through which you become released from the bondage of life belongs to the higher religions. I don't think I see anything like that in aboriginal mythology.

MOYERS: What is the source of it?

CAMPBELL: I don't know. It would probably come from people of spiritual power and depth who experienced their lives as being inadequate to the spiritual aspect or dimension of their being.

MOYERS: You say that elites create myths, that shamans and artists and others who take the journey into the unknown come back to create these myths. But what about ordinary folks? Don't they create the stories of Paul Bunyan, for example?

CAMPBELL: Yes, but that is not a myth. That doesn't hit the level of myth. The prophets and what in India are called the "rishis" are said to have *heard* the scriptures. Now anybody might open his ears, but not everyone has the capacity actually to hear the scriptures.

MOYERS: "He who has ears to hear, let him hear."

CAMPBELL: There has to be a training to help you open your ears so that you can begin to hear metaphorically instead of concretely. Freud and Jung both felt that myth is grounded in the unconscious.

Anyone writing a creative work knows that you open, you yield yourself, and the book talks to you and builds itself. To a certain extent, you become the carrier of something that is given to you from what have been called the Muses—or, in biblical language, "God." This is no fancy, it is a fact. Since the inspiration comes from the unconscious, and since the unconscious minds of the people of any single small society have much in common, what the shaman or seer brings forth is something that is waiting to be brought forth in everyone. So when one hears the seer's story, one responds, "Aha! This is my story. This is something that I had always wanted to say but wasn't able to say." There has to be a dialogue, an interaction between the seer and the community. The seer who sees things that people in the community don't want to hear is just ineffective. Sometimes they will wipe him out.

MOYERS: So when we talk about folk tales, we are talking not about myths but about stories that ordinary folks tell in order to entertain themselves or express some level of existence that is below that of the great spiritual pilgrims.

CAMPBELL: Yes, the folk tale is for entertainment. The myth is for spiritual instruction. There's a fine saying in India with respect to these two orders of myths, the folk idea and the elementary idea. The folk aspect is called *desi*, which means "provincial," having to do with your society. That is for young people. It's through that that the young person is brought into the society and is taught to go out and kill monsters. "Okay, here's a soldier suit, we've got the job for you." But there's also the elementary idea. The Sanskrit name for that is *marga*, which means "path." It's the trail back to yourself. The myth comes from the imagination, and it leads back to it. The society teaches you what the myths are, and then it disengages you so that in your meditations you can follow the path right in.

Civilizations are grounded on myth. The civilization of the Middle Ages was grounded on the myth of the Fall in the Garden, the redemption on the cross, and the carrying of the grace of redemption to man through the sacraments.

The cathedral was the center of the sacrament, and the castle was the center protecting the cathedral. There you have the two forms of government—the government of the spirit and the government of the physical life, both in accord with the one source, namely the grace of the crucifixion.

MOYERS: But within those two spheres ordinary people told little tales of leprechauns and witches.

CAMPBELL: There are three centers of what might be called mythological and folkloristic creativity in the Middle Ages. One is the cathedral and all that is associated with monasteries and hermitages. A second is the castle. The third is the cottage, where the people are. The cathedral, the castle, and the cottage—you go to any of the areas of high civilization, and you will see the same—the temple, the palace, and the town. They are different generating centers, but in so far as this is one civilization, they are all operating in the same symbolic field.

MOYERS: Same symbolic field?

CAMPBELL: The symbolic field is based on the experiences of people in a particular community, at that particular time and place. Myths are so intimately bound to the culture, time, and place that unless the symbols, the metaphors, are kept alive by constant recreation through the arts, the life just slips away from them.

MOYERS: Who speaks in metaphors today?

CAMPBELL: All poets. Poetry is a metaphorical language.

MOYERS: A metaphor suggests potential.

CAMPBELL: Yes, but it also suggests the actuality that hides behind the visible aspect. The metaphor is the mask of God through which eternity is to be experienced.

MOYERS: You speak of the poets and artists. What about the clergy?

CAMPBELL: I think our clergy is really not doing its proper work. It does not speak about the connotations of the metaphors but is stuck with the ethics of good and evil.

MOYERS: Why haven't the priests become the shamans of American society?

CAMPBELL: The difference between a priest and a shaman is that the priest is a functionary and the shaman is someone who has had an experience. In our tradition it is the monk who seeks the experience, while the priest is the one who has studied to serve the community.

I had a friend who attended an international meeting of the Roman Catholic meditative orders, which was held in Bangkok. He told me that the Catholic monks had no problems under-standing the Buddhist monks, but that it was the clergy of the two religions who were unable to understand each other.

The person who has had a mystical experience knows that all the symbolic expressions of it are faulty. The symbols don't render the experience, they suggest it. If you haven't had the experience, how can you know what it is? Try to explain the joy of skiing to somebody living in the tropics who has never even seen snow. There has to be an experience to catch the message, some clue—otherwise you're not hearing what is being said.

MOYERS: The person who has the experience has to project it in the best way he can with images. It seems to me that we have lost the art in our society of thinking in images.

CAMPBELL: Oh, we definitely have. Our thinking is largely discursive, verbal, linear. There is more reality in an image than in a word.

MOYERS: Do you ever think that it is this absence of the religious experience of ecstasy, of joy, this denial of transcendence in our society, that has turned so many young people to the use of drugs?

CAMPBELL: Absolutely. That is the way in.

MOYERS: The way in?

CAMPBELL: To an experience.

MOYERS: And religion can't do that for you, or art can't do it?

CAMPBELL: It could, but it is not doing it now. Religions are addressing social problems and ethics instead of the mystical experience.

MOYERS: So you think religion's great calling is the experience?

CAMPBELL: One of the wonderful things in the Catholic ritual is going to communion. There you are taught that this *is* the body and blood of the Savior. And you take it to you, and you turn inward, and there Christ is working within you. This is a way of inspiring a meditation on experiencing the spirit in you. You see people coming back from communion, and they are inward-turned, they really are.

In India, I have seen a red ring put around a stone, and then the stone becomes regarded as an incarnation of the mystery. Usually you think of things in practical terms, but you could think of anything in terms of its mystery. For example, this is a watch, but it is also a thing in being. You could put it down, draw a ring around it, and regard it in that dimension. That is the point of what is called consecration.

MOYERS: What do you mean? What can you make of the watch you're wearing? What kind of mystery does it reveal?

CAMPBELL: It is a thing, isn't it?

MOYERS: Yes.

CAMPBELL: Do you really know what a thing is? What supports it? It is something in time and space. Think how mysterious it is that anything should be. The watch becomes the center for a meditation, the center of the intelligible mystery of being, which is everywhere. This watch is now the center of the universe. It is the still point in the turning world.

MOYERS: Where does the meditation take you?

CAMPBELL: Oh, it depends on how talented you are.

MOYERS: You talk about the "transcendent." What is the transcendent? What happens to someone in the transcendent?

CAMPBELL: "Transcendent" is a technical, philosophical term, translated in two different ways. In Christian theology, it refers to God as being beyond or outside the field of nature. That is a materialistic way of talking about the transcendent, because God is thought of as a kind of spiritual fact existing somewhere out there. It was Hegel who spoke of our anthropomorphic god as the gaseous vertebrate—such an idea of God as many Christians hold. Or he is thought of as a bearded old man with a not very pleasant temperament. But "transcendent" properly means that which is beyond all concepts. Kant tells us that all of our experiences are bounded by time and space. They take place within space, and they take place in the course of time.

Time and space form the sensibilities that bound our experiences. Our senses are enclosed in the field of time and space, and our minds are enclosed in a frame of the categories of thought. But the ultimate thing (which is no thing) that we are trying to get in touch with is not so enclosed. We enclose it as we try to think of it.

The transcendent transcends all of these categories of thinking. Being and nonbeing—those are categories. The word "God" properly refers to what transcends all thinking, but the word "God" itself is something thought about.

Now you can personify God in many, many ways. Is there one god? Are there many gods? Those are merely categories of thought. What you are talking and trying to think about *transcends* all that.

One problem with Yahweh, as they used to say in the old Christian Gnostic texts, is that he forgot he was a metaphor. He thought he was a fact. And when he said, "I am God," a voice was heard to say, "You are mistaken, Samael." "Samael" means "blind god": blind to the infinite Light of which he is a local historical manifestation. This is known as the blasphemy of Jehovah—that he thought he was God.

MOYERS: You are saying that God can't be known.

CAMPBELL: I mean that whatever is ultimate is beyond the categories of being and nonbeing. Is it or is it not? As the Buddha is reported to have said: "It both is and is not; neither is, nor is not." God as the ultimate mystery of being is beyond thinking.

There is a wonderful story in one of the Upanishads about the god Indra. Now, it happened at this time that a great monster had enclosed all the waters of the earth, so there was a terrible drought, and the world was in a very bad condition. It took Indra quite a while to realize that he had a box of thunderbolts and that all he had to do was drop a thunderbolt on the monster and blow him up. When he did that, the waters flowed, and the world was refreshed, and Indra said, "What a great boy am I."

So, thinking, "What a great boy am I," Indra goes up to the cosmic mountain, which is the central mountain of the world, and decides to build a palace worthy of such as he. The main carpenter of the gods goes to work on it, and in very quick order he gets the palace into pretty good condition. But every time Indra comes to inspect it, he has bigger ideas about how splendid and grandiose the palace should be. Finally, the carpenter says, "My god, we are both immortal, and there is no end to his desires. I am caught for eternity." So he decides to go to Brahma, the creator god, and complain.

Brahma sits on a lotus, the symbol of divine energy and divine grace. The lotus grows from the navel of Vishnu, who is the sleeping god, whose dream is the universe. So the carpenter comes to the edge of the great lotus pond of the universe and tells his story to Brahma. Brahma says, "You go home. I will fix this up." Brahma gets off his lotus and kneels down to address sleeping Vishnu. Vishnu just makes a gesture and says something like, "Listen, fly, something is going to happen."

Next morning, at the gate of the palace that is being built, there appears a beautiful blue-black boy with a lot of children around him, just admiring his beauty. The porter at the gate of the new palace goes running to Indra, and Indra says, "Well, bring in the boy." The boy is brought in, and Indra, the king god, sitting on his throne, says, "Young man, welcome. And what brings you to my palace?"

"Well," says the boy with a voice like thunder rolling on the horizon, "I have been told that you are building such a palace as no Indra before you ever built."

And Indra says, "Indras before me, young man—what are you talking about?"

The boy says, "Indras before you. I have seen them come and go, come and go. Just think, Vishnu sleeps in the cosmic ocean, and the lotus of the universe grows from his navel. On the lotus sits Brahma, the creator. Brahma opens his eyes, and a world comes into being, governed by an Indra. Brahma closes his eyes, and a world goes out of being. The life of a Brahma is four hundred and thirty-two thousand years. When he dies, the lotus goes back, and another lotus is formed, and another Brahma. Then think of the galaxies beyond galaxies in infinite space, each a lotus, with a Brahma sitting on it, opening his eyes, closing his eyes. And Indras? There may be wise men in your court who would volunteer to count the drops of water in the oceans of the world or the grains of sand on the beaches, but no one would count those Brahmin, let alone those Indras."

While the boy is talking, an army of ants parades across the floor. The boy laughs when he sees them, and Indra's hair stands on end, and he says to the boy, "Why do you laugh?"

The boy answers, "Don't ask unless you are willing to be hurt."

Indra says, "I ask. Teach." (That, by the way, is a good Oriental idea: you don't teach until you are asked. You don't force your mission down people's throats.)

And so the boy points to the ants and says, "Former Indras all. Through many lifetimes they rise from the lowest conditions to highest illumination. And then they drop their thunderbolt on a monster, and they think, 'What a good boy am I.' And down they go again."

While the boy is talking, a crotchety old yogi comes into the palace with a banana leaf parasol. He is naked except for a loincloth, and on his chest is a little disk of hair, and half the hairs in the middle have all dropped out.

The boy greets him and asks him just what Indra was about to ask. "Old man, what is your name? Where do you come from? Where is your family? Where is your house? And what is the meaning of this curious constellation of hair on your chest?"

"Well," says the old fella, "my name is Hairy. I don't have a house. Life is too short for that. I just have this parasol. I don't have a family. I just meditate on Vishnu's feet, and think of eternity, and how passing time is. You know, every time an Indra dies, a world disappears—these things just flash by like that. Every time an Indra dies, one hair drops out of this circle on my chest. Half the hairs are gone now. Pretty soon they will all be gone. Life is short. Why build a house?"

Then the two disappear. The boy was Vishnu, the Lord Protector, and the old yogi was Shiva, the creator and destroyer of the world, who had just come for the instruction of Indra, who is simply a god of history but thinks he is the whole show.

Indra is sitting there on the throne, and he is completely

disillusioned, completely shot. He calls the carpenter and says, "I'm quitting the building of this palace. You are dismissed." So the carpenter got his intention. He is dismissed from the job, and there is no more house building going on.

Indra decides to go out and be a yogi and just meditate on the lotus feet of Vishnu. But he has a beautiful queen named Indrani. And when Indrani hears of Indra's plan, she goes to the priest of the gods and says, "Now he has got the idea in his head of going out to become a yogi."

"Well," says the priest, "come in with me, darling, and we will sit down, and I will fix this up."

So they sit down before the king's throne, and the priest says, "Now, I wrote a book for you many years ago on the art of politics. You are in the position of the king of the gods. You are a manifestation of the mystery of Brahma in the field of time. This is a high privilege. Appreciate it, honor it, and deal with life as though you were what you really are. And besides, now I am going to write you a book on the art of love so that you and your wife will know that in the wonderful mystery of the two that are one, the Brahma is radiantly present also."

And with this set of instructions, Indra gives up his idea of going out and becoming a yogi and finds that, in life, he can represent the eternal as a symbol, you might say, of the Brahma.

So each of us is, in a way, the Indra of his own life. You can make a choice, either to throw it all off and go into the forest to meditate, or to stay in the world, both in the life of your job, which is the kingly job of politics and achievement, and in the love life with your wife and family. Now, this is a very nice myth, it seems to me.

MOYERS: And it says much of what modern science is discovering, that time is endless—

CAMPBELL: —and there are galaxies, galaxies, galaxies, and our God—our personification of God and his son and the mystery—is for this little set of time.

MOYERS: Culture, though, has always influenced our thinking about ultimate matters.

CAMPBELL: Culture can also teach us to go past its concepts. That is what is known as initiation. A true initiation is when the guru tells you, "There is no Santa Claus." Santa Claus is metaphoric of a relationship between parents and children. The relationship does exist, and so it can be experienced, but there is no Santa Claus. Santa Claus was simply a way of clueing children into the appreciation of a relationship.

Life is, in its very essence and character, a terrible mystery—this whole business of living by killing and eating. But it is a childish attitude to say no to life with all its pain, to say that this is something that should not have been.

MOYERS: Zorba says, "Trouble? Life is trouble."

CAMPBELL: Only death is no trouble. People ask me, "Do you have optimism about the world?" And I say, "Yes, it's great just the way it is. And you are not going to fix it up. Nobody has ever made it any better. It is never going to be any better. This is it, so take it or leave it. You are not going to correct or improve it."

MOYERS: Doesn't that lead to a rather passive attitude in the face of evil?

CAMPBELL: You yourself are participating in the evil, or you are not alive. Whatever you do is evil for somebody. This is one of the ironies of the whole creation.

MOYERS: What about this idea of good and evil in mythology, of life as a conflict between the forces of darkness and the forces of light?

CAMPBELL: That is a Zoroastrian idea, which has come over into Judaism and Christianity. In other traditions, good and evil are relative to the position in which you are standing. What is good for one is evil for the other. And you play your part, not withdrawing from the world when you realize how horrible it is, but seeing that this horror is simply the foreground of a wonder: a *mysterium tremendum et fascinans.*

"All life is sorrowful" is the first Buddhist saying, and so it is. It wouldn't be life if there were not temporality involved, which is sorrow—loss, loss, loss. You've got to say yes to life and see it as magnificent this way; for this is surely the way God intended it.

MOYERS: Do you really believe that?

CAMPBELL: It is joyful just as it is. I don't believe there was anybody who intended it, but this is the way it is. James Joyce has a memorable line: "History is a nightmare from which I am trying to awake." And the way to awake from it is not to be afraid, and to recognize that all of this, as it is, is a manifestation of the horrendous power that is of all creation. The ends of things are always painful. But pain is part of there being a world at all.

MOYERS: But if you accepted that as an ultimate conclusion, you wouldn't try to form any laws or fight any battles or—

CAMPBELL: I didn't say that.

MOYERS: Isn't that the logical conclusion to draw from accepting everything as it is?

CAMPBELL: That is not the *necessary* conclusion to draw. You could say, "I will participate in this life, I will join the army, I will go to war," and so forth.

MOYERS: "I will do the best I can."

CAMPBELL: "I will participate in the game. It is a wonderful, wonderful opera—except that it hurts."

Affirmation is difficult. We always affirm with conditions. I affirm the world on condition that it gets to be the way Santa Claus told me it ought to be. But affirming it the way it is— that's the hard thing, and that is what rituals are about. Ritual is group participation in the most hideous act, which is the act of life—namely, killing and eating another living thing. We do it together, and this is the way life is. The hero is the one who comes to participate in life courageously and decently, in the way of nature, not in the way of personal rancor, disappointment, or revenge.

The hero's sphere of action is not the transcendent but here, now, in the field of time, of good and evil—of the pairs of opposites. Whenever one moves out of the transcendent, one comes into a field of opposites. One has eaten of the tree of knowledge, not only of good and evil, but of male and female, of right and wrong, of this and that, and of light and dark. Everything in the field of time is dual: past and future, dead and alive, being and nonbeing. But the ultimate pair in the imagination are male and female, the male being aggressive, and the female being receptive, the male being the warrior, the female the dreamer. We have the realm of love and the realm of war, Freud's Eros and Thanatos.

Heraclitus said that for God all things are good and right and just, but for man some things are right and others are not. When you are a man, you are in the field of time and decisions. One of the problems of life is to live with the realization of both terms, to say, "I know the center, and I know that good and evil are simply temporal aberrations and that, in God's view, there is no difference."

MOYERS: That is the idea in the Upanishads: "Not female, nor yet male is it, neither is it neuter. Whatever body it assumes, through that body it is served."

CAMPBELL: That is right. So Jesus says, "Judge not that you may not be judged." That is to say, put yourself back in the position of Paradise before you thought in terms of good and evil. You don't hear this much from the pulpits. But one of the great challenges of life is to say "yea" to that person or that act or that condition which in your mind is most abominable.

MOYERS: Most abominable?

CAMPBELL: There are two aspects to a thing of this kind. One is your judgment in the field of action, and the other is your judgment as a metaphysical observer. You can't say there shouldn't be poisonous serpents—that's the way life is. But in the field of action, if you see a poisonous serpent about to bite somebody, you kill it. That's not saying no to the serpent, that's saying no to that situation. There's a wonderful verse in the Rig Veda that says, "On the tree"—that's the tree of life, the tree of your own life—"there are two birds, fast friends. One eats the fruit of the tree, and the other, not eating, watches." Now, the one eating the fruit of the tree is killing the fruit. Life lives on life, that's what it's all about. A little myth from India tells the story of the great god Shiva, the lord whose dance is the universe. He had as his consort the goddess Parvathi, daughter of the mountain king. A monster came to him and said, "I want your wife as my mistress." Shiva was indignant, so he simply opened his third eye, and lightning bolts struck the earth, there was smoke and fire, and when the smoke cleared, there was another monster, lean, with hair like the hair of a lion flying to the four directions. The first monster saw that the lean monster was about to eat him up. Now, what do you do when you're in a situation like that? Traditional advice says to throw yourself on the mercy of the deity. So the monster said, "Shiva, I throw myself on your mercy." Now, there are rules for this god game. When someone throws himself on your mercy, then you yield mercy.

So Shiva said, "I yield my mercy. Lean monster, don't eat him."

"Well," said the lean monster, "what do I do? I'm hungry. You made me hungry, to eat this guy up."

"Well," said Shiva, "eat yourself."

So the lean monster started on his feet and came chomping up, chomping up—this is an image of life living on life. Finally, there was nothing left of the lean monster but a face. Shiva looked at the face and said, "I've never seen a greater demonstration of what life's all about than this. I will call you Kirtimukha—face of glory." And you will see that mask, that face of glory, at the portals to Shiva shrines and also to Buddha shrines. Shiva said to the face, "He who will not bow to you is unworthy to come to me." You've got to say yes to this miracle of life as it is, not on the condition that it follow your rules. Otherwise, you'll never get through to the metaphysical dimension.

Once in India I thought I would like to meet a major guru or teacher face to face. So I went to see a celebrated teacher named Sri Krishna Menon, and the first thing he said to me was, "Do you have a question?"

The teacher in this tradition always answers questions. He doesn't tell you anything you are not yet ready to hear. So I said, "Yes, I have a question. Since in Hindu thinking everything in the universe is a manifestation of divinity itself, how should we say no to anything in the world? How should we say no to brutality, to stupidity, to vulgarity, to thoughtlessness?"

And he answered, "For you and for me—the way is to say yes."

We then had a wonderful talk on this theme of the affirmation of all things. And it confirmed me in the feeling I had had that who are we to judge? It seems to me that this is one of the great teachings, also, of Jesus.

MOYERS: In classic Christian doctrine the material world is to be despised, and life is to be redeemed in the hereafter, in heaven, where our rewards come. But you say that if you affirm that which you deplore, you are affirming the very world which is our eternity at the moment.

CAMPBELL: Yes, that is what I'm saying. Eternity isn't some later time. Eternity isn't even a long time. Eternity has nothing to do with time. Eternity is that dimension of here and now that all thinking in temporal terms cuts off. And if you don't get it here, you won't get it anywhere. The problem with heaven is that you will be having such a good time there, you won't even think of eternity. You'll just have this unending delight in the beatific vision of God. But the experience of eternity right here and now, in all things, whether thought of as good or as evil, is the function of life.

MOYERS: This is it.

CAMPBELL: This is it.

III

THE FIRST STORYTELLERS

The animal envoys of the Unseen Power no longer serve, as in primeval times, to teach and to guide mankind. Bears, lions, elephants, ibexes, and gazelles are in cages in our zoos. Man is no longer the newcomer in a world of unexplored plains and forests, and our immediate neighbors are not wild beasts but other human beings, contending for goods and space on a planet that is whirling without end around the fireball of a star. Neither in body nor in mind do we inhabit the world of those hunting races of the Paleolithic millennia, to whose lives and life ways we nevertheless owe the very forms of our bodies and structures of our minds. Memories of their animal envoys still must sleep, somehow, within us; for they wake a little and stir when we venture into wilderness. They wake in terror to thunder. And again they wake, with a sense of recognition, when we enter any one of those great painted caves. Whatever the inward darkness may have been to which the shamans of those caves descended in their trances, the same must lie within ourselves, nightly visited in sleep.

—JOSEPH CAMPBELL,
The Way of the Animal Powers

MOYERS: Do you think the poet Wordsworth was right when he wrote, "Our birth is but a sleep and a forgetting:/The soul that rises with us, our life's star,/Hath had elsewhere its setting,/And cometh from afar"? Do you think that is so?

CAMPBELL: I do. Not in entire forgetfulness—that is to say, the nerves in our body carry the memories that shaped the organization of our nervous system to certain environmental circumstances and to the demands of an organism.

MOYERS: What do our souls owe to ancient myths?

CAMPBELL: The ancient myths were designed to harmonize the mind and the body. The mind can ramble off in strange ways and want things that the body does not want. The myths and rites were means of putting the mind in accord with the body and the way of life in accord with the way that nature dictates.

MOYERS: So these old stories live in us?

CAMPBELL: They do indeed. The stages of human development are the same today as they were in the ancient times. As a child, you are brought up in a world of discipline, of obedience, and you are dependent on others. All this has to be transcended when you come to maturity, so that you can live not in dependency but with self-responsible authority. If you can't cross that threshold, you have the basis for neuroses. Then comes the one after you have gained your world, of yielding it—the crisis of dismissal, disengagement.

MOYERS: And ultimately death?

CAMPBELL: And ultimately death. That's the ultimate disengagement. So myth has to serve both aims, that of inducting the young person into the life of his world—that's the function of the folk idea—then disengaging him. The folk idea unshells the elementary idea, which guides you to your own inward life.

MOYERS: And these myths tell me how others have made the passage, and how I can make the passage?

CAMPBELL: Yes, and also what are the beauties of the way. I feel this now, moving into my own last years, you know—the myths help me to go with it.

MOYERS: What kind of myths? Give me one that has actually helped you.

CAMPBELL: The tradition in India, for instance, of actually changing your whole way of dress, even changing your name, as you pass from one stage to another. When I retired from teaching, I knew that I had to create a new way of life, and I changed my manner of thinking about my life, just in terms of that notion —moving out of the sphere of achievement into the sphere of enjoyment and appreciation and relaxing to the wonder of it all.

MOYERS: And then there is that final passage through the dark gate?

CAMPBELL: Well, that is no problem at all. The problem in middle life, when the body has reached its climax of power and begins to decline, is to identify yourself not with the body, which is falling away, but with the consciousness of which it is a vehicle. This is something I learned from myths. What am I? Am I the bulb that carries the light, or am I the light of which the bulb is a vehicle?

One of the psychological problems in growing old is the fear of death. People resist the door of death. But this body is a vehicle of consciousness, and if you can identify with the consciousness, you can watch this body go like an old car. There goes the fender, there goes the tire, one thing after another— but it's predictable. And then, gradually, the whole thing drops off, and consciousness rejoins consciousness. It is no longer in this particular environment.

MOYERS: So these myths have something to say about growing old. I asked that because so many of the myths are of these beautiful youth.

CAMPBELL: The Greek myths are. When we think about mythology, we usually think either of the Greek mythology or of the biblical mythology. There is a kind of humanization of the myth material in both of these cultures. There is a very strong accent on the human, and in the Greek myths, especially, on the humanity and glory of the beautiful youth.

But they appreciate age as well. You have the wise old man and the sage as respected characters in the Greek world.

MOYERS: And the other cultures?

CAMPBELL: They don't stress the beauty of youth to that extent.

MOYERS: You say that the image of death is the beginning of mythology. What do you mean?

CAMPBELL: The earliest evidence of anything like mythological thinking is associated with graves.

MOYERS: And they suggest that men and women saw life, and then they didn't see it, so they wondered about it?

CAMPBELL: It must have been something like that. You only have to imagine what your own experience would be. The grave burials with their weapons and sacrifices to ensure a continued life—these certainly suggest that there was a person who was alive and warm before you who is now lying there, cold, and beginning to rot. Something was there that isn't there. Where is it now?

MOYERS: When do you think humans first discovered death?

CAMPBELL: They first discovered death when they were first humans, because they died. Now, animals have the experience of watching their companions dying. But, as far as we know, they have no further thoughts about it. And there is no evidence that humans thought about death in a significant way until the Neanderthal period, when weapons and animal sacrifices occur with burials.

MOYERS: What did these sacrifices represent?

CAMPBELL: That I wouldn't know.

MOYERS: Only a guess.

CAMPBELL: I try not to guess. You know, we have a tremendous amount of information about this subject, but there is a place where the information stops. And until you have writing, you don't know what people were thinking. All you have are significant remains of one kind or another. You can extrapolate backward, but that is dangerous. However, we do know that burials always involve the idea of the continued life beyond the visible one, of a plane of being that is behind the visible plane, and that is somehow supportive of the visible one to which we have to relate. I would say that is the basic theme of all mythology—that there is an invisible plane supporting the visible one.

MOYERS: What we don't know supports what we do know.

CAMPBELL: Yes. And this idea of invisible support is connected with one's society, too. Society was there before you, it is there after you are gone, and you are a member of it. The myths that link you to your social group, the tribal myths, affirm that you are an organ of the larger organism. Society itself is an organ of a larger organism, which is the landscape, the world in which the tribe moves. The main theme in ritual is the linking of the individual to a larger morphological structure than that of his own physical body.

Man lives by killing, and there is a sense of guilt connected with that. Burials suggest that my friend has died, and he survives. The animals that I have killed must also survive. Early hunters usually had a kind of animal divinity—the technical name would be the animal master, the animal who is the master animal. The animal master sends the flocks to be killed.

You see, the basic hunting myth is of a kind of covenant between the animal world and the human world. The animal gives its life willingly, with the understanding that its life transcends its physical entity and will be returned to the soil or to the mother through some ritual of restoration. And this ritual of restoration is associated with the main hunting animal. To the Indians of the American plains, it was the buffalo. On the Northwest coast the great festivals have to do with the run of salmon coming in. When you go to South Africa, the eland, the magnificent antelope, is the principal animal.

MOYERS: And the principal animal is—

CAMPBELL: —is the one that furnishes the food.

MOYERS: So in the early hunting societies there grew up between human beings and animals a bonding that required one to be consumed by the other.

CAMPBELL: That is the way life is. Man is a hunter, and the hunter is a beast of prey. In the myths, the beast of prey and the animal who is preyed upon play two significant roles. They represent two aspects of life—the aggressive, killing, conquering, creating aspect of life, and the one that is the matter or, you might say, the subject matter.

MOYERS: Life itself. What happens in the relationship between the hunter and the hunted?

CAMPBELL: As we know from the life of the Bushmen and from the relation of the native Americans to the buffalo, it is one of reverence, of respect. For example, the Bushmen of Africa live in a desert world. It's a very hard life, and the hunt in such an environment is a very difficult hunt. There is very little wood for massive, powerful bows. The Bushmen have tiny little bows, and the extent of the arrow's flight is hardly more than thirty yards. The arrow has a very weak penetration. It can hardly do more than break the animal's skin. But the Bushmen apply a prodigiously powerful poison to the point of the arrow so that these beautiful animals, the elands, die in pain over a day and a half. After the animal has been shot and is dying painfully of the poison, the hunters have to fulfill certain taboos of not doing this and not doing that in a kind of "participation mystique," a mystical participation in the death of the animal, whose meat has become their life, and whose death they have brought about. There's an identification, a mythological identification. Killing is not simply slaughter, it's a ritual act, as eating is when you say grace before meals. A ritual act is a recognition of your dependency on the voluntary giving of this food to you by the animal who has given its life. The hunt is a ritual.

MOYERS: And a ritual expresses a spiritual reality.

CAMPBELL: It expresses that this is in accord with the way of nature, not simply with my own personal impulse.

I am told that when the Bushmen tell their animal stories, they actually mimic the mouth formations of the different animals, pronouncing the words as though the animals themselves were pronouncing them. They had an intimate knowledge of these creatures, and friendly neighborly relationships.

And then they killed some of them for food. I know ranch people who have a pet cow in addition to their ranch animals. They won't eat the meat of that cow because there is a kind of cannibalism in eating the meat of a friend. But the aborigines were eating the meat of their friends all the time. Some kind of psychological compensation has to be achieved, and the myths help in doing that.

MOYERS: How?

CAMPBELL: These early myths help the psyche to participate without a sense of guilt or fright in the necessary act of life.

MOYERS: And these great stories consistently refer to this dynamic in one way or the other—the hunt, the hunter, the hunted, and the animal as friend, as a messenger from God.

CAMPBELL: Right. Normally the animal preyed upon becomes the animal that is the messenger of the divine.

MOYERS: And you wind up as the hunter killing the messenger.

CAMPBELL: Killing the god.

MOYERS: Does that cause guilt?

CAMPBELL: No, guilt is what is wiped out by the myth. Killing the animal is not a personal act. You are performing the work of nature.

MOYERS: Guilt is wiped out by the myth?

CAMPBELL: Yes.

MOYERS: But you must at times feel some reluctance upon closing in for the kill. You don't really want to kill that animal.

CAMPBELL: The animal is the father. You know what the Freudians say, that the first enemy is the father, if you are a man. If you are a boy, every enemy is potentially, psychologically associated with the father image.

MOYERS: Do you think that the animal became the father image of God?

CAMPBELL: Yes. It is a fact that the religious attitude toward the principal animal is one of reverence and respect, and not only that—submission to the inspiration of that animal. The animal is the one that brings the gifts—tobacco, the mystical pipe, and so on.

MOYERS: Do you think this troubled early man—to kill the animal that is a god, or the messenger of a god?

CAMPBELL: Absolutely—that is why you have the rites.

MOYERS: What kind of rites?

CAMPBELL: Rituals of appeasement and of thanks to the animal. For example, when the bear is killed, there is a ceremony of feeding the bear a piece of its own flesh. And then there will be a little ceremony with the bear's skin placed over a kind of rack, as though he were present—and he is present, he serves his own meat for dinner. A fire is burning—and the fire is the goddess. Then there is a conversation between the mountain god, which is the bear, and the fire goddess.

MOYERS: What do they say?

CAMPBELL: Who knows? No one hears them, but there is a little socializing going on there.

MOYERS: If the cave bears were not appeased, the animals wouldn't appear, and the primitive hunters would starve to death. They began to perceive some kind of power on which they were dependent, a power greater than their own.

CAMPBELL: Yes. That is the power of the animal master, the willingness of the animals to participate in this game. You find among hunting people all over the world a very intimate, appreciative relationship to the principal food animal. Now, when we sit down to a meal, we thank God for giving us the food. These people thanked the animal.

MOYERS: So appeasing the animal with this ritual honoring the animal would be like bribing the butcher at the supermarket.

CAMPBELL: No, I don't think it would be bribing at all. It is thanking a friend for cooperating in a mutual relationship. And if you didn't thank him, the species would become offended.

There are rituals that have been described for killing animals. Before the hunter goes to kill, he will draw on the hilltop a picture of the animal that he is about to kill. And that hilltop will be in such a place that the first rays of the rising sun will strike it. When the sun rises, the hunter is waiting there with a little team of people to perform the rites. And when the light strikes the animal picture, the hunter's arrow flies right along that light beam and hits the drawn animal, and the woman who is present to assist him raises her hands and shouts. Then the hunter goes out and kills the animal. And the arrow will be just where it was in the picture. The next morning when the sun rises, the hunter erases the animal. This is something that was done in the name of the natural order, not in the name of his personal intention.

Now, there is another story from a totally different sphere of society, of the samurai, the Japanese warrior, who had the duty to avenge the murder of his overlord. When he cornered the man who had murdered his overlord, and he was about to deal with him with his samurai sword, the man in the corner, in the passion of terror, spat in the warrior's face. And the warrior sheathed the sword and walked away.

MOYERS: Why?

CAMPBELL: Because he was made angry, and if he had killed that man in anger, then it would have been a personal act. And he had come to do another kind of act, an impersonal act of vengeance.

MOYERS: Do you think this kind of impersonality played some part in the psyche of the hunter on the Great Plains?

CAMPBELL: Yes, definitely. Because isn't it a moral problem to kill somebody and eat that person? You see, these people didn't think of animals the way we do, as some subspecies. Animals are our equals at least, and sometimes our superiors.

The animal has powers that the human doesn't have. The shaman, for instance, will often have an animal familiar, that is to say, the spirit of some animal species that will be his support and his teacher.

MOYERS: But if humans begin to be able to imagine and see beauty and create beauty out of the relationship, then they become superior to the animals, do they not?

CAMPBELL: Well, I don't think they are thinking as much about superiority as equality. They ask the animals for advice, and the animal becomes the model for how to live. In that case, it is superior. And sometimes the animal becomes the giver of a ritual, as in the legends of the origins of the buffalo. For example, you can see this equality in the basic legend of the Blackfoot tribe, which is the origin legend of their buffalo dance rituals by which they invoke the cooperation of the animals in this play of life.

MOYERS: What was that?

CAMPBELL: Well, this story arises from the problem of how you find food for a large tribal group. One way of acquiring meat for the winter would be to drive a buffalo herd over a rock cliff so that they would all tumble over and could be slaughtered easily at the foot of the cliff. This is known as a buffalo fall.

This story is of a Blackfoot tribe, long, long ago, who couldn't get the buffalo to go over the cliff. The buffalo would approach the cliff and then turn aside. So it looked as though the tribe wasn't going to have any meat for that winter.

One day, the daughter of one of the houses got up early in the morning to draw the water for the family and happened to look up to the cliff. There on the cliff were the buffalo. And she said, "Oh, if you would only come over, I would marry one of you."

To her surprise, they all began coming over. Now, that was surprise number one. Surprise number two was when one of the old buffalo, the shaman of the herd, comes and says, "All right, girlie, off we go."

"Oh, no," she says.

"Oh, yes," he says, "you made your promise. We've kept our side of the bargain. Look at all my relatives here—dead. Now off we go."

Well, the family gets up in the morning and they look around, and where is Minnehaha? The father looks around on the ground —you know how Indians are, he can see by the footprints—and he says, "She's gone off with a buffalo. And I'm going to get her back."

So he puts on his walking moccasins, his bow and arrow, and so forth, and goes out over the plains. He has gone quite a distance when he feels he better sit down and rest. So he sits down, and he is thinking about what he should do now, when along comes the magpie, one of those clever birds that has shamanic qualities.

MOYERS: Magical qualities.

CAMPBELL: Yes. And the Indian says to him, "O beautiful bird, did my daughter run away with a buffalo? Have you seen her? Would you hunt around and see if you can find her out on the plains somewhere?"

And the magpie says, "Well, there is a lovely girl with the buffalo right now, over there, just a bit away."

"Well," says the man, "will you go tell her that her daddy is here at the buffalo wallow?"

So the magpie flies over and finds the girl who is there among the buffalo. They're all asleep, and she is knitting or something of the kind. And the magpie comes over, and he says, "Your father is over at the wallow waiting for you."

"Oh," she says, "this is terrible. This is very dangerous. These buffalo are going to kill us. You tell him to wait, and I'll be over. I'll try to work this out."

Now, her buffalo husband is behind her, and he wakes up and takes off his horn, and says, "Go to the wallow and get me a drink."

So she takes the horn and goes over, and there is her father. He grabs her by the arm and says, "Come!"

But she says, "No, no, no! This is real danger. The whole herd will be right after us. I have to work this thing out. Now, let me just go back."

So she gets the water and goes back. And the buffalo says, "Fe, fi, fo, fum, I smell the blood of an Indian"—you know, that sort of thing. And she says, no, nothing of the kind. And he says, "Yes indeed!" And he gives a buffalo bellow, and all the buffalo get up, and they all do a slow buffalo dance with tails raised, and they go over, and they trample that poor man to death, so that he disappears entirely. He is just all broken up to pieces. All gone. The girl is crying, and her buffalo husband says, "So you are crying."

"Yes," she says, "he is my daddy."

"Well," he says, "but what about us? There are our children, at the bottom of the cliff, our wives, our parents—and you cry about your daddy." Well, apparently he was a kind of compassionate buffalo, and he said, "Okay, if you can bring your daddy back to life again, I will let you go."

So she turns to the magpie and says, "Please pick around a little bit and see if you can find a bit of Daddy." And the magpie does so, and he comes up finally with a vertebra, just one little bone. And the girl says, "That's enough." And she puts the bone down on the ground and covers it with her blanket and sings a revivifying song, a magical song with great power. And presently—yes, there is a man under the blanket. She looks. "That's Daddy all right!" But he is not breathing yet. She sings a few more stanzas of whatever the song was, and he stands up.

The buffalo are amazed. And they say, "Well, why don't you do this for us? We'll teach you our buffalo dance, and when you will have killed our families, you do this dance and sing this song, and we will all come back to live again."

And that is the basic idea—that through the ritual that dimension is reached that transcends temporality and out of which life comes and back into which it goes.

MOYERS: What happened a hundred years ago when the white man came and slaughtered this animal of reverence?

CAMPBELL: That was a sacramental violation. You can see in many of the early nineteenth-century paintings by George Catlin of the Great Western Plains in his day literally hundreds of thousands of buffalo all over the place. And then, through the next half century, the frontiersmen, equipped with repeating rifles, shot down whole herds, taking only the skins to sell and leaving the bodies there to rot. This was a sacrilege.

MOYERS: It turned the buffalo from a "thou"—

CAMPBELL: —to an "it."

MOYERS: The Indians addressed the buffalo as "thou," an object of reverence.

CAMPBELL: The Indians addressed all of life as a "thou"—the trees, the stones, everything. You can address anything as a "thou," and if you do it, you can feel the change in your own psychology. The ego that sees a "thou" is not the same ego that sees an "it." And when you go to war with people, the problem of the newspapers is to turn those people into "its."

MOYERS: This happens in marriage, too, doesn't it? And happens with children, too.

CAMPBELL: Sometimes the "thou" turns into an "it," and you don't know what the relationship is. The Indian relationship to animals is in contrast to our relationship to animals, where we see animals as a lower form of life. In the Bible we are told that we are the masters. For hunting people, as I said, the animal is in many ways superior. A Pawnee Indian said: "In the beginning of all things, wisdom and knowledge were with the animal. For Tirawa, the One Above, did not speak directly to man. He sent certain animals to tell mankind that he showed himself through the beast. And that from them, and from the stars and the sun and the moon, man should learn."

MOYERS: So it is in this time of hunting man that we begin to sense a stirring of the mythic imagination, the wonder of things.

CAMPBELL: Yes. There is a burst of magnificent art and all the evidence you need of a mythic imagination in full form.

MOYERS: Do you ever look at these primitive art objects and think not of the art but of the man or woman standing there painting or creating? I find that I speculate—who was he or she?

CAMPBELL: This is what hits you when you go into those ancient caves. What was in their minds as they created these images? How did they get up there? And how did they see anything? The only light they had was a little flickering torch.

And with respect to the problem of beauty—is this beauty intended? Or is it something that is the natural expression of a beautiful spirit? Is the beauty of the bird's song intentional? In what sense is it intentional? Or is it the expression of the bird, the beauty of the bird's spirit, you might say? I think that way very often about this art. To what degree was the intention of the artist what we would call "aesthetic" or to what degree expressive? And to what degree is the art something that they had simply learned to do that way?

When a spider makes a beautiful web, the beauty comes out of the spider's nature. It's instinctive beauty. How much of the beauty of our own lives is about the beauty of being alive? How much of it is conscious and intentional? That is a big question.

MOYERS: Tell me what you remember when you first looked upon those painted caves.

CAMPBELL: You don't want to leave. Here you come into an enormous chamber, like a great cathedral, with all these painted animals. The darkness is inconceivable. We were there with electric lights, but in a couple of instances the man who was showing us through turned off the lights, and you were never in darker darkness in your life. It was—I don't know, just a complete knockout. You don't know where you are, whether you are looking north, south, east, or west. All orientation is gone, and you are in a darkness that never saw the sun. Then they turn the lights on again, and you see these gloriously painted animals. And they are painted with the vitality of ink on silk in a Japanese painting—you know, just like that. A bull that will be twenty feet long, and painted so that its haunches will be represented by a swelling in the rock. They take account of the whole thing.

MOYERS: You call them temple caves.

CAMPBELL: Yes.

MOYERS: Why?

CAMPBELL: A temple is a landscape of the soul. When you walk into a cathedral, you move into a world of spiritual images. It is the mother womb of your spiritual life—mother church. All the forms around are significant of spiritual value.

Now, in a cathedral, the imagery is in anthropomorphic form. God and Jesus and the saints and all are in human form. And in the caves the images are in animal form. But it's the same thing, believe me. The form is secondary. The message is what is important.

MOYERS: And the message of the caves?

CAMPBELL: The message of the caves is of a relationship of time to eternal powers that is somehow to be experienced in that place.

MOYERS: What were these caves used for?

CAMPBELL: Scholars speculate that they had to do with the initiation of boys into the hunt. Boys had to learn not only to hunt but how to respect the animals, and what rituals to perform, and how in their own lives no longer to be little boys but to be men. Those hunts, you see, were very, very dangerous. These caves are the original men's rite sanctuaries where the boys became no longer their mothers' sons but their fathers' sons.

MOYERS: What would happen to me as a child if I went through one of these rites?

CAMPBELL: Well, we don't know what they did in the caves, but we know what the aborigines do in Australia. Now, when a boy gets to be a little bit ungovernable, one fine day the men come in, and they are naked except for stripes of white bird down that they've stuck on their bodies using their own blood for glue. They are swinging the bull-roarers, which are the voices of spirits, and the men arrive as spirits.

The boy will try to take refuge with his mother, and she will pretend to try to protect him. But the men just take him away. A mother is no good from then on, you see. You can't go back to Mother, you're in another field.

Then the boys are taken out to the men's sacred ground, and they're really put through an ordeal—circumcision, subincision, the drinking of men's blood, and so forth. Just as they had drunk mother's milk as children, so now they drink men's blood. They're being turned into men. While this is going on, they are being shown enactments of mythological episodes from the great myths. They are instructed in the mythology of the tribe. Then, at the end of this, they are brought back to the village, and the girl whom each is to marry has already been selected. The boy has now come back as a man.

He has been removed from his childhood, and his body has been scarified, and circumcision and subincision have been en-acted. Now he has a man's body. There's no chance of relapsing back to boyhood after a show like that.

MOYERS: You don't go back to Mother.

CAMPBELL: No, but in our life we don't have anything like that. You can have a man forty-five years old still trying to be obedient to his father. So he goes to a psychoanalyst, who does the job for him.

MOYERS: Or he goes to the movies.

CAMPBELL: That might be our counterpart to mythological re-enactments—except that we don't have the same kind of thinking going into the production of a movie that goes into the production of an initiation ritual.

MOYERS: No, but given the absence of initiation rituals, which have largely disappeared from our society, the world of imagi-nation as projected on that screen serves, even if in a faulty way, to tell that story, doesn't it?

CAMPBELL: Yes, but what is unfortunate for us is that a lot

of the people who write these stories do not have the sense of their responsibility. These stories are making and breaking lives. But the movies are made simply to make money. The kind of responsibility that goes into a priesthood with a ritual is not there. That is one of our problems today.

MOYERS: We have none of those rites today, do we?

CAMPBELL: I'm afraid we don't. So the youngsters invent them themselves, and you have these raiding gangs, and so forth—that is self-rendered initiation.

MOYERS: So myth relates directly to ceremony and tribal ritual, and the absence of myth can mean the end of ritual.

CAMPBELL: A ritual is the enactment of a myth. By participating in a ritual, you are participating in a myth.

MOYERS: What does the absence of these myths mean to young boys today?

CAMPBELL: Well, the confirmation ritual is the counterpart today of these rites. As a Catholic boy, you choose your confirmed name, the name you are going to be confirmed by. But instead of scarifying you and knocking your teeth out and all, the bishop gives you a smile and a slap on the cheek. It has been reduced to that. Nothing has happened to you. The Jewish counterpart is the bar mitzvah. Whether it actually works to effect a psychological transformation will depend on the individual case, I suppose. But in those old days there was no problem. The boy came out with a different body, and he had really gone through something.

MOYERS: What about the female? Most of the figures in the temple caves are male. Was this a kind of secret society for males?

CAMPBELL: It wasn't a secret society, it was that the boys had to go through it. Now of course we don't know exactly what happened to the female in this period because there is very little evidence to tell us. But in primary cultures today the girl becomes a woman with her first menstruation. It happens to her. Nature does it to her. And so she has undergone the transformation, and what is her initiation? Typically it is to sit in a little hut for a certain number of days and realize what she is.

MOYERS: How does she do that?

CAMPBELL: She sits there. She is now a woman. And what is a woman? A woman is a vehicle of life. Life has overtaken her. Woman is what it is all about—the giving of birth and the giving of nourishment. She is identical with the earth goddess in her powers, and she has got to realize that about herself. The boy does not have a happening of this kind, so he has to be turned into a man and voluntarily become a servant of something greater than himself.

MOYERS: This is where the mythic imagination, as far as we know, began to operate.

CAMPBELL: Yes.

MOYERS: What were the chief themes of that era? Death?

CAMPBELL: The mystery of death is one of them—which balances the theme of the mystery of life. It is the same mystery in its two aspects. The next theme is the relationship of this to the animal world, which dies and lives again.

Then there is the motif of procuring food. The relationship of the woman to the nature of the outer world is there. Then we have to take into account the problem of the transformation of children into adults. That transformation is a fundamental concern throughout the ritual life of people. We have it today. There is the problem of turning ungovernable children, who express just the naive impulses of nature, into members of the society. That takes a lot of doing. These people could not tolerate anybody who wouldn't follow the rules. The society couldn't support them. They would kill them.

MOYERS: Because they were a threat to the health of the whole?

CAMPBELL: Well, of course. They were like cancers, something that was tearing the body apart. These tribal groups were living on the edge all the time.

MOYERS: And yet out on the edge they began to ask fundamental questions.

CAMPBELL: Yes. But the attitude toward dying wasn't like ours at all. The notion of a transcendent world was really taken seriously.

MOYERS: One important part of ancient ritual was that it made you a member of the tribe, a member of the community, a member of society. The history of Western culture has been the steadily widening separation of the self from society. "I" first, the individual first.

CAMPBELL: I wouldn't say that that's characteristic of Western culture all the way because the separation is not a separation just of a raw biological entity. There has always been the spiritual import until very lately. Now, when you see old newsreels of the installation of the President of the United States, you see him wearing a top hat. President Wilson, even in his time, was wearing a top hat. He did not wear a top hat in his usual life. But, as President, he has a ritual aspect to his presence. Now it's Johnny-come-lately walking in right off the golf course, you know, and sitting down with you and talking about whether we're going to have atom bombs. It's another style. There's been a reduction of ritual. Even in the Roman Catholic Church, my God—they've translated the Mass out of ritual language and into a language that has a lot of domestic associations. The Latin of the Mass was a language that threw you *out* of the field of domesticity. The altar was turned so that the priest's back was to you, and with him you addressed yourself outward. Now they've turned the altar around—it looks like Julia Child giving a demonstration—all homey and cozy.

MOYERS: And they play a guitar.

CAMPBELL: They play a guitar. They've forgotten that the function of ritual is to pitch you out, not to wrap you back in where you have been all the time.

MOYERS: And the ritual of a marriage ceremony pitches you out to the other.

CAMPBELL: It certainly does. But the rituals that once conveyed an inner reality are now merely form. That's true in the rituals of society as well as the personal rituals of marriage.

MOYERS: So I can see why in some respects religious instruction has become obsolete to a lot of people.

CAMPBELL: With respect to ritual, it must be kept alive. So much of our ritual is dead. It's extremely interesting to read of the primitive, elementary cultures—how they transform the folk tales, the myths, all the time in terms of the circumstances. People move from an area where, let's say, the vegetation is the main support, out into the plains. Most of our Plains Indians in the period of the horse-riding Indians had originally been of the Mississippian culture. They lived along the Mississippi in settled dwelling towns and agriculturally based villages.

And then they receive the horse from the Spaniards, which makes it possible to venture out into the plains and handle the great hunt of the buffalo herds. At this time, the mythology transforms from a vegetation mythology to a buffalo mythology. You can see the structure of the earlier vegetation mythologies underlying the mythologies of the Dakota Indians and the Pawnee Indians and the Kiowa, and so forth.

MOYERS: You're saying that the environment shapes the story?

CAMPBELL: The people respond to the environment, you see. But now we have a tradition that doesn't respond to the environment—it comes from somewhere else, from the first millennium B.C. It has not assimilated the qualities of our modern culture and the new things that are possible and the new vision of the universe.

Myth must be kept alive. The people who can keep it alive are artists of one kind or another. The function of the artist is the mythologization of the environment and the world.

MOYERS: You mean artists are the mythmakers of our day?

CAMPBELL: The mythmakers of earlier days were the counterparts of our artists.

MOYERS: They do the paintings on the walls, they perform the rituals.

CAMPBELL: Yes. There's an old romantic idea in German, *das Volk dichtet*, which says that the ideas and poetry of the traditional cultures come out of the folk. They do not. They come out of an elite experience, the experience of people particularly gifted, whose ears are open to the song of the universe. These people speak to the folk, and there is an answer from the folk, which is then received as an interaction. But the first impulse in the shaping of a folk tradition comes from above, not from below.

MOYERS: In these early elementary cultures, as you call them, who would have been the equivalent of the poets today?

CAMPBELL: The shamans. The shaman is the person, male or female, who in his late childhood or early youth has an overwhelming psychological experience that turns him totally inward. It's a kind of schizophrenic crack-up. The whole unconscious opens up, and the shaman falls into it. This shaman experience has been described many, many times. It occurs all the way from Siberia right through the Americas down to Tierra del Fuego.

MOYERS: And ecstasy is a part of it.

CAMPBELL: It is.

MOYERS: The trance dance, for example, in the Bushman society.

CAMPBELL: Now, there's a fantastic example of something. The Bushmen live in a desert world. It's a very hard life, a life of great, great tension. The male and female sexes are, in a disciplined way, separate. Only in the dance do the two come together. And they come together this way. The women sit in a circle or in a little group and beat their thighs, setting a pace for the men dancing around them. The women are the center around which the men dance. And they control the dance and what goes on with the men through their own singing and beating of the thighs.

MOYERS: What's the significance, that the woman is controlling the dance?

CAMPBELL: Well, the woman is life, and the man is the servant of life. That's the basic idea in these things. During the course of the circling, which they do all night long, one of the men will suddenly pass out. He experiences what we might call a possession. But it is described as a flash, a kind of thunderbolt or lightning bolt, which passes from the pelvic area right up the spine into the head.

MOYERS: It is described in your book *The Way of the Animal Powers*—here:

CAMPBELL: "When people sing, I dance. I enter the earth. I go in at a place like a place where people drink water. I travel a long way, very far." He's entranced now, and this is a description of an experience. "When I emerge, I am already climbing. I'm climbing threads, the threads that lie over there in the south. I climb one and leave it, then I climb another one. Then I leave it and climb another. . . . And when you arrive at God's place, you make yourself small. You have become small. You come in small to God's place. You do what you have to do there. Then you return to where everyone is, and you hide your face. You hide your face so you won't see anything. You come and come and come and finally you enter your body again. All the people who have stayed behind are waiting for you—they fear you. You enter, enter the earth, and you return to enter the skin of your body. . . . And you say 'he-e-e-e!' That is the sound of your return to your body. Then you begin to sing. The *ntum*-masters are there around." *Ntum* is the supernatural power. "They take powder and blow it—Phew! Phew!—in your face. They take hold of your head and blow about the sides of your face. This is how you manage to be alive again. Friends, if they don't do that to you, you die. . . . You just die and are dead. Friends, this is what it does, this *ntum* that I do, this *ntum* here that I dance."

My God! This guy's had an experience of another whole realm of consciousness! In these experiences they are, as it were, flying through the air.

MOYERS: He then becomes the shaman.

CAMPBELL: Not in this culture. He becomes the trance dancer. All the men are potentially tranced.

MOYERS: Is there something like this common in the experience of our culture? I'm thinking particularly of the born-again experience in our Southern culture.

CAMPBELL: There must be. This is an actual experience of transit through the earth to the realm of mythological imagery, to God, to the seat of power. I don't know what the born-again Christian experience is. I suppose medieval visionaries who saw visions of God and brought back stories of that would have had a comparable experience.

MOYERS: There's a sense of ecstasy, isn't there, in this experience?

CAMPBELL: As reported, it's always of ecstasy.

MOYERS: Have you ever seen such a rite? Such a happening? Have you ever known that kind of ecstasy or witnessed it?

CAMPBELL: No, I have not. I have friends who have been in Haiti a good deal and actually participated in voodoo ceremonials there where people become possessed. And there are dances where the ecstasy is simulated. There was an old idea of going berserk in war, of exciting warriors before they go to battle. They should actually be in a madness while they're in battle—the battle frenzy.

MOYERS: Is this the only way one can experience the unconscious?

CAMPBELL: No, the other way occurs as a breakthrough for people who have not been thinking that way—and then it comes to them, bang, like that.

MOYERS: And the one who had this psychological experience, this traumatic experience, this ecstasy, would become the interpreter for others of things not seen.

CAMPBELL: He would become the interpreter of the heritage of mythological life, you might say, yes.

MOYERS: And what draws him into that?

CAMPBELL: The best example I know which might help to answer that is the experience of Black Elk.

Black Elk was a young Sioux boy around nine years old. Now, this happened before the American cavalry had encountered the Sioux, who were the great people of the plains. The boy became sick, psychologically sick. His family tells the typical shaman story. The child begins to tremble and is immobilized. The family is terribly concerned about it, and they send for a shaman who has had the experience in his own youth, to come as a kind of psychoanalyst and pull the youngster out of it. But instead of relieving the boy of the deities, the shaman is adapting him to the deities and the deities to himself. It's a different problem from that of psychoanalysis. I think it was Nietzsche who said, "Be careful lest in casting out the devils you cast out the best thing that's in you." Here, the deities who have been encountered—powers, let's call them—are retained. The connection is maintained, not broken. And these men then become the spiritual advisers and gift-givers to their people.

Well, what happened with this young boy was that he had a prophetic vision of the terrible future of his tribe. It was a vision of what he called "the hoop" of the nation. In the vision, Black Elk saw that the hoop of his nation was one of many hoops, which is something that we haven't learned at all well yet. He saw the cooperation of all the hoops, all the nations in grand procession. But more than that, the vision was an experience of himself as going through the realms of spiritual imagery that were of his culture and assimilating their import. It comes to one great statement, which for me is a key statement to the understanding of myth and symbols. He says, "I saw myself on the central mountain of the world, the highest place, and I had a vision because I was seeing in the sacred manner of the world." And the sacred central mountain was Harney Peak in South Dakota. And then he says, "But the central mountain is everywhere."

That is a real mythological realization. It distinguishes between the local cult image, Harney Peak, and its connotation as the center of the world. The center of the world is the *axis mundi*, the central point, the pole around which all revolves. The central point of the world is the point where stillness and movement are together. Movement is time, but stillness is eternity. Realizing how this moment of your life is actually a moment of eternity, and experiencing the eternal aspect of what you're doing in the temporal experience—this is the mythological experience.

So is the central mountain of the world Jerusalem? Rome? Benares? Lhasa? Mexico City?

MOYERS: This Indian boy was saying there is a shining point where all lines intersect.

CAMPBELL: That's exactly what he was saying.

MOYERS: And he was saying God has no circumference?

CAMPBELL: There is a definition of God which has been repeated by many philosophers. God is an intelligible sphere—a sphere known to the mind, not to the senses—whose center is everywhere and whose circumference is nowhere. And the center, Bill, is right where you're sitting. And the other one is right where I'm sitting. And each of us is a manifestation of that mystery. That's a nice mythological realization that sort of gives you a sense of who and what you are.

MOYERS: So it's a metaphor, an image of reality.

CAMPBELL: Yes. What you have here is what might be translated into raw individualism, you see, if you didn't realize that the center was also right there facing you in the other person. This is the mythological way of being an individual. You are the central mountain, and the central mountain is everywhere.

IV

SACRIFICE
AND BLISS

If you follow your bliss, you put yourself on a kind of track that has been there all the while, waiting for you, and the life that you ought to be living is the one you are living. Wherever you are—if you are following your bliss, you are enjoying that refreshment, that life within you, all the time.

MOYERS: What impresses me as I read what you have written about the impact of the environment on storytelling is that these people—the people on the plains, the hunters, the people in the forest, the planters—are participating in their landscape. They are part of their world, and every feature of their world becomes sacred to them.

CAMPBELL: The sanctification of the local landscape is a fundamental function of mythology. You can see this very clearly with the Navaho, who will identify a northern mountain, a southern mountain, an eastern mountain, a western mountain, and a central mountain. In a Navaho hogan, the door always faces east. The fireplace is in the center, which becomes a cosmic center, with the smoke coming up through the hole in the ceiling so that the scent of the incense goes to the nostrils of the gods.

The landscape, the dwelling place, becomes an icon, a holy picture. Wherever you are, you are related to the cosmic order.

Again, when you see a Navaho sand painting, there will be a surrounding figure—it may represent a mirage or the rainbow or what not, but there will always be a surrounding figure with an opening in the east so that the new spirit can pour in. When the Buddha sat under the bo tree, he faced east—the direction of the rising sun.

MOYERS: On my first visit to Kenya, I went alone to one of the ancient sites of a primitive camp on what used to be the shore of a lake, and stayed there until night fell, feeling a sense of the presence of all creation—sensing underneath that night sky, in that vast place, that I belonged to something ancient, something very much still alive.

CAMPBELL: I think it's Cicero who says that when you go into a great tall grove, the presence of a deity becomes known to you. There are sacred groves everywhere. Going into the forest as a little boy, I can remember worshiping a tree, a great big old tree, thinking, "My, my, what you've known and been." I think this sense of the presence of creation is a basic mood of man. But we live now in a city. It's all stone and rock, manufactured by human hands. It's a different kind of world to grow up in when you're out in the forest with the little chipmunks and the great owls. All these things are around you as presences, representing forces and powers and magical possibilities of life that are not yours and yet are all part of life, and that opens it out to you. Then you find it echoing in yourself, because you are nature. When a Sioux Indian would take the calumet, the pipe, he would hold it up stem to the sky so that the sun could take the first puff. And then he'd address the four directions always. In that frame of mind, when you're addressing yourself to the horizon, to the world that you're in, then you're in your place in the world. It's a different way to live.

MOYERS: You write in *The Mythic Image* about the center of

transformation, the idea of a sacred place where the temporal walls may dissolve to reveal a wonder. What does it mean to have a sacred place?

CAMPBELL: This is an absolute necessity for anybody today. You must have a room, or a certain hour or so a day, where you don't know what was in the newspapers that morning, you don't know who your friends are, you don't know what you owe anybody, you don't know what anybody owes to you. This is a place where you can simply experience and bring forth what you are and what you might be. This is the place of creative incubation. At first you may find that nothing happens there. But if you have a sacred place and use it, something eventually will happen.

MOYERS: This sacred place does for you what the plains did for the hunter.

CAMPBELL: For them the whole world was a sacred place. But our life has become so economic and practical in its orientation that, as you get older, the claims of the moment upon you are so great, you hardly know where the hell you are, or what it is you intended. You are always doing something that is required of you. Where is your bliss station? You have to try to find it. Get a phonograph and put on the music that you really love, even if it's corny music that nobody else respects. Or get the book you like to read. In your sacred place you get the "thou" feeling of life that these people had for the whole world in which they lived.

MOYERS: We have talked about the impact of the landscape on the people. But what about the effect of people on the landscape?

CAMPBELL: People claim the land by creating sacred sites, by mythologizing the animals and plants—they invest the land with spiritual powers. It becomes like a temple, a place for meditation. For example, the Navaho did a marvelous job in mythologizing animals. In the Navaho sand paintings, you see these little animals, each with its own value. Now, these animals are not shown naturalistically. They are stylized. And the stylization refers to their spiritual, not to their merely physical, characteristics. There is a big fly, for example, that will sometimes fly down and sit on your shoulder when you are walking along in the desert. In the Navaho myths he is known as Big Fly, also as Little Wind. He whispers to the young heroes the answers to all the questions that their fathers put to them when they are being tested. Big Fly is the voice of the holy spirit revealing hidden wisdom.

MOYERS: And the purpose of all this?

CAMPBELL: To claim the land. To turn the land where they lived into a place of spiritual relevance.

MOYERS: So when Moses looked out on the Promised Land, he was simply doing what other spiritual leaders had done for their own people. He was claiming that land.

CAMPBELL: Yes. You remember the story of Jacob's dream. When Jacob awakes, the place becomes Bethel, the house of God. Jacob has claimed that place with a certain spiritual significance. This is the place where God sowed his energies.

MOYERS: Do sacred sites still exist on this continent today?

CAMPBELL: Mexico City was a sacred site, one of the great cities in the world before the Spanish tore it apart. When the Spanish first saw Mexico City, or Tenochtitlán, it was a greater city than any city in Europe. And it was a sacred city, with great temples. Now the Catholic cathedral is right where the temple of the sun used to be. That's an example of land-claiming by the Christians. You see, they are transforming the same landscape into their landscape by putting their temple where the other temple was.

Our Pilgrim fathers, for example, named sites after biblical centers. And somebody in upper New York State had the *Odyssey* and *Iliad* in his mind—Ithaca, Utica, and one classical name after another.

MOYERS: In a sense, people are anointing the land where they believe there is energy which empowers them. There is an organic relationship between the land and the structures people build upon it.

CAMPBELL: Yes, but that ended with the coming of the metropolis.

MOYERS: In New York now, the competition is over who can build the tallest building.

CAMPBELL: This is a kind of architectural triumph. It is the statement of the city that we are a financial power center, and look what we can do. It is a kind of virtuoso acrobatic stunt.

MOYERS: Where are the sacred places today?

CAMPBELL: They don't exist. There are a few historical spots where people may go to think about something important that happened there. For example, we may go visit the Holy Land, because that's the land of our religious origins. But every land should be a holy land. One should find the symbol in the landscape itself of the energies of the life there. That's what all early traditions do. They sanctify their own landscape.

That's what the early settlers of Iceland did, for example, in the eighth and ninth centuries. They established their different settlements in a relationship of 432,000 Roman feet to each other (432,000 is an important mythological number known to many traditions). The whole organization of the Icelandic landscape was in terms of such cosmic relationships, so that wherever you go in Iceland, you are, so to say (if you know your mythology), in accord with the universe. This is the same kind of mythology that you have in Egypt, but in Egypt the symbology took a different shape because Egypt is not circular, Egypt is long. So there you have the sky goddess as a Sacred Cow, two feet in the south and two feet in the north—a rectangular idea, so to speak. But the spiritual symbolization of our own civilization is basically lost to us. That's why it's so wonderful to go to the lovely little French town of Chartres where the cathedral still dominates, and you hear the bells ring when night turns to day, and when morning turns to noon, and again when day turns to night.

I consider Chartres my parish. I've been there often. When I was a student in Paris, I spent one whole weekend in the cathedral, studying every single figure there. I was there so much that the concierge came up to me one noontime and said, "Would you like to go up with me and ring the bells?" I said, "I sure would." So we climbed the tower up to the great bronze bell. There was a little platform like a seesaw. He stood on one end of the seesaw, and I stood on the other end of the seesaw, and there was a little bar there for us to hold on to. He gave the thing a push, and then he was on it, and I was on it. And we started going up and down, and the wind was blowing through our hair, up there in the cathedral, and then it began ringing underneath us—"Bong, bong, bong." It was one of the most thrilling adventures of my life.

When it was all over, he brought me down, and he said, "I want to show you where my room is." Well, in a cathedral you have the nave, then the transept, and then the apse, and around the apse is the choir screen. He took me through a little door in the middle of the choir screen, and there was his little bed and a little table with a lamp on it. When I looked out through the screen, there was the window of the Black Madonna—and that was where he lived. Now, there was a man living by constant meditation. That was a very moving, beautiful thing. I've been to Chartres time and time again since.

MOYERS: And what do you find there?

CAMPBELL: It takes me back to a time when these spiritual principles informed the society. You can tell what's informing a society by what the tallest building is. When you approach a medieval town, the cathedral is the tallest thing in the place. When you approach an eighteenth-century town, it is the political palace that's the tallest thing in the place. And when you approach a modern city, the tallest places are the office buildings, the centers of economic life.

If you go to Salt Lake City, you see the whole thing illustrated right in front of your face. First the temple was built, right in the center of the city. This is the proper organization because the temple is the spiritual center from which everything flows in all directions. Then the political building, the Capitol, was built beside it, and it's taller than the temple. And now the tallest thing is the office building that takes care of the affairs of both the temple and the political building. That's the history of Western civilization. From the Gothic through the princely periods of the sixteenth, seventeenth, eighteenth centuries, to this economic world that we're in now.

MOYERS: So when you go to Chartres—

CAMPBELL: —I'm back in the Middle Ages. I'm back in the world that I was brought up in as a child, the Roman Catholic spiritual-image world, and it is magnificent.

MOYERS: You're not a man who swims long in nostalgia. It's not just the past that moves you when you go there, is it?

CAMPBELL: No, it's the present. That cathedral talks to me about the spiritual information of the world. It's a place for meditation, just walking around, just sitting, just looking at those beautiful things.

MOYERS: The cathedral at Chartres which you love so much also expresses a relationship of the human to the cosmos, doesn't it?

CAMPBELL: Yes. The cathedral is in the form of a cross, with the altar in the middle there. It's a symbolic structure. Now many churches are built as though they were theaters. Visibility is important. In the cathedral, there is no interest in visibility at all. Most of what goes on goes on out of your sight. But the symbol is what's important there, not just watching the show. Everybody knows the show by heart. You've seen it ever since you were a six-year-old child.

MOYERS: Why keep going to the cathedral, then?

CAMPBELL: That's the whole business of myth. Why do we like to talk about these things again? Because it puts us back in touch with the essential archetypology of our spiritual life. Going through a ritual day after day keeps you on the line.

MOYERS: But we don't do that now.

CAMPBELL: We've lost touch with that kind of concern. The goal of early life was to live in constant consciousness of the spiritual principle. In the Assyrian palaces, you'll see a composite beast with the head of a man, the body of a lion, the wings of the eagle, and the feet of a bull: four signs of the zodiac that have been put together and made into door guardians.

Those same four beasts, which are associated with the vision of Ezekiel, become the four evangelists in the Christian tradition. You remember the prayer: "Matthew, Mark, Luke, and John, bless the bed that I sleep on." In this prayer, you are in the middle, where Christ is, and the four points of the compass around you are the four posts of your bed.

Now, this mandala represents the Christ appearing from beyond Space-Time. Those four beasts represent the veil of Space-Time, veiling eternity, and the Christ in the center is the breakthrough, the second birth, the coming of the Lord of the World from the womb of the universal goddess, Space-Time.

MOYERS: You say that a cathedral such as Chartres symbolizes the knowledge of a ground of meaning that transcends the law and is present architecturally not only in the forms of majestic stone but also in the great silence surrounding and inhabiting those forms.

CAMPBELL: All final spiritual reference is to the silence beyond sound. The word made flesh is the first sound. Beyond that sound is the transcendent unknown, the unknowable. It can be spoken of as the great silence, or as the void, or as the transcendent absolute.

MOYERS: When I listen to you talk about how myths connect us to our sacred places, and how landscapes connected primal human beings to the universe, I begin to think that the supernatural, at least as you understand it, is really only the natural.

CAMPBELL: The idea of the supernatural as being something over and above the natural is a killing idea. In the Middle Ages this was the idea that finally turned that world into something like a wasteland, a land where people were living inauthentic lives, never doing a thing they truly wanted to because the supernatural laws required them to live as directed by their clergy. In a wasteland, people are fulfilling purposes that are not properly theirs but have been put upon them as inescapable laws. This is a killer. The twelfth-century troubadour poetry of courtly love was a protest against this supernaturally justified violation of life's joy in truth. So too the Tristan legend and at least one of the great versions of the legend of the Grail, that of Wolfram von Eschenbach. The spirit is really the bouquet of life. It is not something breathed into life, it comes out of life. This is one of the glorious things about the mother-goddess religions, where the world is the body of the Goddess, divine in itself, and divinity isn't something ruling over and above a fallen nature. There was something of this spirit in the medieval cult of the Virgin, out of which all the beautiful thirteenth-century French cathedrals arose.

However, our story of the Fall in the Garden sees nature as corrupt; and that myth corrupts the whole world for us. Because nature is thought of as corrupt, every spontaneous act is sinful and must not be yielded to. You get a totally different civilization and a totally different way of living according to whether your myth presents nature as fallen or whether nature is in itself a manifestation of divinity, and the spirit is the revelation of the divinity that is inherent in nature.

MOYERS: Who interprets the divinity inherent in nature for us today? Who are our shamans? Who interprets unseen things for us?

CAMPBELL: It is the function of the artist to do this. The artist is the one who communicates myth for today. But he has to be an artist who understands mythology and humanity and isn't simply a sociologist with a program for you.

MOYERS: What about those others who are ordinary, those who are not poets or artists, or who have not had a transcendent ecstasy? How do we know of these things?

CAMPBELL: I'll tell you a way, a very nice way. Sit in a room and read—and read and read. And read the right books by the right people. Your mind is brought onto that level, and you have a nice, mild, slow-burning rapture all the time. This realization of life can be a constant realization in your living. When you find an author who really grabs you, read everything he has done. Don't say, "Oh, I want to know what So-and-so did"—and don't bother at all with the best-seller list. Just read what this one author has to give you. And then you can go read what he had read. And the world opens up in a way that is consistent with a certain point of view. But when you go from one author to another, you may be able to tell us the date when each wrote such and such a poem—but he hasn't said anything to you.

MOYERS: So shamans functioned in early societies as artists do now. They play a much more important role than simply being—

CAMPBELL: They played the role the priesthood traditionally plays in our society.

MOYERS: Then shamans were priests?

CAMPBELL: There's a major difference, as I see it, between a shaman and a priest. A priest is a functionary of a social sort. The society worships certain deities in a certain way, and the priest becomes ordained as a functionary to carry out that ritual. The deity to whom he is devoted is a deity that was there before he came along. But the shaman's powers are symbolized in his own familiars, deities of his own personal experience. His authority comes out of a psychological experience, not a social ordination.

MOYERS: The shaman has been somewhere I haven't, and he explains it to me.

CAMPBELL: Also, as in the case of Black Elk, the shaman may translate some of his visions into ritual performances for his people. That's bringing the inner experience into the outer life of the people themselves.

MOYERS: This was the beginning of a religion?

CAMPBELL: Personally, I think that's how religions began. But that's just a guess. We don't really know.

MOYERS: A Jesus goes into the wilderness, experiences a psychological transformation, comes back, and says to people, "Follow me." And this happens in these elementary cultures?

CAMPBELL: That's the evidence we have. We find a shamanic aspect in practically all the hunting cultures.

MOYERS: Why, particularly, in the hunting cultures?

CAMPBELL: Because they're individual. The hunter is an individual in a way that no farmer will ever be. Toiling in the fields and waiting for nature to tell you when you're going to do it is one thing, but going off on a hunt—every hunt is a different hunt from the last one. And the hunters are trained in individual skills that require very special talents and abilities.

MOYERS: So what happened to the shaman in human evolution?

CAMPBELL: When this big emphasis came on the settled village life, the shaman lost power. In fact, there's a wonderful set of stories and myths of some of the Southwestern American Indians, the Navaho and Apache, who were originally hunting peoples who came down into an area where agriculture had been developed and took on an agricultural system of life. In their stories of the beginnings, there is typically an amusing episode where the shamans are disgraced and the priests take over. The shamans say something that offends the sun, and the sun disappears, and then they say, "Oh, I can bring the sun back." Then they do all their tricks, and these are cynically, comically described. But their tricks don't bring the sun back. The shamans are reduced, then, to a shaman society, a kind of clown society. They are magicians of a special power, but their power is now subordinate to a larger society.

MOYERS: We talked about the effect of the hunting plain on mythology, this space clearly bounded by a circular horizon with the great dome of heaven above. But what about the people who lived in the dense foliage of the jungle? There's no dome of the sky, no horizon, no sense of perspective—just trees, trees, trees.

CAMPBELL: Colin Turnbull tells an interesting story of bringing a pygmy who had never been out of the forest onto a mountaintop. Suddenly they came from the trees onto the hill, and there was an extensive plain stretching out before them. The poor little fellow was utterly terrified. He had no way of judging perspective or distance. He thought that the animals grazing on the plain in the distance were just across the way and were so small that they were ants. He was just totally baffled, and rushed back into the forest.

MOYERS: Geography has done a great deal to shape our culture and our idea of religion. The god of the desert is not the god of the plains—

CAMPBELL: —or the god of the rain forest—the gods, plural, of the rain forest. When you're out in the desert with one sky and one world, then you might have one deity, but in a jungle, where there's no horizon and you never see anything more than ten or twelve yards away from you, you don't have that idea anymore.

MOYERS: So are they projecting their idea of God on the world?

CAMPBELL: Yes, of course.

MOYERS: Their geography shapes their image of divinity, and then they project it out and call it God.

CAMPBELL: Yes. The god idea is always culturally conditioned, always. And even when a missionary brings what he thinks is God, his god, that god is transformed in terms of what the people are able to think of as a divinity.

There is an amusing story about a British missionary in Hawaii who was paid a visit by a priestess of the goddess Pele. Now, a priestess of Pele would be, in a sense, a minor incarnation of Pele herself. So the missionary was actually talking to a goddess there. He said, "I have come to bring you the message of God." And the priestess said, "Oh, that's your god, Pele's mine."

MOYERS: Is the idea "Thou shalt have no other gods before me" purely a Hebraic idea?

CAMPBELL: I've not found it anywhere else.

MOYERS: Why only one god?

CAMPBELL: This I do not understand. I do understand the accent on the local social deity for people who are living in a desert. Your whole commitment is to the society which is protecting you. Society is always patriarchal. Nature is always matrilineal.

MOYERS: Do you think goddess religions emerged because in the domestication of the human race women played such a dominant role in the planting and harvesting activities of those early societies?

CAMPBELL: There is no doubt about it. At that moment, the

women become the most important members of the society in terms of magic power.

MOYERS: It had been the man hunting—

CAMPBELL: Yes, and now it moves over into the woman. Since her magic is that of giving birth and nourishment, as the earth does, her magic supports the magic of the earth. In the early tradition, she is the first planter. It is only later, when the plow is invented in the high culture systems, that the male takes over the agricultural lead again. And then the simulation of coitus, with the plow plowing the earth, becomes a dominant myth figure.

MOYERS: So these differing approaches to myth are what you mean by the "way of the animal powers," the "way of the seeded earth," the "way of the celestial lights," and the "way of man."

CAMPBELL: These have to do with the symbolic system through which the normal human condition of the time is symbolized and organized and given knowledge of itself.

MOYERS: And what it values?

CAMPBELL: The values will be a result of the conditions that govern life. For instance, the hunter is always directed outward to the animal. His life depends on the relationship to the animals. His mythology is outward turned. But the planting mythology, which has to do with the cultivation of the plant, the planting of the seed, the death of the seed, so to say, and the coming of the new plant, is more inward turned. With the hunters, the animals inspired the mythology. When a man wanted to gain power and knowledge, he would go into the forest and fast and pray, and an animal would come and teach him.

With the planters, the plant world is the teacher. The plant world is identical in its life sequences with the life of man. So you see, there's an inward relationship there.

MOYERS: What happened to the mythic imagination as human

beings turned from the hunting of animals to the planting of seeds?

CAMPBELL: There is a dramatic and total transformation, not just of the myths but of the psyche itself, I think. You see, an animal is a total entity, he is within a skin. When you kill that animal, he's dead—that's the end of him. There is no such thing as a self-contained individual in the vegetal world. You cut a plant, and another sprout comes. Pruning is helpful to a plant. The whole thing is just a continuing inbeingness.

Another idea associated with the tropical forests is that out of rot comes life. I have seen wonderful redwood forests with great, huge stumps from enormous trees that were cut down decades ago. Out of them are coming these bright new little children who are part of the same plant. Also, if you cut off the limb of a plant, another one comes. Tear off the limb of an animal, and unless it is a certain kind of lizard, it doesn't grow again.

So in the forest and planting cultures, there is a sense of death as not death somehow, that death is required for new life. And the individual isn't quite an individual, he is a branch of a plant. Jesus uses this image when he says, "I am the vine, and you are the branches." That vineyard image is a totally different one from the separate animals. When you have a planting culture, there is a fostering of the plant that is going to be eaten.

MOYERS: What stories did this experience of the planter inspire?

CAMPBELL: The motif of the plants that you eat having grown from the cut-up and buried body of a sacrificed deity or ancestral personage occurs all over the place, but particularly in the Pacific cultures.

These plant stories actually penetrate what we normally think of as a hunting area in the Americas. The North American culture is a very strong example of the interaction of hunting and planting cultures. The Indians were chiefly hunters, but they were also growing maize. One Algonquin story about the origin of maize tells of a boy who has a vision. In this vision, he sees a young man who comes to him with green plumes on his head and who invites the boy to a wrestling match. He wins and comes again and wins again, and so on. But one day the young man tells the boy that next time the boy must kill him and bury him and take care of the place where he has been buried. The boy then does what he has been told to do, and kills and buries the beautiful youth. In time, the boy returns and sees the corn growing where the plumed young man has been buried, or planted, you might say.

Now, this boy had been concerned for his father, who was a hunter but old. The boy was wondering whether there might be some other way to get food besides hunting. The vision came to him out of his intention. And the boy says to his father at the end of the tale, "We no longer need to go out hunting now." That must have been a moment of great awakening for these people.

MOYERS: But the idea is that the plumed man in the vision has to die and be buried before the plant can grow from the remains of his body. Does that story run through one myth after another in the planting cultures?

CAMPBELL: It does. A duplicate of this story comes up throughout Polynesia, for instance. There is a girl who loves to bathe in a certain pool. A great eel is also swimming around in the pool, and day after day he scrapes across her thigh as she is bathing. Then one fine day he turns into a young man and becomes her lover for a moment. Then he goes away and comes back again, and goes away and comes back again. But one time when he comes, he says, just as the plumed man in the Algonquin story had said, "Now, next time I come to visit you, you must kill me, cut off my head, and bury it." She does so, and there grows from the buried head a coconut tree. And when you pick a coconut, you can see it is just the size of a head. You can even see eyes and the little nodules that simulate the head. If we are to believe what most of our American anthropologists tell us, there is no connection between the Pacific cultures and the cultures of middle America from which our planting myths have come.

MOYERS: So we have the same story springing up in cultures unrelated to each other. What does that say about it?

CAMPBELL: That is one of the amazing things about these myths. I have been dealing with this stuff all my life, and I am still stunned by the accuracies of the repetitions. It is almost like a reflex in another medium of the same thing, the same story. Instead of corn, or maize, it's a coconut.

MOYERS: The stunning thing to me about these stories from the planting cultures is that for the first time we have people arising from the womb of the earth. The womb keeps appearing again and again and again in so many of these stories.

CAMPBELL: It is particularly conspicuous in legends of the American Southwest, where the first people come out of the earth. They come forth out of the hole of emergence, and that becomes the sacred place, the world axial center. It is associated with a certain mountain.

The story is that there were people down in the depths who weren't yet really people, who didn't even know they were people. One of them breaks a taboo that nobody knew was a taboo, and the floodwaters begin coming in. They have to ascend, to get out by a rope through the hole in the ceiling of the world —and then they are in another world. In one story, the shamans become aggressive in their thinking and insult the sun and moon, which then disappear, so everybody is in the dark.

The shamans say, oh, they can get the sun back, and they swallow trees and bring the trees out through their bellies, and they bury themselves in the ground with only their eyes sticking out, and do all these great shamanic magic tricks. But the tricks don't work. The sun doesn't come back.

Then the priests say, well now, let the people try. And the

people consist of all the animals. These animal people stand in a circle, and they dance and they dance, and it is the dance of the people that brings forth the hill that grows then into a mountain and becomes the elevated center of the world, out of which all the human people come.

And then comes an interesting thing, just as in the Old Testament—all we have heard is the story of this particular group, the Navaho, let's say. But when they come out, the Pueblo people are already there. It's like the problem of where did Adam's sons get their wives? There is the creation of these people, and the rest of the world is somehow there by another accident.

MOYERS: This is the idea of the Chosen People.

CAMPBELL: Sure it is. Every people is a chosen people in its own mind. And it is rather amusing that their name for themselves usually means mankind. They have odd names for the other people—like Funny Face, or Twisted Nose.

MOYERS: The Indians from the northeast woods of America told of a woman who fell from the sky and gave birth to twins. The Indians of the Southwest told a story of twins born to a virgin mother.

CAMPBELL: Yes. The woman from the sky originally comes from a hunting-culture base, and the woman of the earth comes from the planting culture. The twins represent two contrary principles, but quite different contrary principles from those represented by Cain and Abel in the Bible. In the Iroquois story, one twin is Sprout or Plant Boy, and the other is named Flint. Flint so damages his mother when he is born that she dies. Now, Flint and Plant Boy represent the two traditions. Flint is used for the blade to kill animals, so the twin named Flint represents the hunting tradition, and Plant Boy, of course, represents the planting principle.

In the biblical tradition, the plant boy is Cain and the flint boy is Abel, who is really a herder rather than a hunter. So in the Bible, you have the herder against the planter, and the planter is the one who is abominated. This is the myth of hunting people or herding people who have come into a planting-culture world and denigrate the people whom they have conquered.

MOYERS: It sounds like a great range war in the old West.

CAMPBELL: Yes. In the biblical tradition, it is always the second son who is the winner, the good one. The second son is the newcomer—namely the Hebrews. The older son, or the Canaanites, were living there before. Cain represents the agriculturally based city position.

MOYERS: These stories explain a great deal about contemporary conflicts, don't they?

CAMPBELL: Yes, they do indeed. It's fascinating to compare the coming together of an invading planting society or an invading hunting or herding people in conflict with planters. The counterparts are exactly the same across the planet—two systems in conflict and conjunction.

MOYERS: You said that the woman who fell from the sky was already pregnant and the woman who gave birth on earth to twins was already pregnant. What does it say to you that in so many of these cultures there are legends of virgins giving birth to heroes who die and are resurrected?

CAMPBELL: The death and resurrection of a savior figure is a common motif in all of these legends. For example, in the story of the origin of maize, you have this benign figure who appears to the young boy in a vision, and gives him maize, and dies. The plant comes from his body. Somebody has had to die in order for life to emerge. I begin to see this incredible pattern of death giving rise to birth, and birth giving rise to death. Every generation has to die in order that the next generation can come.

MOYERS: You write, "Out of the rocks of fallen wood and leaves, fresh sprouts arise, from which the lesson appears to have been that from death springs life, and out of death new birth. And the grim conclusion drawn was that the way to increase life is to increase death. Accordingly, the entire equatorial belt of this globe has been characterized by a frenzy of sacrifice—vegetable, animal and human sacrifice."

CAMPBELL: There is a ritual associated with the men's societies in New Guinea that actually enacts the planting-society myth of death, resurrection, and cannibalistic consumption. There is a sacred field with drums going, and chants going, and then pauses. This goes on for four or five days, on and on. Rituals are boring, you know, they just wear you out, and then you break through to something else.

At last comes the great moment. There has been a celebration of real sexual orgy, the breaking of all rules. The young boys who are being initiated into manhood are now to have their first sexual experience. There is a great shed of enormous logs supported by two uprights. A young woman comes in ornamented as a deity, and she is brought to lie down in this place beneath the great roof. The boys, six or so, with the drums going and chanting going, one after another, have their first experience of intercourse with the girl. And when the last boy is with her in full embrace, the supports are withdrawn, the logs drop, and the couple is killed. There is the union of male and female again, as they were in the beginning, before the separation took place. There is the union of begetting and death. They are both the same thing.

Then the little couple is pulled out and roasted and eaten that very evening. The ritual is the repetition of the original act of the killing of a god followed by the coming of food from the dead savior. In the sacrifice of the Mass, you are taught that this is the body and blood of the Savior. You take it to you, and you turn inward, and there he works within you.

MOYERS: What is the truth to which the rituals point?

CAMPBELL: The nature of life itself has to be realized in the acts of life. In the hunting cultures, when a sacrifice is made, it is, as it were, a gift or a bribe to the deity that is being invited to do something for us or to give us something. But when a figure is sacrificed in the planting cultures, that figure itself is the god. The person who dies is buried and becomes the food. Christ is crucified, and from his body the food of the spirit comes.

The Christ story involves a sublimation of what originally was a very solid vegetal image. Jesus is on Holy Rood, the tree, and he is himself the fruit of the tree. Jesus is the fruit of eternal life, which was on the second forbidden tree in the Garden of Eden. When man ate of the fruit of the first tree, the tree of the knowledge of good and evil, he was expelled from the Garden. The Garden is the place of unity, of nonduality of male and female, good and evil, God and human beings. You eat the duality, and you are on the way out. The tree of coming back to the Garden is the tree of immortal life, where you know that I and the Father are one.

Getting back into that Garden is the aim of many a religion. When Yahweh threw man out of the Garden, he put two cherubim at the gate, with a flaming sword between. Now, when you approach a Buddhist shrine, with the Buddha seated under the tree of immortal life, you will find at the gate two guardians—those are the cherubim, and you're going between them to the tree of immortal life. In the Christian tradition, Jesus on the cross is on a tree, the tree of immortal life, and he is the fruit of the tree. Jesus on the cross, the Buddha under the tree—these are the same figures. And the cherubim at the gate—who are they? At the Buddhist shrines you'll see one has his mouth open, the other has his mouth closed—fear and desire, a pair of opposites. If you're approaching a garden like that, and those two figures there are real to you and threaten you, if you have fear for your life, you are still outside the garden. But if you are no longer attached to your ego existence, but see the ego existence as a function of a larger, eternal totality, and you favor the larger against the smaller, then you won't be afraid of those two figures, and you will go through.

We're kept out of the Garden by our own fear and desire in relation to what we think to be the goods of our life.

MOYERS: Have all men at all times felt some sense of exclusion from an ultimate reality, from bliss, from delight, from perfection, from God?

CAMPBELL: Yes, but then you also have moments of ecstasy. The difference between everyday living and living in those moments of ecstasy is the difference between being outside and inside the Garden. You go past fear and desire, past the pair of opposites.

MOYERS: Into harmony?

CAMPBELL: Into transcendence. This is an essential experience of any mystical realization. You die to your flesh and are born into your spirit. You identify yourself with the consciousness and life of which your body is but the vehicle. You die to the vehicle and become identified in your consciousness with that of which the vehicle is the carrier. That is the God.

What you get in the vegetation traditions is this notion of identity behind the surface display of duality. Behind all these manifestations is the one radiance, which shines through all things. The function of art is to reveal this radiance through the created object. When you see the beautiful organization of a fortunately composed work of art, you just say, "Aha!" Somehow it speaks to the order in your own life and leads to the realization of the very things that religions are concerned to render.

MOYERS: That death is life, and life is death, and that the two are in accord?

CAMPBELL: That you have to balance between death and life—they are two aspects of the same thing, which is being, becoming.

MOYERS: And that is in all of these stories?

CAMPBELL: All of them. I know no story in which death is

rejected. The old idea of being sacrificed is not what we think at all. The Mayan Indians had a kind of basketball game in which, at the end, the captain of the winning team was sacrificed on the field by the captain of the losing team. His head was cut off. Going to your sacrifice as the winning stroke of your life is the essence of the early sacrificial idea.

MOYERS: This idea of sacrifice, especially of the winner being sacrificed, is so foreign to our world. Our ruling motif today is winner take all.

CAMPBELL: In this Mayan ritual, the name of the game was to become worthy to be sacrificed as a god.

MOYERS: Do you think it is true that he who loses his life gains his life?

CAMPBELL: That is what Jesus says.

MOYERS: Do you believe it is true?

CAMPBELL: I do—if you lose it in the name of something. There is a report by the seventeenth-century Jesuit missionaries in eastern Canada of a young Iroquois brave who has just been captured by an enemy tribe. He is being brought to be tortured to death. The Northeastern Indians had a custom of systematic torture of their male captives. The ordeal was to be suffered without flinching. That was the final test of real manhood. And so this young Iroquois is being brought in to endure this horrible ordeal; but, to the Jesuits' amazement, it is as though he were coming to celebrate his wedding. He is decorated and loudly singing. His captors are treating him as though they were his welcoming hosts and he their honored guest. And he is playing the game along with them, knowing all the while to what end he is being conducted. The French priests describing the occasion are simply appalled by what they interpret as the heartless mockery of such a reception, characterizing the youth's captors as a company of savage brutes. But no! Those people were to be the young brave's sacrificial priests. This was to be a sacrifice of the altar and, by analogy, that boy was the like of Jesus. The French priests themselves, every day, were celebrating Mass, which is a replication of the brutal sacrifice of the cross.

There is an equivalent scene described in the apocryphal Christian Acts of John, immediately before Jesus goes to be crucified. This is one of the most moving passages in Christian literature. In the Matthew, Mark, Luke and John gospels, it is simply mentioned that, at the conclusion of the celebration of the Last Supper, Jesus and his disciples sang a hymn before he went forth. But in the Acts of John, we have a word-for-word account of the whole singing of the hymn. Just before going out into the garden at the end of the Last Supper, Jesus says to the company, "Let us dance!" And they all hold hands in a circle, and as they circle around him, Jesus sings, "Glory be to thee, Father!"

To which the circling company responds, "Amen."

"Glory be to thee, Word!"

And again, "Amen."

"I would be born and I would bear!"

"Amen."

"I would eat and I would be eaten!"

"Amen."

"Thou that dancest, see what I do, for thine is this passion of the manhood, which I am about to suffer!"

"Amen."

"I would flee and I would stay!"

"Amen."

"I would be united and I would unite!"

"Amen."

"A door am I to thee that knocketh at me. . . . A way am I to thee, a wayfarer." And when the dance is ended, he walks out into the garden to be taken and crucified.

When you go to your death that way, as a god, in the knowledge of the myth, you are going to your eternal life. So what is there in that to be sad about? Let us make it magnificent—as it is. Let us celebrate it.

MOYERS: The god of death is the lord of the dance.

CAMPBELL: The god of death is at the same time the lord of sex.

MOYERS: What do you mean?

CAMPBELL: It's amazing: one after another, you discover these gods who are at once of death and of generation. The death god, Ghede, of the Haitian Voodoo tradition, is also the sex god. The Egyptian god Osiris was the judge and lord of the dead, and the lord of the regeneration of life. It is a basic theme—that which dies is born. You have to have death in order to have life.

This is the origin of the head hunt in Southeast Asia, particularly in Indonesia. The head hunt is a sacred act, a sacred killing. Before a young man can be permitted to marry and become a father, he must go forth and have his kill. Unless there is death, there cannot be birth. The significance of that is that every generation has to die in order that the next generation can come. As soon as you beget or give birth to a child, you are the dead one. The child is the new life, and you are simply the protector of that new life.

MOYERS: Your time has come.

CAMPBELL: That is why there is the deep psychological association of begetting and dying.

MOYERS: Is there some relationship between what you are saying and the fact that a parent will give his or her life for a child?

CAMPBELL: There is a magnificent essay by Schopenhauer in which he asks, how is it that a human being can so participate in the peril or pain of another that without thought, spontaneously, he sacrifices his own life to the other? How can it happen that what we normally think of as the first law of nature and self-preservation is suddenly dissolved?

In Hawaii some four or five years ago there was an extraordinary event that represents this problem. There is a place there called the Pali, where the trade winds from the north come rushing through a great ridge of mountains. People like to go up there to get their hair blown about or sometimes to commit suicide—you know, something like jumping off the Golden Gate Bridge.

One day, two policemen were driving up the Pali road when they saw, just beyond the railing that keeps the cars from rolling over, a young man preparing to jump. The police car stopped, and the policeman on the right jumped out to grab the man but caught him just as he jumped, and he was himself being pulled over when the second cop arrived in time and pulled the two of them back.

Do you realize what had suddenly happened to that policeman who had given himself to death with that unknown youth? Everything else in his life had dropped off—his duty to his family, his duty to his job, his duty to his own life—all of his wishes and hopes for his lifetime had just disappeared. He was about to die.

Later, a newspaper reporter asked him, "Why didn't you let go? You would have been killed." And his reported answer was, "I couldn't let go. If I had let that young man go, I couldn't have lived another day of my life." How come?

Schopenhauer's answer is that such a psychological crisis represents the breakthrough of a metaphysical realization, which is that you and that other are one, that you are two aspects of the one life, and that your apparent separateness is but an effect of the way we experience forms under the conditions of space and time. Our true reality is in our identity and unity with all life. This is a metaphysical truth which may become spontaneously realized under circumstances of crisis. For it is, according to Schopenhauer, the truth of your life.

The hero is the one who has given his physical life to some order of realization of that truth. The concept of love your neighbor is to put you in tune with this fact. But whether you love your neighbor or not, when the realization grabs you, you may risk your life. That Hawaiian policeman didn't know who the young man was to whom he had given himself. Schopenhauer declares that in small ways you can see this happening every day, all the time, moving life in the world, people doing selfless things to and for each other.

MOYERS: So when Jesus says, "Love thy neighbor as thyself," he is saying in effect, "Love thy neighbor because he *is* yourself."

CAMPBELL: There is a beautiful figure in the Oriental tradition, the bodhisattva, whose nature is boundless compassion, and from whose fingertips there is said to drip ambrosia down to the lowest depths of hell.

MOYERS: And the meaning of that?

CAMPBELL: At the very end of the *Divine Comedy*, Dante realizes that the love of God informs the whole universe down to the lowest pits of hell. That's very much the same image. The bodhisattva represents the principle of compassion, which is the healing principle that makes life possible. Life is pain, but compassion is what gives it the possibility of continuing. The bodhisattva is one who has achieved the realization of immortality yet voluntarily participates in the sorrows of the world. Voluntary participation in the world is very different from just getting born into it. That's exactly the theme of Paul's statement about Christ in his Epistle to the Philippians: that Jesus "did not think God-hood something to be held to but took the form of a servant here on the earth, even to death on the cross." That's a voluntary participation in the fragmentation of life.

MOYERS: So you would agree with Abelard in the twelfth century, who said that Jesus' death on the cross was not as ransom paid, or as a penalty applied, but that it was an act of atonement, at-one-ment, with the race.

CAMPBELL: That's the most sophisticated interpretation of why Christ had to be crucified, or why he elected to be crucified. An earlier one was that the sin in the Garden of Eden had committed mankind to the Devil, and God had to redeem man from the pawnbroker, the Devil. So he offered his own son, Jesus, as the redemption. Pope Gregory gave this interpretation of Jesus as the bait that hooked the Devil. That's the redemption idea. In another version, God was so offended by the act of impudence in the Garden that he became wrathful and threw man out of his field of mercy, and then the only thing that could atone man with God was a sacrifice that would be as great in its importance as the sin had been. No mere man could make such a sacrifice, so the son of God himself became man in order to pay the debt.

But Abelard's idea was that Christ came to be crucified to evoke in man's heart the sentiment of compassion for the suffering of life, and so to remove man's mind from blind commitment to the goods of this world. It is in compassion with Christ that we turn to Christ, and the injured one becomes our Savior.

This is reflected in the medieval idea of the injured king, the Grail King, suffering from his incurable wound. The injured one again becomes the savior. It is the suffering that evokes the humanity of the human heart.

MOYERS: So you would agree with Abelard that mankind yearning for God and God yearning for mankind met in compassion at that cross?

CAMPBELL: Yes. As soon as there is time, there is suffering. You can't have a future unless you have a past, and if you are in love with the present, it becomes past, whatever it is. Loss, death, birth, loss, death—and so on. By contemplating the cross, you are contemplating a symbol of the mystery of life.

MOYERS: That is why there is so much pain associated with the true religious transformation or conversion. It is not easy to lose yourself.

CAMPBELL: The New Testament teaches dying to one's self, literally suffering the pain of death to the world and its values. This is the vocabulary of the mystics. Now, suicide is also a symbolic act. It casts off the psychological posture that you happen to be in at the time, so that you may come into a better one. You die to your current life in order to come to another of some kind. But, as Jung says, you'd better not get caught in a symbolic situation. You don't have to die, really, physically. All you have to do is die spiritually and be reborn to a larger way of living.

MOYERS: But it seems so foreign to our experience today. Religion is easy. You put it on as if you are putting on a coat and going out to the movies.

CAMPBELL: Yes, most churches are for nice social gatherings. You like the people there, they are respectable people, they are old friends, and the family has known them for a long time.

MOYERS: What has happened to this mythic idea of the self-sacrificing savior in our culture today?

CAMPBELL: During the Vietnam War, I remember seeing on the television young men in helicopters going out to rescue one or another of their companions, at great risk to themselves. They didn't have to rescue that greatly endangered young man. And so there I saw this same thing working, the same willingness of which Schopenhauer wrote, of sacrificing one's own life for another. Men sometimes confess they love war because it puts them in touch with the experience of being alive. In going to the office every day, you don't get that experience, but suddenly, in war, you are ripped back into being alive. Life is pain; life is suffering; and life is horror—but, by God, you are alive. Those young men in Vietnam were truly alive in braving death for their fellows.

MOYERS: But a man said to me once after years of standing on the platform of the subway, "I die a little bit down there every day, but I know I am doing so for my family." There are small acts of heroism, too, that occur without regard to the notoriety that you attract for it. For example, a mother does it by the isolation she endures on behalf of the family.

CAMPBELL: Motherhood is a sacrifice. On our veranda in Hawaii the birds come to feed. Each year there have been one or two mother birds. When you see a mother bird, plagued by her progeny for food, with five baby birds, some of them bigger than she is, flopping all over her—"Well," you think, "this is the symbol of motherhood, this giving of your substance and every damn thing to your progeny." That is why the mother becomes the symbol of Mother Earth. She is the one who has given birth to us and on whom we live and on whose body we find our food.

MOYERS: As you talk, I think of another figure in *The Way of the Animal Powers* that struck me as Christlike. Do you remember that savior figure from the creation legend of the Pima Indians?

CAMPBELL: Yes. It is an instructive story. He is the classic savior figure who brings life to mankind, and mankind then tears him to pieces. You know the old saying: Save a man's life and make an enemy for life.

MOYERS: When the world is created, he emerges from the center of the earth and later leads his people from underground, but they turn against him, killing him not once but several times—

CAMPBELL: —even pulverizing him.

MOYERS: But he always returns to life. At last he goes into the mountains where the trails become so confused, no one can follow him. Now, that is a Christlike figure, isn't it?

CAMPBELL: Yes, it is. And here also is the labyrinth motif. The trails are deliberately confused, but if you know the secret of the labyrinth, you can go and pay its inhabitant a visit.

MOYERS: And if you have faith, you can follow Jesus.

CAMPBELL: You can. Very often one of the things that one learns as a member of the mystery religions is that the labyrinth, which blocks, is at the same time the way to eternal life. This is the final secret of myth—to teach you how to penetrate the labyrinth of life in such a way that its spiritual values come through.

That is the problem of Dante's *Divine Comedy*, too. The crisis comes in the "middle of the way of our life," when the body is beginning to fade, and another whole constellation of themes comes breaking into your dream world. Dante says that, in the middle year of his life, he was lost in a dangerous wood. And he was threatened there by three animals, symbolizing pride, desire, and fear. Then Virgil, the personification of poetic insight, appeared and conducted him through the labyrinth of hell, which is the place of those fixed to their desires and fears, who can't pass through to eternity. Dante was carried through to the beatific vision of God. On a smaller scale, in this Pima Indian story, we have the same mythological image. The Pima Indians were among the simplest Indian cultures in North America. And here they have, in their own way, made use of this highly sophisticated image, which matches Dante.

MOYERS: You have written that "the sign of the cross has to be looked upon as a sign of an eternal affirmation of all that ever was or shall ever be. It symbolizes not only the one historic moment on Calvary but the mystery through all time and space of God's presence and participation in the agony of all living things."

CAMPBELL: The big moment in the medieval myth is the awakening of the heart to compassion, the transformation of passion into compassion. That is the whole problem of the Grail stories, compassion for the wounded king. And out of that you also get the notion that Abelard offered as an explanation of the crucifixion: that the Son of God came down into this world to be crucified to awaken our hearts to compassion, and thus to turn our minds from the gross concerns of raw life in the world to the specifically human values of self-giving in shared suffering. In that sense the wounded king, the maimed king of the Grail legend, is a counterpart of the Christ. He is there to evoke compassion and thus bring a dead wasteland to life. There is a mystical notion there of the spiritual function of suffering in this world. The one who suffers is, as it were, the Christ, come before us to evoke the one thing that turns the human beast of prey into a valid human being. That one thing is compassion. This is the theme that James Joyce takes over and develops in *Ulysses*—the awakening of his hero, Stephen Dedalus, to manhood through a shared compassion with Leopold Bloom. That was the awakening of his heart to love and the opening of the way.

In Joyce's next great work, *Finnegans Wake*, there is a mysterious number that constantly recurs. It is 1132. It occurs as a date, for example, and inverted as a house address, 32 West 11th Street. In every chapter, some way or another, 1132 appears. When I was writing *A Skeleton Key to Finnegans Wake*, I tried every way I knew to imagine, "What the dickens is this number 1132?" Then I recalled that in *Ulysses*, while Bloom is wandering about the streets of Dublin, a ball drops from a tower to indicate noon, and he thinks, "The law of falling bodies, 32 feet per sec per sec." Thirty-two, I thought, must be the number of the Fall; 11 then might be the renewal of the decade, 1, 2, 3, 4, 5, 6, 7, 8, 9, 10—but then 11, and you start over again. There were a number of other suggestions in *Ulysses* that made me think, "Well, what we have here is perhaps the number of the Fall, 32, and Redemption, 11; sin and forgiveness, death and renewal." *Finnegans Wake* has to do with an event that occurred in Phoenix Park, which is a major park in Dublin. The phoenix is the bird that burns itself to death and then comes to life renewed. Phoenix Park thus becomes the Garden of Eden where the Fall took place, and where the cross was planted on the skull of Adam: *O felix culpa* ("O Phoenix culprit!" says Joyce). And so we have death and redemption. That seemed a pretty good answer, and that's the one I gave in *A Skeleton Key*.

But while preparing a class one evening for my students in comparative mythology, I was rereading St. Paul's Epistle to the Romans and came across a curious sentence that seemed to epitomize everything Joyce had had in mind in *Finnegans Wake*. St. Paul had written, "For God has consigned all men to disobedience, that he may show his mercy to all." You cannot be so disobedient that God's mercy will not be able to follow you, so give him a chance. "Sin bravely," as Luther said, and see how much of God's mercy you can invoke. The great sinner is the great awakener of God to compassion. This idea is an essential one in relation to the paradoxology of morality and the values of life.

So I said to myself, "Well, gee, this is really what Joyce is talking about." So I wrote it down in my Joyce notebook: "Romans, Chapter 11, verse 32." Can you imagine my surprise? There was that same number again, 1132, right out of the Good Book! Joyce had taken that paradox of the Christian faith as the motto of the greatest masterwork of his life. And there he describes ruthlessly the depths of the private and public monstrosities of human life and action in the utterly sinful course of human history. It's all there—told with love.

MOYERS: Can Westerners grasp the mystical experience that leaves theology behind? If you're locked to the image of God in a culture where science determines your perceptions of reality, how can you experience this ultimate ground that the shamans talk about?

CAMPBELL: Well, people do experience it. Those in the Middle Ages who experienced it were usually burned as heretics. One of the great heresies in the West is the heresy that Christ pronounced when he said, "I and the Father are one." He was crucified for saying that. In the Middle Ages, nine hundred years after Christ, a great Sufi mystic said, "I and my beloved are one," and he, too, was crucified. As he was going to the cross, he prayed, "O my Lord, if you had taught these people what you have taught me, they would not be doing this to me. And if you had not taught me, this would not be happening to me. Blessed is the Lord and all his works." Another of the Sufi mystics said, "The function of the orthodox community is to give the mystic his desire, which is a union with God, through mortification and death."

MOYERS: What has undercut this experience today?

CAMPBELL: It's characteristic of democracy that majority rule is understood as being effective not only in politics but also in thinking. In thinking, of course, the majority is always wrong.

MOYERS: Always wrong?

CAMPBELL: In matters of this kind, yes. The majority's function in relation to the spirit is to try to listen and to open up to someone who's had an experience beyond that of food, shelter, progeny, and wealth.

Have you ever read Sinclair Lewis' *Babbitt*?

MOYERS: Not in a long time.

CAMPBELL: Remember the last line? "I have never done the thing that I wanted to in all my life." That is a man who never followed his bliss. Well, I actually heard that line when I was teaching at Sarah Lawrence. Before I was married, I used to eat out in the restaurants of town for my lunch and dinners. Thursday night was the maid's night off in Bronxville, so that many of the families were out in restaurants. One fine evening I was in my favorite restaurant there, and at the next table there was a father, a mother, and a scrawny boy about twelve years old. The father said to the boy, "Drink your tomato juice."

And the boy said, "I don't want to."

Then the father, with a louder voice, said, "Drink your tomato juice."

And the mother said, "Don't make him do what he doesn't want to do."

The father looked at her and said, "He can't go through life doing what he wants to do. If he does only what he wants to do, he'll be dead. Look at me. I've never done a thing I wanted to in all my life."

And I thought, "My God, there's Babbitt incarnate!"

That's the man who never followed his bliss. You may have a success in life, but then just think of it—what kind of life was it? What good was it—you've never done the thing you wanted to do in all your life. I always tell my students, go where your body and soul want to go. When you have the feeling, then stay with it, and don't let anyone throw you off.

MOYERS: What happens when you follow your bliss?

CAMPBELL: You come to bliss. In the Middle Ages, a favorite image that occurs in many, many contexts is the wheel of fortune. There's the hub of the wheel, and there is the revolving rim of the wheel. For example, if you are attached to the rim of the wheel of fortune, you will be either above going down or at the bottom coming up. But if you are at the hub, you are in the same place all the time. That is the sense of the marriage vow —I take you in health or sickness, in wealth or poverty: going up or going down. But I take you as my center, and you are my bliss, not the wealth that you might bring me, not the social prestige, but you. That is following your bliss.

MOYERS: How would you advise somebody to tap that spring of eternal life, that bliss that is right there?

CAMPBELL: We are having experiences all the time which may on occasion render some sense of this, a little intuition of where your bliss is. Grab it. No one can tell you what it is going to be. You have to learn to recognize your own depth.

MOYERS: When did you know yours?

CAMPBELL: Oh, when I was a kid. I never let anybody pull me off course. My family helped me, all the time, just to do the thing I really, deeply, most wanted to do. I didn't even realize there was a problem.

MOYERS: How can those of us who are parents help our children recognize their bliss?

CAMPBELL: You have to know your child and be attentive to

the child. You can help. When I taught at Sarah Lawrence, I would have an individual conference with every one of my students at least once a fortnight, for a half hour or so. Now, if you're talking on about the things that students ought to be reading, and suddenly you hit on something that the student really responds to, you can see the eyes open and the complexion change. The life possibility has opened there. All you can say to yourself is, "I hope this child hangs on to that." They may or may not, but when they do, they have found life right there in the room with them.

MOYERS: And one doesn't have to be a poet to do this.

CAMPBELL: Poets are simply those who have made a profession and a lifestyle of being in touch with their bliss. Most people are concerned with other things. They get themselves involved in economic and political activities, or get drafted into a war that isn't the one they're interested in, and it may be difficult to hold to this umbilical under those circumstances. That is a technique each one has to work out for himself somehow.

But most people living in that realm of what might be called occasional concerns have the capacity that is waiting to be awakened to move to this other field. I know it, I have seen it happen in students.

When I taught in a boys' prep school, I used to talk to the boys who were trying to make up their minds as to what their careers were going to be. A boy would come to me and ask, "Do you think I can do this? Do you think I can do that? Do you think I can be a writer?"

"Oh," I would say, "I don't know. Can you endure ten years of disappointment with nobody responding to you, or are you thinking that you are going to write a best seller the first crack? If you have the guts to stay with the thing you really want, no matter what happens, well, go ahead."

Then Dad would come along and say, "No, you ought to study law because there is more money in that, you know." Now, that is the rim of the wheel, not the hub, not following your bliss.

Are you going to think of fortune, or are you going to think of your bliss?

I came back from Europe as a student in 1929, just three weeks before the Wall Street crash, so I didn't have a job for five years. There just wasn't a job. That was a great time for me.

MOYERS: A great time? The depth of the Depression? What was wonderful about it?

CAMPBELL: I didn't feel poor, I just felt that I didn't have any money. People were so good to each other at that time. For example, I discovered Frobenius. Suddenly he hit me, and I had to read everything Frobenius had written. So I simply wrote to a bookselling firm that I had known in New York City, and they sent me these books and told me I didn't have to pay for them until I got a job—four years later.

There was a wonderful old man up in Woodstock, New York, who had a piece of property with these little chicken coop places he would rent out for twenty dollars a year or so to any young person he thought might have a future in the arts. There was no running water, only here and there a well and a pump. He declared he wouldn't install running water because he didn't like the class of people it attracted. That is where I did most of my basic reading and work. It was great. I was following my bliss.

Now, I came to this idea of bliss because in Sanskrit, which is the great spiritual language of the world, there are three terms that represent the brink, the jumping-off place to the ocean of transcendence: *Sat, Chit, Ananda.* The word "*Sat*" means being. "*Chit*" means consciousness. "*Ananda*" means bliss or rapture. I thought, "I don't know whether my consciousness is proper consciousness or not; I don't know whether what I know of my being is my proper being or not; but I do know where my rapture is. So let me hang on to rapture, and that will bring me both my consciousness and my being." I think it worked.

MOYERS: Do we ever know the truth? Do we ever find it?

CAMPBELL: Each person can have his own depth, experience,

and some conviction of being in touch with his own *sat-chit-ananda*, his own being through consciousness and bliss. The religious people tell us we really won't experience bliss until we die and go to heaven. But I believe in having as much as you can of this experience while you are still alive.

MOYERS: Bliss is now.

CAMPBELL: In heaven you will be having such a marvelous time looking at God that you won't get your own experience at all. That is not the place to have the experience—here is the place to have it.

MOYERS: Do you ever have this sense when you are following your bliss, as I have at moments, of being helped by hidden hands?

CAMPBELL: All the time. It is miraculous. I even have a superstition that has grown on me as the result of invisible hands coming all the time—namely, that if you do follow your bliss you put yourself on a kind of track that has been there all the while, waiting for you, and the life that you ought to be living is the one you are living. When you can see that, you begin to meet people who are in the field of your bliss, and they open the doors to you. I say, follow your bliss and don't be afraid, and doors will open where you didn't know they were going to be.

MOYERS: Have you ever had sympathy for the man who has no invisible means of support?

CAMPBELL: Who has no *in*visible means? Yes, he is the one that evokes compassion, the poor chap. To see him stumbling around when all the waters of life are right there really evokes one's pity.

MOYERS: The waters of eternal life are right there? Where?

CAMPBELL: Wherever you are—if you are following your bliss, you are enjoying that refreshment, that life within you, all the time.

V

THE HERO'S
ADVENTURE

*Furthermore, we have not even to risk the adventure alone,
for the heroes of all time have gone before us. The labyrinth is
thoroughly known. We have only to follow the thread of the
hero path, and where we had thought to find an abomination,
we shall find a god. And where we had thought to slay another,
we shall slay ourselves. Where we had thought to travel
outward, we will come to the center of our own existence. And
where we had thought to be alone, we will be with all the
world.*

—JOSEPH CAMPBELL

MOYERS: Why are there so many stories of the hero in mythology?

CAMPBELL: Because that's what's worth writing about. Even
in popular novels, the main character is a hero or heroine who
has found or done something beyond the normal range of
achievement and experience. A hero is someone who has given
his or her life to something bigger than oneself.

MOYERS: So in all of these cultures, whatever the local costume the hero might be wearing, what is the deed?

CAMPBELL: Well, there are two types of deed. One is the physical deed, in which the hero performs a courageous act in battle or saves a life. The other kind is the spiritual deed, in which the hero learns to experience the supernormal range of human spiritual life and then comes back with a message.

The usual hero adventure begins with someone from whom something has been taken, or who feels there's something lacking in the normal experiences available or permitted to the members of his society. This person then takes off on a series of adventures beyond the ordinary, either to recover what has been lost or to discover some life-giving elixir. It's usually a cycle, a going and a returning.

But the structure and something of the spiritual sense of this adventure can be seen already anticipated in the puberty or initiation rituals of early tribal societies, through which a child is compelled to give up its childhood and become an adult—to die, you might say, to its infantile personality and psyche and come back as a responsible adult. This is a fundamental psychological transformation that everyone has to undergo. We are in childhood in a condition of dependency under someone's protection and supervision for some fourteen to twenty-one years —and if you're going on for your Ph.D., this may continue to perhaps thirty-five. You are in no way a self-responsible, free agent, but an obedient dependent, expecting and receiving punishments and rewards. To evolve out of this position of psychological immaturity to the courage of self-responsibility and assurance requires a death and a resurrection. That's the basic motif of the universal hero's journey—leaving one condition and finding the source of life to bring you forth into a richer or mature condition.

MOYERS: So even if we happen not to be heroes in the grand sense of redeeming society, we still have to take that journey inside ourselves, spiritually and psychologically.

CAMPBELL: That's right. Otto Rank in his important little book *The Myth of the Birth of the Hero* declares that everyone is a hero in birth, where he undergoes a tremendous psychological as well as physical transformation, from the condition of a little water creature living in a realm of amniotic fluid into an air-breathing mammal which ultimately will be standing. That's an enormous transformation, and had it been consciously undertaken, it would have been, indeed, a heroic act. And there was a heroic act on the mother's part, as well, who had brought this all about.

MOYERS: Then heroes are not all men?

CAMPBELL: Oh, no. The male usually has the more conspicuous role, just because of the conditions of life. He is out there in the world, and the woman is in the home. But among the Aztecs, for example, who had a number of heavens to which people's souls would be assigned according to the conditions of their death, the heaven for warriors killed in battle was the same for mothers who died in childbirth. Giving birth is definitely a heroic deed, in that it is the giving over of oneself to the life of another.

MOYERS: Don't you think we've lost that truth in this society of ours, where it's deemed more heroic to go out into the world and make a lot of money than it is to raise children?

CAMPBELL: Making money gets more advertisement. You know the old saying: if a dog bites a man, that's not a story, but if a man bites a dog, you've got a story there. So the thing that happens and happens and happens, no matter how heroic it may be, is not news. Motherhood has lost its novelty, you might say.

MOYERS: That's a wonderful image, though—the mother as hero.

CAMPBELL: It has always seemed so to me. That's something I learned from reading these myths.

MOYERS: It's a journey—you have to move out of the known, conventional safety of your life to undertake this.

CAMPBELL: You have to be transformed from a maiden to a mother. That's a big change, involving many dangers.

MOYERS: And when you come back from your journey, with the child, you've brought something for the world.

CAMPBELL: Not only that, you've got a life job ahead of you. Otto Rank makes the point that there is a world of people who think that their heroic act in being born qualifies them for the respect and support of their whole community.

MOYERS: But there's still a journey to be taken after that.

CAMPBELL: There's a large journey to be taken, of many trials.

MOYERS: What's the significance of the trials, and tests, and ordeals of the hero?

CAMPBELL: If you want to put it in terms of intentions, the trials are designed to see to it that the intending hero should be really a hero. Is he really a match for this task? Can he overcome the dangers? Does he have the courage, the knowledge, the capacity, to enable him to serve?

MOYERS: In this culture of easy religion, cheaply achieved, it seems to me we've forgotten that all three of the great religions teach that the trials of the hero journey are a significant part of life, that there's no reward without renunciation, without paying the price. The Koran says, "Do you think that you shall enter the Garden of Bliss without such trials as came to those who passed before you?" And Jesus said in the gospel of Matthew, "Great is the gate and narrow is the way which leadeth to life, and few there be who find it." And the heroes of the Jewish tradition undergo great tests before they arrive at their redemption.

CAMPBELL: If you realize what the real problem is—losing yourself, giving yourself to some higher end, or to another—you realize that this itself is the ultimate trial. When we quit thinking primarily about ourselves and our own self-preservation, we undergo a truly heroic transformation of consciousness.

And what all the myths have to deal with is transformations of consciousness of one kind or another. You have been thinking one way, you now have to think a different way.

MOYERS: How is consciousness transformed?

CAMPBELL: Either by the trials themselves or by illuminating revelations. Trials and revelations are what it's all about.

MOYERS: Isn't there a moment of redemption in all of these stories? The woman is saved from the dragon, the city is spared from obliteration, the hero is snatched from danger in the nick of time.

CAMPBELL: Well, yes. There would be no hero deed unless there were an achievement. We can have the hero who fails, but he's usually represented as a kind of clown, someone pretending to more than he can achieve.

MOYERS: How is a hero different from a leader?

CAMPBELL: That is a problem Tolstoy dealt with in *War and Peace*. Here you have Napoleon ravaging Europe and now about to invade Russia, and Tolstoy raises this question: Is the leader really a leader, or is he simply the one out in front on a wave? In psychological terms, the leader might be analyzed as the one who perceived what could be achieved and did it.

MOYERS: It has been said that a leader is someone who discerned the inevitable and got in front of it. Napoleon was a leader, but he wasn't a hero in the sense that what he accomplished was grand for humanity's sake. It was for France, the glory of France.

CAMPBELL: Then he is a French hero, is he not? This is the problem for today. Is the hero of a given state or people what we need today, when the whole planet should be our field of concern? Napoleon is the nineteenth-century counterpart of Hitler in the twentieth. Napoleon's ravaging of Europe was horrific.

MOYERS: So you could be a local god and fail the test on a larger cosmic level?

CAMPBELL: Yes. Or you could be a local god, but for the people whom that local god conquered, you could be the enemy. Whether you call someone a hero or a monster is all relative to where the focus of your consciousness may be.

MOYERS: So we have to be careful not to call a deed heroic when, in a larger, mythological sense, it simply doesn't work that way.

CAMPBELL: Well, I don't know. The deed could be absolutely a heroic deed—a person giving his life for his own people, for example.

MOYERS: Ah, yes. The German soldier who dies—

CAMPBELL: —is as much a hero as the American who was sent over there to kill him.

MOYERS: So does heroism have a moral objective?

CAMPBELL: The moral objective is that of saving a people, or saving a person, or supporting an idea. The hero sacrifices himself for something—that's the morality of it. Now, from another position, of course, you might say that the idea for which he sacrificed himself was something that should not have been respected. That's a judgment from the other side, but it doesn't destroy the intrinsic heroism of the deed performed.

MOYERS: That's a different angle on heroes from what I got as a young boy, when I read the story of Prometheus going after fire and bringing it back, benefiting humanity and suffering for it.

CAMPBELL: Yes, Prometheus brings fire to mankind and consequently civilization. The fire theft, by the way, is a universal mythic theme. Often, it's a trickster animal or bird that steals the fire and then passes it along to a relay team of birds or animals who run with it. Sometimes the animals are burned by the flames as they pass the fire along, and this is said to account for their different colorings. The fire theft is a very popular, worldwide story.

MOYERS: The people in each culture are trying to explain where fire came from?

CAMPBELL: The story isn't really trying to explain it, it has to do more with the value of fire. The fire theft sets man apart from the animals. When you're in the woods at night, you light a fire, and that keeps the animals away. You can see their eyes shining, but they're outside the fire range.

MOYERS: So they're not telling the story just to inspire others or to make a moral point.

CAMPBELL: No, it's to evaluate the fire, its importance to us, and to say something about what has set man apart from the beasts.

MOYERS: Does your study of mythology lead you to conclude that a single human quest, a standard pattern of human aspiration and thought, constitutes for all mankind something that we have in common, whether we lived a million years ago or will live a thousand years from now?

CAMPBELL: There's a certain type of myth which one might call the vision quest, going in quest of a boon, a vision, which has the same form in every mythology. That is the thing that I tried to present in the first book I wrote, *The Hero with a Thousand Faces*. All these different mythologies give us the same essential quest. You leave the world that you're in and go into a depth or into a distance or up to a height. There you come to what was missing in your consciousness in the world you formerly inhabited. Then comes the problem either of staying with that, and letting the world drop off, or returning with that boon and trying to hold on to it as you move back into your social world again. That's not an easy thing to do.

MOYERS: So the hero goes *for* something, he doesn't just go along for the ride, he's not simply an adventurer?

CAMPBELL: There are both kinds of heroes, some that choose to undertake the journey and some that don't. In one kind of adventure, the hero sets out responsibly and intentionally to perform the deed. For instance, Odysseus' son Telemachus was told by Athena, "Go find your father." That father quest is a major hero adventure for young people. That is the adventure of finding what your career is, what your nature is, what your source is. You undertake that intentionally. Or there is the legend of the Sumerian sky goddess, Inanna, who descended into the underworld and underwent death to bring her beloved back to life.

Then there are adventures into which you are thrown—for example, being drafted into the army. You didn't intend it, but you're in now. You've undergone a death and resurrection, you've put on a uniform, and you're another creature.

One kind of hero that often appears in Celtic myths is the princely hunter, who has followed the lure of a deer into a range of forest that he has never been in before. The animal there undergoes a transformation, becoming the Queen of the Faerie Hills, or something of that kind. This is a type of adventure in which the hero has no idea what he is doing but suddenly finds himself in a transformed realm.

MOYERS: Is the adventurer who takes that kind of trip a hero in the mythological sense?

CAMPBELL: Yes, because he is always ready for it. In these stories, the adventure that the hero is ready for is the one he gets. The adventure is symbolically a manifestation of his character. Even the landscape and the conditions of the environment match his readiness.

MOYERS: In George Lucas' *Star Wars*, Solo begins as a mercenary and ends up a hero, coming in at the last to save Luke Skywalker.

CAMPBELL: Yes. There Solo has done the hero act of sacrificing himself for another.

MOYERS: Do you think that a hero is created out of guilt? Was Solo guilty because he had abandoned Skywalker?

CAMPBELL: It depends on what system of ideas you want to apply. Solo was a very practical guy, at least as he thought of himself, a materialist. But he was a compassionate human being at the same time and didn't know it. The adventure evoked a quality of his character that he hadn't known he possessed.

MOYERS: So perhaps the hero lurks in each one of us when we don't know it?

CAMPBELL: Our life evokes our character. You find out more about yourself as you go on. That's why it's good to be able to put yourself in situations that will evoke your higher nature rather than your lower. "Lead us not into temptation."

Ortega y Gasset talks about the environment and the hero in his *Meditations on Don Quixote*. Don Quixote was the last hero of the Middle Ages. He rode out to encounter giants, but instead of giants, his environment produced windmills. Ortega points out that this story takes place about the time that a mechanistic interpretation of the world came in, so that the environment was no longer spiritually responsive to the hero. The hero is today running up against a hard world that is in no way responsive to his spiritual need.

MOYERS: A windmill.

CAMPBELL: Yes, but Quixote saved the adventure for himself by inventing a magician who had just transformed the giants he had gone forth to encounter into windmills. You can do that, too, if you have a poetic imagination. Earlier, though, it was not a mechanistic world in which the hero moved but a world alive and responsive to his spiritual readiness. Now it has become to such an extent a sheerly mechanistic world, as interpreted through our physical sciences, Marxist sociology, and behavioristic psychology, that we're nothing but a predictable pattern of wires responding to stimuli. This nineteenth-century interpretation has squeezed the freedom of the human will out of modern life.

MOYERS: In the political sense, is there a danger that these myths of heroes teach us to look at the deeds of others as if we were in an amphitheater or coliseum or a movie, watching others perform great deeds while consoling ourselves to impotence?

CAMPBELL: I think this is something that has overtaken us only recently in this culture. The one who watches athletic games instead of participating in athletics is involved in a surrogate achievement. But when you think about what people are actually undergoing in our civilization, you realize it's a very grim thing to be a modern human being. The drudgery of the lives of most of the people who have to support families—well, it's a life-extinguishing affair.

MOYERS: But I think I would take that to the plagues of the twelfth century and the fourteenth century—

CAMPBELL: Their mode of life was much more active than ours. We sit in offices. It's significant that in our civilization the problem of the middle-aged is conspicuous.

MOYERS: You're beginning to get personal!

CAMPBELL: I'm beyond middle age, so I know a little bit about this. Something that's characteristic of our sedentary lives is that there is or may be intellectual excitement, but the body is not in it very much. So you have to engage intentionally in mechanical exercises, the daily dozen and so forth. I find it very difficult to enjoy such things, but there it is. Otherwise, your whole body says to you, "Look, you've forgotten me entirely. I'm becoming just a clogged stream."

MOYERS: Still, it's feasible to me that these stories of heroes could become sort of a tranquilizer, invoking in us the benign passivity of watching instead of acting. And the other side of it is that our world seems drained of spiritual values. People feel impotent. To me, that's the curse of modern society, the impotence, the ennui that people feel, the alienation of people from the world order around them. Maybe we need some hero who will give voice to our deeper longing.

CAMPBELL: This is exactly T. S. Eliot's *The Waste Land* that you are describing, a sociological stagnation of inauthentic lives and living that has settled upon us, and that evokes nothing of our spiritual life, our potentialities, or even our physical courage—until, of course, it gets us into one of its inhuman wars.

MOYERS: You're not against technology, are you?

CAMPBELL: Not at all. When Daedalus, who can be thought of as the master technician of most ancient Greece, put the wings he had made on his son Icarus, so that he might fly out of and escape from the Cretan labyrinth which he himself had invented, he said to him: "Fly the middle way. Don't fly too high, or the sun will melt the wax on your wings, and you will fall. Don't fly too low, or the tides of the sea will catch you." Daedalus himself flew the middle way, but he watched his son become ecstatic and fly too high. The wax melted, and the boy fell into the sea. For some reason, people talk more about Icarus than about Daedalus, as though the wings themselves had been responsible for the young astronaut's fall. But that is no case against industry and science. Poor Icarus fell into the water— but Daedalus, who flew the middle way, succeeded in getting to the other shore.

A Hindu text says, "A dangerous path is this, like the edge

of a razor." This is a motif that occurs in medieval literature, also. When Lancelot goes to rescue Guinevere from captivity, he has to cross a stream on a sword's edge with his bare hands and feet, a torrent flowing underneath. When you are doing something that is a brand-new adventure, breaking new ground, whether it is something like a technological breakthrough or simply a way of living that is not what the community can help you with, there's always the danger of too much enthusiasm, of neglecting certain mechanical details. Then you fall off. "A dangerous path is this." When you follow the path of your desire and enthusiasm and emotion, keep your mind in control, and don't let it pull you compulsively into disaster.

MOYERS: One of the intriguing points of your scholarship is that you do not believe science and mythology conflict.

CAMPBELL: No, they don't conflict. Science is breaking through now into the mystery dimensions. It's pushed itself into the sphere the myth is talking about. It's come to the edge.

MOYERS: The edge being—

CAMPBELL: —the edge, the interface between what can be known and what is never to be discovered because it is a mystery that transcends all human research. The source of life—what is it? No one knows. We don't even know what an atom is, whether it is a wave or a particle—it is both. We don't have any idea of what these things are.

That's the reason we speak of the divine. There's a transcendent energy source. When the physicist observes subatomic particles, he's seeing a trace on a screen. These traces come and go, come and go, and we come and go, and all of life comes and goes. That energy is the informing energy of all things. Mythic worship is addressed to that.

MOYERS: Do you have a favorite mythic hero?

CAMPBELL: When I was a boy, I had two heroes. One was Douglas Fairbanks; the other was Leonardo da Vinci. I wanted to be a synthesis of the two. Today, I don't have a single hero at all.

MOYERS: Does our society?

CAMPBELL: It did have. It had the Christ. And then America had men like Washington and Jefferson and, later, men like Daniel Boone. But life today is so complex, and it is changing so fast, that there is no time for anything to constellate itself before it's thrown over again.

MOYERS: We seem to worship celebrities today, not heroes.

CAMPBELL: Yes, and that's too bad. A questionnaire was once sent around one of the high schools in Brooklyn which asked, "What would you like to be?" Two thirds of the students responded, "A celebrity." They had no notion of having to give of themselves in order to achieve something.

MOYERS: Just to be known.

CAMPBELL: Just to be known, to have fame—name and fame. It's too bad.

MOYERS: But does a society need heroes?

CAMPBELL: Yes, I think so.

MOYERS: Why?

CAMPBELL: Because it has to have constellating images to pull together all these tendencies to separation, to pull them together into some intention.

MOYERS: To follow some path.

CAMPBELL: I think so. The nation has to have an intention somehow to operate as a single power.

MOYERS: What did you think of the outpouring over John Lennon's death? Was he a hero?

CAMPBELL: Oh, he definitely was a hero.

THE POWER OF MYTH

MOYERS: Explain that in the mythological sense.

CAMPBELL: In the mythological sense, he was an innovator. The Beatles brought forth an art form for which there was a readiness. Somehow, they were in perfect tune with their time. Had they turned up thirty years before, their music would have fizzled out. The public hero is sensitive to the needs of his time. The Beatles brought a new spiritual depth into popular music which started the fad, let's call it, for meditation and Oriental music. Oriental music had been over here for years, as a curiosity, but now, after the Beatles, our young people seem to know what it's about. We are hearing more and more of it, and it's being used in terms of its original intention as a support for meditations. That's what the Beatles started.

MOYERS: Sometimes it seems to me that we ought to feel pity for the hero instead of admiration. So many of them have sacrificed their own needs for others.

CAMPBELL: They all have.

MOYERS: And very often what they accomplish is shattered by the inability of the followers to see.

CAMPBELL: Yes, you come out of the forest with gold and it turns to ashes. That's a well-known fairy-tale motif.

MOYERS: There's that haunting incident in the story of Odysseus, when the ship tears apart and the members of the crew are thrown overboard, and the waves toss Odysseus over. He clings to a mast and finally lands on shore, and the text says, "Alone at last. Alone at last."

CAMPBELL: Well, that adventure of Odysseus is a little complicated to try to talk about very briefly. But that particular adventure where the ship is wrecked is at the Island of the Sun—that's the island of highest illumination. If the ship had not been wrecked, Odysseus might have remained on the island and become, you might say, the sort of yogi who, on achieving full enlightenment, remains there in bliss and never returns. But the Greek idea of making the values known and enacted in life brings him back. Now, there was a taboo on the Island of the Sun, namely, that one should not kill and eat any of the oxen of the Sun. Odysseus' men, however, were hungry, so they slaughtered the cattle of the Sun, which is what brought about their shipwreck. The lower consciousness was still functioning while they were up there in the sphere of the highest spiritual light. When you're in the presence of such an illumination, you are not to think, "Gee, I'm hungry. Get me a roast beef sandwich." Odysseus' men were not ready or eligible for the experience which had been given to them.

That's a model story of the earthly hero's attaining to the highest illumination but then coming back.

MOYERS: What are we to make of what you wrote of the bittersweet story of Odysseus when you said, "The tragic sense of that work lies precisely in its deep joy in life's beauty and excellence—the noble loveliness of fair woman, the real worth of manly men. Yet the end of the tale is ashes."

CAMPBELL: You can't say life is useless because it ends in the grave. There's an inspiring line in one of Pindar's poems where he is celebrating a young man who has just won a wrestling championship at the Pythian games. Pindar writes, "Creatures of a day, what is any one? What is he not? Man is but a dream of a shadow. Yet when there comes as a gift of heaven a gleam of sunshine, there rests upon men a radiant light and, aye, a gentle life." That dismal saying, "Vanity, vanity, all is vanity!"— it is not all vanity. This moment itself is no vanity, it is a triumph, a delight. This accent on the culmination of perfection in our moments of triumph is very Greek.

MOYERS: Don't many of the heroes in mythology die to the world? They suffer, they're crucified.

CAMPBELL: Many of them give their lives. But then the myth also says that out of the given life comes a new life. It may not be the hero's life, but it's a new life, a new way of being or becoming.

MOYERS: These stories of the hero vary from culture to culture. Is the hero from the East different from the hero in our culture?

CAMPBELL: It's the degree of the illumination or action that makes them different. There is a typical early culture hero who goes around slaying monsters. Now, that is a form of adventure from the period of prehistory when man was shaping his world out of a dangerous, unshaped wilderness. He goes about killing monsters.

MOYERS: So the hero evolves over time like most other concepts and ideas?

CAMPBELL: He evolves as the culture evolves. Moses is a hero figure, for example. He ascends the mountain, he meets with Yahweh on the summit of the mountain, and he comes back with rules for the formation of a whole new society. That's a typical hero act—departure, fulfillment, return.

MOYERS: Is Buddha a hero figure?

CAMPBELL: The Buddha follows a path very much like that of Christ; only of course the Buddha lived five hundred years earlier. You can match those two savior figures right down the line, even to the roles and characters of their immediate disciples or apostles. You can parallel, for example, Ananda and St. Peter.

MOYERS: Why did you call your book *The Hero with a Thousand Faces*?

CAMPBELL: Because there is a certain typical hero sequence of actions which can be detected in stories from all over the world and from many periods of history. Essentially, it might even be said there is but one archetypal mythic hero whose life has been replicated in many lands by many, many people. A legendary hero is usually the founder of something—the founder of a new age, the founder of a new religion, the founder of a new city, the founder of a new way of life. In order to found something new, one has to leave the old and go in quest of the seed idea, a germinal idea that will have the potentiality of bringing forth that new thing.

The founders of all religions have gone on quests like that. The Buddha went into solitude and then sat beneath the bo tree, the tree of immortal knowledge, where he received an illumination that has enlightened all of Asia for twenty-five hundred years.

After baptism by John the Baptist, Jesus went into the desert for forty days; and it was out of that desert that he came with his message. Moses went to the top of a mountain and came down with the tables of the law. Then you have the one who founds a new city—almost all the old Greek cities were founded by heroes who went off on quests and had surprising adventures, out of which each then founded a city. You might also say that the founder of a life—your life or mine, if we live our own lives, instead of imitating everybody else's life—comes from a quest as well.

MOYERS: Why are these stories so important to the human race?

CAMPBELL: It depends on what kind of story it is. If the story represents what might be called an archetypal adventure—the story of a child becoming a youth, or the awakening to the new world that opens at adolescence—it would help to provide a model for handling this development.

MOYERS: You talk about how stories help us through crises. When I read them as a child, they all had happy endings. It was a time before I learned that life is fraught with plodding, indulgent, and cruel realities. Sometimes I think we buy a ticket to Gilbert and Sullivan, and when we go into the theater, we find the play is by Harold Pinter. Maybe fairy tales make us misfits to reality.

CAMPBELL: Fairy tales are told for entertainment. You've got to distinguish between the myths that have to do with the serious matter of living life in terms of the order of society and of nature, and stories with some of those same motifs that are told for entertainment. But even though there's a happy ending for most fairy tales, on the way to the happy ending, typical mythological motifs occur—for example, the motif of being in deep trouble and then hearing a voice or having somebody come to help you out.

Fairy tales are for children. Very often they're about a little girl who doesn't want to grow up to be a woman. At the crisis of that threshold crossing she's balking. So she goes to sleep until the prince comes through all the barriers and gives her a reason to think it might be nice on the other side after all. Many of the Grimm tales represent the little girl who is stuck. All of these dragon killings and threshold crossings have to do with getting past being stuck.

The rituals of primitive initiation ceremonies are all mythologically grounded and have to do with killing the infantile ego and bringing forth an adult, whether it's the girl or the boy. It's harder for the boy than for the girl, because life overtakes the girl. She becomes a woman whether she intends it or not, but the little boy has to intend to be a man. At the first menstruation, the girl is a woman. The next thing she knows, she's pregnant, she's a mother. The boy first has to disengage himself from his mother, get his energy into himself, and then start forth. That's what the myth of "Young man, go find your father" is all about. In the *Odyssey*, Telemachus lives with his mother. When he's twenty years old, Athena comes and says, "Go find your father." That is the theme all through the stories. Sometimes it's a mystical father, but sometimes, as here in the *Odyssey*, it's the physical father.

A fairy tale is the child's myth. There are proper myths for proper times of life. As you grow older, you need a sturdier mythology. Of course, the whole story of the crucifixion, which is a fundamental image in the Christian tradition, speaks of the coming of eternity into the field of time and space, where there is dismemberment. But it also speaks of the passage from the field of time and space into the field of eternal life. So we crucify our temporal and earthly bodies, let them be torn, and through that dismemberment enter the spiritual sphere which transcends all the pains of earth. There's a form of the crucifix known as "Christ Triumphant," where he is not with head bowed and blood pouring from him, but with head erect and eyes open, as though having come voluntarily to the crucifixion. St. Augustine has written somewhere that Jesus went to the cross as a bridegroom to his bride.

MOYERS: So there are truths for older age and truths for children.

CAMPBELL: Oh, yes. I remember the time Heinrich Zimmer was lecturing at Columbia on the Hindu idea that all life is as a dream or a bubble; that all is *maya*, illusion. After his lecture a young woman came up to him and said, "Dr. Zimmer, that was a wonderful lecture on Indian philosophy! But *maya*—I don't get it—it doesn't speak to me."

"Oh," he said, "don't be impatient! That's not for you yet, darling." And so it is: when you get older, and everyone you've known and originally lived for has passed away, and the world itself is passing, the *maya* myth comes in. But, for young people, the world is something yet to be met and dealt with and loved and learned from and fought with—and so, another mythology.

MOYERS: The writer Thomas Berry says that it's all a question of story. The story is the plot we assign to life and the universe, our basic assumptions and fundamental beliefs about how things work. He says we are in trouble now "because we are in between stories. The old story sustained us for a long time—it shaped our emotional attitudes, it provided us with life's purpose, it energized our actions, it consecrated suffering, it guided education. We awoke in the morning and knew who we were, we could answer the questions of our children. Everything was taken care of because the story was there. Now the old story is not functioning. And we have not yet learned a new."

CAMPBELL: I'm in partial agreement with that—partial because there is an old story that is still good, and that is the story of the spiritual quest. The quest to find the inward thing that you basically are is the story that I tried to render in that little book of mine written forty-odd years ago—*The Hero with a Thousand Faces*. The relationship of myths to cosmology and sociology has got to wait for man to become used to the new world that he is in. The world is different today from what it was fifty years ago. But the inward life of man is exactly the same. So if you put aside for a while the myth of the origin of the world—scientists will tell you what that is, anyway—and go back to the myth of what is the human quest, what are its stages of realization, what are the trials of the transition from childhood to maturity and what does maturity mean, the story is there, as it is in all the religions.

The story of Jesus, for example—there's a universally valid hero deed represented in the story of Jesus. First he goes to the edge of the consciousness of his time when he goes to John the Baptist to be baptized. Then he goes past the threshold into the desert for forty days. In the Jewish tradition the number forty is mythologically significant. The children of Israel spent forty years in the wilderness, Jesus spent forty days in the desert. In the desert, Jesus underwent three temptations. First there was the economic temptation, where the Devil comes to him and says, "You look hungry, young man! Why not change these stones to bread?" And Jesus replies, "Man lives not by bread alone, but by every word out of the mouth of God." And then next we have the political temptation. Jesus is taken to the top of a mountain and shown the nations of the world, and the Devil says to him, "You can control all these if you'll bow down to me," which is a lesson, not well enough made known today, of what it takes to be a successful politician. Jesus refuses. Finally the Devil says, "And so now, you're so spiritual, let's go up to the top of Herod's Temple and let me see you cast yourself down. God will bear you up, and you won't even be bruised." This is what is known as spiritual inflation. I'm so spiritual, I'm above concerns of the flesh and this earth. But Jesus is incarnate, is he not? So he says, "You shall not tempt the Lord, your God." Those are the three temptations of Christ, and they are as relevant today as they were in the year A.D. 30.

The Buddha, too, goes into the forest and has conferences there with the leading gurus of his day. Then he goes past them and, after a season of trials and search, comes to the bo tree, the tree of illumination, where he, likewise, undergoes three temptations. The first is of lust, the second of fear, and the third of submission to public opinion, doing as told.

In the first temptation, the Lord of Lust displayed his three beautiful daughters before the Buddha. Their names were Desire, Fulfillment, and Regrets—Future, Present, and Past. But the Buddha, who had already disengaged himself from attachment to his sensual character, was not moved.

Then the Lord of Lust turned himself into the Lord of Death and flung at the Buddha all the weapons of an army of monsters. But the Buddha had found in himself that still point within, which is of eternity, untouched by time. So again, he was not moved, and the weapons flung at him turned into flowers of worship.

Finally the Lord of Lust and Death transformed himself into the Lord of Social Duty and argued, "Young man, haven't you read the morning papers? Don't you know what there is to be done today?" The Buddha responded by simply touching the earth with the tips of the fingers of his right hand. Then the voice of the goddess mother of the universe was heard, like thunder rolling on the horizon, saying, "This, my beloved son, has already so given of himself to the world that there is no one here to be ordered about. Give up this nonsense." Whereupon the elephant on which the Lord of Social Duty was riding bowed in worship of the Buddha, and the entire company of the Antagonist dissolved like a dream. That night, the Buddha achieved illumination, and for the next fifty years remained in the world as teacher of the way to the extinction of the bondages of egoism.

Now, those first two temptations—of desire and of fear—are the same that Adam and Eve are shown to have experienced in the extraordinary painting by Titian (now in the Prado), conceived when he was ninety-four years old. The tree is, of course, the mythological world axis, at the point where time and eternity, movement and rest, are at one, and around which all things revolve. It is here represented only in its temporal aspect, as the tree of the knowledge of good and evil, profit and loss, desire and fear. At the right is Eve, who sees the tempter in the form of a child, offering the apple, and she is moved by desire. Adam, however, from the opposite point of view, sees the serpent-legs of the ambiguous tempter and is touched with fear. Desire and fear: these are the two emotions by which all life in the world is governed. Desire is the bait, death is the hook.

Adam and Eve were moved; the Buddha was not. Eve and Adam brought forth life and were cursed of God; the Buddha taught release from life's fear.

MOYERS: And yet with the child—with life—come danger, fear, suffering?

CAMPBELL: Here I am now, in my eighties, and I'm writing a work that is to be of several volumes. I want very much to live until I finish this work. I want that child. So that puts me in fear of death. If I had no desire to complete that book, I wouldn't mind dying. Now, both the Buddha and Christ found salvation beyond death, and returned from the wilderness to choose and instruct disciples, who then brought their message to the world.

The messages of the great teachers—Moses, the Buddha, Christ, Mohammed—differ greatly. But their visionary journeys are much the same. At the time of his election, Mohammed was an illiterate camel-caravan master. But every day he would leave his home in Mecca and go out to a mountain cave to meditate. One day a voice called to him, "Write!" and he listened, and we have the Koran. It's an old, old story.

MOYERS: In each case receivers of the boon have done some rather grotesque things with their interpretation of the hero's message.

CAMPBELL: There are some teachers who decide they won't teach at all because of what society will do with what they've found.

MOYERS: What if the hero returns from his ordeal, and the world doesn't want what he brings back?

CAMPBELL: That, of course, is a normal experience. It isn't always so much that the world doesn't want the gift, but that it doesn't know how to receive it and how to institutionalize it—

MOYERS: —how to keep it, how to renew it.

CAMPBELL: Yes, how to help keep it going.

MOYERS: I've always liked that image of life being breathed back into the dry bones, back into the ruins and the relics.

CAMPBELL: There is a kind of secondary hero to revitalize the tradition. This hero reinterprets the tradition and makes it valid as a living experience today instead of a lot of outdated clichés. This has to be done with all traditions.

MOYERS: So many of the religions began with their own hero stories. The whole of the Orient has been blessed with the teaching of the good law brought back by Buddha, and the Occident has been blessed by the laws Moses brought back from Sinai. The tribal or local heroes perform their deeds for a single folk, and universal heroes like Mohammed, Jesus, and Buddha bring the message from afar. These heroes of religion came back with the wonder of God, not with a blueprint of God.

CAMPBELL: Well, you find an awful lot of laws in the Old Testament.

MOYERS: But that's the transformation of religion to theology. Religion begins with the sense of wonder and awe and the attempt to tell stories that will connect us to God. Then it becomes a set of theological works in which everything is reduced to a code, to a creed.

CAMPBELL: That's the reduction of mythology to theology. Mythology is very fluid. Most of the myths are self-contradictory. You may even find four or five myths in a given culture, all giving different versions of the same mystery. Then theology comes along and says it has got to be just this way. Mythology is poetry, and the poetic language is very flexible.

Religion turns poetry into prose. God is literally up there, and this is literally what he thinks, and this is the way you've got to behave to get into proper relationship with that god up there.

MOYERS: You don't have to believe that there was a King Arthur to get the significance of those stories, but Christians say we have to believe there was a Christ, or the miracles don't make sense.

CAMPBELL: They are the same miracles that Elijah performed. There's a whole body of miracles that float, like particles in the air, and a man of a certain type of achievement comes along, and all these things cluster around him. These stories of miracles let us know simply that this remarkable man preached of a spiritual order that is not to be identified with the merely physical order, so he could perform spiritual magic. It doesn't follow that he actually did any of these things, although of course it's possible. Three or four times I've seen what appear to be magical effects occur: men and women of power can do things that you wouldn't think possible. We don't really know what the limits of the possible might be. But the miracles of legend need not necessarily have been facts. The Buddha walked on water, as did Jesus. The Buddha ascended to heaven and returned.

MOYERS: I remember a lecture in which you drew a circle, and you said, "That's your soul."

CAMPBELL: Well, that was simply a pedagogical stunt. Plato

has said somewhere that the soul is a circle. I took this idea to suggest on the blackboard the whole sphere of the psyche. Then I drew a horizontal line across the circle to represent the line of separation of the conscious and unconscious. The center from which all our energy comes I represented as a dot in the center of the circle, below the horizontal line. An infant has no intention that doesn't come from its own little body requirements. That's the way life begins. An infant is mostly the impulse of life. Then the mind comes along and has to figure out what it's all about, what is it I want? And how do I get it?

Now, above the horizontal line there is the ego, which I represent as a square: that aspect of our consciousness that we identify as our center. But, you see, it's very much off center. We think that this is what's running the show, but it isn't.

MOYERS: What's running the show?

CAMPBELL: What's running the show is what's coming up from way down below. The period when one begins to realize that one isn't running the show is adolescence, when a whole new system of requirements begins announcing itself from the body. The adolescent hasn't the slightest idea how to handle all this, and cannot but wonder what it is that's pushing him—or even more mysteriously, pushing her.

MOYERS: It seems fairly evident that we arrive here as infants with some kind of memory box down there.

CAMPBELL: Well, it's surprising how much memory there is down there. The infant knows what to do when a nipple's in its mouth. There is a whole system of built-in action which, when we see it in animals, we call instinct. That is the biological ground. But then certain things can happen that make it repulsive or difficult or frightening or sinful to do some of the things that one is impelled to do, and that is when we begin to have our most troublesome psychological problems.

Myths primarily are for fundamental instruction in these matters. Our society today is not giving us adequate mythic instruction of this kind, and so young people are finding it difficult to get their act together. I have a theory that, if you can find out where a person is blocked, it should be possible to find a mythological counterpart for that particular threshold problem.

MOYERS: We hear people say, "Get in touch with yourself." What do you take that to mean?

CAMPBELL: It's quite possible to be so influenced by the ideals and commands of your neighborhood that you don't know what you really want and could be. I think that anyone brought up in an extremely strict, authoritative social situation is unlikely ever to come to the knowledge of himself.

MOYERS: Because you're told what to do.

CAMPBELL: You're told exactly what to do, every bit of the time. You're in the army now. So this is what we do here. As a child in school, you're always doing what you're told to do, and so you count the days to your holidays, since that's when you're going to be yourself.

MOYERS: What does mythology tell us about how to get in touch with that other self, that real self?

CAMPBELL: The first instruction would be to follow the hints of the myth itself and of your guru, your teacher, who should know. It's like an athlete going to a coach. The coach tells him how to bring his own energies into play. A good coach doesn't tell a runner exactly how to hold his arms or anything like that. He watches him run, then helps him to correct his own natural mode. A good teacher is there to watch the young person and recognize what the possibilities are—then to give advice, not commands. The command would be, "This is the way I do it, so you must do it this way, too." Some artists teach their students that way. But the teacher in any case has to talk it out, to give some general clues. If you don't have someone to do that for you, you've got to work it all out from scratch—like reinventing the wheel.

A good way to learn is to find a book that seems to be dealing with the problems that you're now dealing with. That will certainly give you some clues. In my own life I took my instruction from reading Thomas Mann and James Joyce, both of whom had applied basic mythological themes to the interpretation of the problems, questions, realizations, and concerns of young men growing up in the modern world. You can discover your own guiding-myth motifs through the works of a good novelist who himself understands these things.

MOYERS: That's what intrigues me. If we are fortunate, if the gods and muses are smiling, about every generation someone comes along to inspire the imagination for the journey each of us takes. In your day it was Joyce and Mann. In our day it often seems to be movies. Do movies create hero myths? Do you think, for example, that a movie like *Star Wars* fills some of that need for a model of the hero?

CAMPBELL: I've heard youngsters use some of George Lucas' terms—"the Force" and "the dark side." So it must be hitting somewhere. It's a good sound teaching, I would say.

MOYERS: I think that explains in part the success of *Star Wars*. It wasn't just the production value that made that such an exciting film to watch, it was that it came along at a time when people needed to see in recognizable images the clash of good and evil. They needed to be reminded of idealism, to see a romance based upon selflessness rather than selfishness.

CAMPBELL: The fact that the evil power is not identified with any specific nation on this earth means you've got an abstract power, which represents a principle, not a specific historical situation. The story has to do with an operation of principles, not of this nation against that. The monster masks that are put on people in *Star Wars* represent the real monster force in the modern world. When the mask of Darth Vader is removed, you see an unformed man, one who has not developed as a human individual. What you see is a strange and pitiful sort of undifferentiated face.

MOYERS: What's the significance of that?

CAMPBELL: Darth Vader has not developed his own humanity. He's a robot. He's a bureaucrat, living not in terms of himself but in terms of an imposed system. This is the threat to our lives that we all face today. Is the system going to flatten you out and deny you your humanity, or are you going to be able to make use of the system to the attainment of human purposes? How do you relate to the system so that you are not compulsively serving it? It doesn't help to try to change it to accord with your system of thought. The momentum of history behind it is too great for anything really significant to evolve from that kind of action. The thing to do is learn to live in your period of history as a human being. That's something else, and it can be done.

MOYERS: By doing what?

CAMPBELL: By holding to your own ideals for yourself and, like Luke Skywalker, rejecting the system's impersonal claims upon you.

MOYERS: When I took our two sons to see *Star Wars*, they did the same thing the audience did at that moment when the voice of Ben Kenobi says to Skywalker in the climactic moment of the last fight, "Turn off your computer, turn off your machine and do it yourself, follow your feelings, trust your feelings." And when he did, he achieved success, and the audience broke out into applause.

CAMPBELL: Well, you see, that movie communicates. It is in a language that talks to young people, and that's what counts. It asks, Are you going to be a person of heart and humanity—because that's where the life is, from the heart—or are you going to do whatever seems to be required of you by what might be called "intentional power"? When Ben Kenobi says, "May the

Force be with you," he's speaking of the power and energy of life, not of programmed political intentions.

MOYERS: I was intrigued by the definition of the Force. Ben Kenobi says, "The Force is an energy field created by all living things. It surrounds us, it penetrates us, it binds the galaxy together." And I've read in *The Hero with a Thousand Faces* similar descriptions of the world navel, of the sacred place, of the power that is at the moment of creation.

CAMPBELL: Yes, of course, the Force moves from within. But the force of the Empire is based on an intention to overcome and master. *Star Wars* is not a simple morality play, it has to do with the powers of life as they are either fulfilled or broken and suppressed through the action of man.

MOYERS: The first time I saw *Star Wars*, I thought, "This is a very old story in a very new costume." The story of the young man called to adventure, the hero going out facing the trials and ordeals, and coming back after his victory with a boon for the community—

CAMPBELL: Certainly Lucas was using standard mythological figures. The old man as the adviser made me think of a Japanese sword master. I've known some of those people, and Ben Kenobi has a bit of their character.

MOYERS: What does the sword master do?

CAMPBELL: He is a total expert in swordsmanship. The Oriental cultivation of the martial arts goes beyond anything I've ever encountered in American gymnasiums. There is a psychological as well as a physiological technique that go together there. This character in *Star Wars* has that quality.

MOYERS: There's something mythological, too, in that the hero is helped by a stranger who shows up and gives him some instrument—

CAMPBELL: He gives him not only a physical instrument but a psychological commitment and a psychological center. The commitment goes past your mere intention system. You are one with the event.

MOYERS: My favorite scene was when they were in the garbage compactor, and the walls were closing in, and I thought, "That's like the belly of the whale that swallowed Jonah."

CAMPBELL: That's where they were, down in the belly of the whale.

MOYERS: What's the mythological significance of the belly?

CAMPBELL: The belly is the dark place where digestion takes place and new energy is created. The story of Jonah in the whale is an example of a mythic theme that is practically universal, of the hero going into a fish's belly and ultimately coming out again, transformed.

MOYERS: Why must the hero do that?

CAMPBELL: It's a descent into the dark. Psychologically, the whale represents the power of life locked in the unconscious. Metaphorically, water is the unconscious, and the creature in the water is the life or energy of the unconscious, which has overwhelmed the conscious personality and must be disempowered, overcome and controlled.

In the first stage of this kind of adventure, the hero leaves the realm of the familiar, over which he has some measure of control, and comes to a threshold, let us say the edge of a lake or sea, where a monster of the abyss comes to meet him. There are then two possibilities. In a story of the Jonah type, the hero is swallowed and taken into the abyss to be later resurrected—a variant of the death-and-resurrection theme. The conscious personality here has come in touch with a charge of unconscious energy which it is unable to handle and must now suffer all the trails and revelations of a terrifying night-sea journey, while learning how to come to terms with this power of the dark and emerge, at last, to a new way of life.

The other possibility is that the hero, on encountering the power of the dark, may overcome and kill it, as did Siegfried and St. George when they killed the dragon. But as Siegfried learned, he must then taste the dragon blood, in order to take to himself something of that dragon power. When Siegfried has killed the dragon and tasted the blood, he hears the song of nature. He has transcended his humanity and reassociated himself with the powers of nature, which are the powers of our life, and from which our minds remove us.

You see, consciousness thinks it's running the shop. But it's a secondary organ of a total human being, and it must not put itself in control. It must submit and serve the humanity of the body. When it does put itself in control, you get a man like Darth Vader in *Star Wars*, the man who goes over to the consciously intentional side.

MOYERS: The dark figure.

CAMPBELL: Yes, that's the figure that in Goethe's *Faust* is represented by Mephistopheles.

MOYERS: But I can hear someone saying, "Well, that's all well and good for the imagination of a George Lucas or for the scholarship of a Joseph Campbell, but that isn't what happens in my life."

CAMPBELL: You bet it is—and if he doesn't recognize it, it may turn him into Darth Vader. If the person insists on a certain program, and doesn't listen to the demands of his own heart, he's going to risk a schizophrenic crackup. Such a person has put himself off center. He has aligned himself with a program for life, and it's not the one the body's interested in at all. The world is full of people who have stopped listening to themselves or have listened only to their neighbors to learn what they ought to do, how they ought to behave, and what the values are that they should be living for.

MOYERS: Given what you know about human beings, is it conceivable that there is a port of wisdom beyond the conflicts of truth and illusion by which our lives can be put back together again? Can we develop new models?

CAMPBELL: They're already here, in the religions. All religions have been true for their time. If you can recognize the enduring aspect of their truth and separate it from the temporal applications, you've got it.

We've spoken about it right here: the sacrifice of the physical desires and fears of the body to that which spiritually supports the body; is the body learning to know and express its own deepest life in the field of time? One way or another, we all have to find what best fosters the flowering of our humanity in this contemporary life, and dedicate ourselves to that.

MOYERS: Not the first cause, but a higher cause?

CAMPBELL: I would say, a more inward cause. "Higher" is just up there, and there is no "up there." We know that. That old man up there has been blown away. You've got to find the Force inside you. This is why Oriental gurus are so convincing to young people today. They say, "It is in you. Go and find it."

MOYERS: But isn't it only the very few who can face the challenge of a new truth and put their lives in accord with it?

CAMPBELL: Not at all! A few may be the teachers and the leaders, but this is something that anybody can respond to, just as anybody has the potential to run out to save a child. It is within everybody to recognize values in his life that are not confined to maintenance of the body and economic concerns of the day.

MOYERS: When I was a boy and read *Knights of the Round Table*, myth stirred me to think that I could be a hero. I wanted to go out and do battle with dragons, I wanted to go into the dark forest and slay evil. What does it say to you that myths can cause the son of an Oklahoma farmer to think of himself as a hero?

CAMPBELL: Myths inspire the realization of the possibility of your perfection, the fullness of your strength, and the bringing of solar light into the world. Slaying monsters is slaying the dark things. Myths grab you somewhere down inside. As a boy, you go at it one way, as I did reading my Indian stories. Later on, myths tell you more, and more, and still more. I think that anyone who has ever dealt seriously with religious or mythic ideas will tell you that we learn them as a child on one level, but then many different levels are revealed. Myths are infinite in their revelation.

MOYERS: How do I slay that dragon in me? What's the journey each of us has to make, what you call "the soul's high adventure"?

CAMPBELL: My general formula for my students is "Follow your bliss." Find where it is, and don't be afraid to follow it.

MOYERS: Is it my work or my life?

CAMPBELL: If the work that you're doing is the work that you chose to do because you are enjoying it, that's it. But if you think, "Oh, no! I couldn't do that!" that's the dragon locking you in. "No, no, I couldn't be a writer," or "No, no, I couldn't possibly do what So-and-so is doing."

MOYERS: In this sense, unlike heroes such as Prometheus or Jesus, we're not going on our journey to save the world but to save ourselves.

CAMPBELL: But in doing that, you save the world. The influence of a vital person vitalizes, there's no doubt about it. The world without spirit is a wasteland. People have the notion of saving the world by shifting things around, changing the rules, and who's on top, and so forth. No, no! Any world is a valid world if it's alive. The thing to do is to bring life to it, and the only way to do that is to find in your own case where the life is and become alive yourself.

MOYERS: When I take that journey and go down there and slay those dragons, do I have to go alone?

CAMPBELL: If you have someone who can help you, that's fine, too. But, ultimately, the last deed has to be done by oneself. Psychologically, the dragon is one's own binding of oneself to one's ego. We're captured in our own dragon cage. The problem of the psychiatrist is to disintegrate that dragon, break him up, so that you may expand to a larger field of relationships. The ultimate dragon is within you, it is your ego clamping you down.

MOYERS: What's my ego?

CAMPBELL: What you think you want, what you will to believe, what you think you can afford, what you decide to love, what you regard yourself as bound to. It may be all much too small, in which case it will nail you down. And if you simply do what your neighbors tell you to do, you're certainly going to be nailed down. Your neighbors are then your dragon as it reflects from within yourself.

Our Western dragons represent greed. However, the Chinese dragon is different. It represents the vitality of the swamps and comes up beating its belly and bellowing, "Haw ha ha haww." That's a lovely kind of dragon, one that yields the bounty of the waters, a great, glorious gift. But the dragon of our Western tales tries to collect and keep everything to himself. In his secret cave he guards things: heaps of gold and perhaps a captured virgin. He doesn't know what to do with either, so he just guards and keeps. There are people like that, and we call them creeps. There's no life from them, no giving. They just glue themselves to you and hang around and try to suck out of you their life.

Jung had a patient who came to him because she felt herself to be alone in the world, on the rocks, and when she drew a picture for him of how she felt, there she was on the shore of a dismal sea, caught in rocks from the waist down. The wind was blowing, and her hair was blowing, and all the gold, all the joy of life, was locked away from her in the rocks. The next picture that she drew, however, followed something that he had said to her. A flash of lightning strikes the rocks, and a golden disk is being lifted out. There is no more gold locked within the rocks. There are golden patches now on the surface. In the course of the conferences that followed, these patches of gold were identified. They were her friends. She wasn't alone. She had locked herself in her own little room and life, yet she had friends. Her recognition of these followed only after the killing of her dragon.

MOYERS: I like what you say about the old myth of Theseus and Ariande. Theseus says to Ariande, "I'll love you forever if you can show me a way to come out of the labyrinth." So she gives him a ball of string, which he unwinds as he goes into the labyrinth, and then follows to find the way out. You say, "All he had was the string. That's all you need."

CAMPBELL: That's all you need—an Ariande thread.

MOYERS: Sometimes we look for great wealth to save us, a great power to save us, or great ideas to save us, when all we need is that piece of string.

CAMPBELL: That's not always easy to find. But it's nice to have someone who can give you a clue. That's the teacher's job, to help you find your Ariande thread.

MOYERS: Like all heroes, the Buddha doesn't show you the truth itself, he shows you the way to truth.

CAMPBELL: But it's got to be your way, not his. The Buddha can't tell you exactly how to get rid of your particular fears, for example. Different teachers may suggest exercises, but they may not be the ones to work for you. All a teacher can do is suggest. He is like a lighthouse that says, "There are rocks over here, steer clear. There is a channel, however, out there."

The big problem of any young person's life is to have models to suggest possibilities. Nietzsche says, "Man is the sick animal."

Man is the animal that doesn't know what to do with itself. The mind has many possibilities, but we can live no more than one life. What are we going to do with ourselves? A living myth presents contemporary models.

MOYERS: Today, we have an endless variety of models. A lot of people end up choosing many and never knowing who they are.

CAMPBELL: When you choose your vocation, you have actually chosen a model, and it will fit you in a little while. After middle life, for example, you can pretty well tell what a person's profession is. Wherever I go, people know I'm a professor. I don't know what it is that I do, or how I look, but I, too, can tell professors from engineers and merchants. You're shaped by your life.

MOYERS: There is a wonderful image in *King Arthur* where the knights of the Round Table are about to enter the search for the Grail in the Dark Forest, and the narrator says, "They thought it would be a disgrace to go forth in a group. So each entered the forest at a separate point of his choice." You've interpreted that to express the Western emphasis upon the unique phenomenon of a single human life—the individual confronting darkness.

CAMPBELL: What struck me when I read that in the thirteenth-century *Queste del Saint Graal* was that it epitomizes an especially Western spiritual aim and ideal, which is, of living the life that is potential in *you* and was never in anyone else as a possibility.

This, I believe, is the great Western truth: that each of us is a completely unique creature and that, if we are ever to give any gift to the world, it will have to come out of our own experience and fulfillment of our own potentialities, not someone else's. In the traditional Orient, on the other hand, and generally in all traditionally grounded societies, the individual is cookie-molded. His duties are put upon him in exact and precise terms, and there's no way of breaking out from them. When you go to a guru to be guided on the spiritual way, he knows just where you are on the traditional path, just where you have to go next, just what you must do to get there. He'll give you his picture to wear, so you can be like him. That wouldn't be a proper Western pedagogical way of guidance. We have to give our students guidance in developing their own pictures of themselves. What each must seek in his life never was, on land or sea. It is to be something out of his own unique potentiality for experience, something that never has been and never could have been experienced by anyone else.

MOYERS: There's the question Hamlet asked, "Are you up to your destiny?"

CAMPBELL: Hamlet's problem was that he wasn't. He was given a destiny too big for him to handle, and it blew him to pieces. That can happen, too.

MOYERS: Which stories from mythology help us understand death?

CAMPBELL: You don't understand death, you learn to acquiesce in death. I would say that the story of Christ assuming the form of a human servant, even to death on the cross, is the principal lesson for us of the acceptance of death. The story of Oedipus and the Sphinx has something to say of this, too. The Sphinx in the Oedipus story is not the Egyptian Sphinx, but a female form with the wings of a bird, the body of an animal, and the breast, neck, and face of a woman. What she represents is the destiny of all life. She has sent a plague over the land, and to lift the plague, the hero has to answer the riddle that she presents: "What is it that walks on four legs, then on two legs, and then on three?" The answer is "Man." The child creeps about on four legs, the adult walks on two, and the aged walk with a cane.

The riddle of the Sphinx is the image of life itself through time—childhood, maturity, age, and death. When without fear you have faced and accepted the riddle of the Sphinx, death has no further hold on you, and the curse of the Sphinx disappears. The conquest of the fear of death is the recovery of life's joy. One can experience an unconditional affirmation of life only when one has accepted death, not as contrary to life but as an aspect of life. Life in its becoming is always shedding death, and on the point of death. The conquest of fear yields the courage of life. That is the cardinal initiation of every heroic adventure—fearlessness and achievement.

I remember reading as a boy of the war cry of the Indian braves riding into battle against the rain of bullets of Custer's men. "What a wonderful day to die!" There was no hanging on there to life. That is one of the great messages of mythology. I, as I now know myself, am not the final form of my being. We must constantly die one way or another to the selfhood already achieved.

MOYERS: Do you have a story that illustrates this?

CAMPBELL: Well, the old English tale of Sir Gawain and the Green Knight is a famous one. One day a green giant came riding on a great green horse into King Arthur's dining hall. "I challenge anyone here," he cried, "to take this great battle-ax that I carry and cut off my head, and then, one year from today, meet me at the Green Chapel, where I shall cut off his head."

The only knight in the hall who had the courage to accept this incongruous invitation was Gawain. He arose from the table, the Green Knight got off his horse, handed Gawain the ax, stuck out his neck, and Gawain with a single stroke chopped off his head. The Green Knight stood up, picked up his head, took back the ax, climbed onto his horse, and as he rode away called back to the astonished Gawain, "I'll see you in a year."

That year everybody was very kind to Gawain. A fortnight or so before the term of the adventure, he rode off to search for the Green Chapel and keep faith with the giant Green Knight. As the date approached, with about three days to go, Gawain found himself before a hunter's cabin, where he asked the way to the Green Chapel. The hunter, a pleasant, genial fellow, met him at the door and replied, "Well, the Chapel is just down the way, a few hundred yards. Why not spend your next three days here with us? We'd love to have you. And when your time comes, your green friend is just down the way."

So Gawain says okay. And the hunter that evening says to him, "Now, early tomorrow I'm going off hunting, but I'll be back in the evening, when we shall exchange our winnings of the day. I'll give you everything I get on the hunt, and you give me whatever will have come to you." They laugh, and that was fine with Gawain. So they all retire to bed.

In the morning, early, the hunter rides off while Gawain is still asleep. Presently, in comes the hunter's extraordinarily beautiful wife, who tickles Gawain under the chin, and wakes him, and passionately invites him to a morning of love. Well, he is a knight of King Arthur's court, and to betray his host is the last thing such a knight can stoop to, so Gawain sternly resists. However, she is insistent and makes more and more of an issue of this thing, until finally she says to him, "Well then, let me give you just one kiss!" So she gives him one large smack. And that was that.

That evening, the hunter arrives with a great haul of all kinds of small game, throws it on the floor, and Gawain gives him one large kiss. They laugh, and that, too, was that.

The second morning, the wife again comes into the room, more passionate than ever, and the fruit of that encounter is two kisses. The hunter in the evening returns with about half as much game as before and receives two kisses, and again they laugh.

On the third morning, the wife is glorious, and Gawain, a young man about to meet his death, has all he can do to keep his head and retain his knightly honor, with this last gift before him of the luxury of life. This time, he accepts three kisses. And when she has delivered these, she begs him, as a token of her love, to accept her garter. "It is charmed," she says, "and will protect you against every danger." So Gawain accepts the garter.

And when the hunter returns with just one silly, smelly fox, which he tosses onto the floor, he receives in exchange three kisses from Gawain—but no garter.

Do we not see what the tests are of this young knight Gawain? They are the same as the first two of Buddha. One is of desire, lust. The other is of the fear of death. Gawain had proved courage enough in just keeping his faith with this adventure. However, the garter was just one temptation too many.

So when Gawain is approaching the Green Chapel, he hears the Green Knight there, whetting the great ax—whiff, whiff, whiff, whiff. Gawain arrives, and the giant simply says to him, "Stretch your neck out here on this block." Gawain does so, and the Green Knight lifts the ax, but then pauses. "No, stretch it out a little more," he says. Gawain does so, and again the giant elevates the great ax. "A little more," he says once again. Gawain does the best he can and then whifffff—only giving Gawain's neck one little scratch. Then the Green Knight, who is in fact the hunter himself transfigured, explains, "That's for the garter."

This, they say, is the origin legend of the order of the Knights of the Garter.

MOYERS: And the moral of the story?

CAMPBELL: The moral, I suppose, would be that the first requirements for a heroic career are the knightly virtues of loyalty, temperance, and courage. The loyalty in this case is of two degrees or commitments: first, to the chosen adventure, but then, also, to the ideals of the order of knighthood. Now, this second commitment seems to put Gawain's way in opposition to the way of the Buddha, who when ordered by the Lord of Duty to perform the social duties proper to his caste, simply ignored the command, and that night achieved illumination as well as release from rebirth. Gawain is a European and, like Odysseus, who remained true to the earth and returned from the Island of the Sun to his marriage with Penelope, he has accepted, as the commitment of his life, not release from but loyalty to the values of life in this world. And yet, as we have just seen, whether following the middle way of the Buddha or the middle way of Gawain, the passage to fulfillment lies between the perils of desire and fear.

A third position, closer than Gawain's to that of the Buddha, yet loyal still to the values of life on this earth, is that of Nietzsche, in *Thus Spake Zarathustra.* In a kind of parable, Nietzsche describes what he calls the three transformations of the spirit. The first is that of the camel, of childhood and youth. The camel gets down on his knees and says, "Put a load on me." This is the season for obedience, receiving instruction and the information your society requires of you in order to live a responsible life.

But when the camel is well loaded, it struggles to its feet and runs out into the desert, where it is transformed into a lion— the heavier the load that had been carried, the stronger the lion will be. Now, the task of the lion is to kill a dragon, and the name of the dragon is "Thou shalt." On every scale of this scaly beast, a "thou shalt" is imprinted: some from four thousand years ago; others from this morning's headlines. Whereas the camel, the child, had to submit to the "thou shalts," the lion, the youth, is to throw them off and come to his own realization.

And so, when the dragon is thoroughly dead, with all its "thou shalts" overcome, the lion is transformed into a child moving out of its own nature, like a wheel impelled from its own hub. No more rules to obey. No more rules derived from the historical needs and tasks of the local society, but the pure impulse to living of a life in flower.

MOYERS: So we return to Eden?

CAMPBELL: To Eden before the Fall.

MOYERS: What are the "thou shalts" of a child that he needs to shed?

CAMPBELL: Every one that inhibits his self-fulfillment. For the camel, the "thou shalt" is a must, a civilizing force. It converts the human animal into a civilized human being. But the period of youth is the period of self-discovery and transformation into a lion. The rules are now to be used at will for life, not submitted to as compelling "thou shalts."

Something of this kind has to be recognized and dealt with by any serious student of art. If you go to a master to study and learn the techniques, you diligently follow all the instructions the master puts upon you. But then comes the time for using the rules in your own way and not being bound by them. That is the time for the lion-deed. You can actually forget the rules because they have been assimilated. You are an artist. Your own innocence now is of one who has become an artist, who has been, as it were, transmuted. You don't behave as the person behaves who has never mastered an art.

MOYERS: You say the time comes. How does a child know when his time has come? In ancient societies, the boy, for example, went through a ritual which told him the time had come. He knew that he was no longer a child and that he had to put off the influences of others and stand on his own. We don't have such a clear moment or an obvious ritual in our society that says to my son, "You are a man." Where is the passage today?

CAMPBELL: I don't have the answer. I figure you must leave it up to the boy to know when he has got his power. A baby bird knows when it can fly. We have a couple of birds' nests right near where we have breakfast in the morning, and we have seen several little families launched. These little things don't make a mistake. They stay on the branch until they know how to fly, and then they fly. I think somehow, inside, a person knows this.

I can give you examples from what I know of students in art studios. There comes a moment when they have learned what the artist can teach them. They have assimilated the craft, and they are ready for their own flight. Some of the artists allow their students to do that. They expect the student to fly off. Others want to establish a school, and the student finds he has got to be nasty to the teacher, or to say bad things about him, in order to get his own flight. But that is the teacher's own fault. He ought to have known it was time for the student to fly. The students I know, the ones who are really valid as students, know when it is time to push off.

MOYERS: There is an old prayer that says, "Lord, teach us when to let go." All of us have to know that, don't we?

CAMPBELL: That's the big problem of the parent. Being a parent is one of the most demanding careers I know. When I think what my father and mother gave up of themselves to launch their family—well, I really appreciate that.

My father was a businessman, and, of course, he would have been very happy to have his son go into business with him and take it on. In fact, I did go into business with Dad for a couple of months, and then I thought, "Geez, I can't do this." And he let me go. There is that testing time in your life when you have got to test yourself out to your own flight.

MOYERS: Myths used to help us know when to let go.

CAMPBELL: Myths formulate things for you. They say, for example, that you have to become an adult at a particular age. The age might be a good average age for that to happen—but actually, in the individual life, it differs greatly. Some people are late bloomers and come to particular stages at a relatively late age. You have to have a feeling for where you are. You've got only one life to live, and you don't have to live it for six people. Pay attention to it.

MOYERS: What about happiness? If I'm a young person and I want to be happy, what do myths tell me about happiness?

CAMPBELL: The way to find out about your happiness is to keep your mind on those moments when you feel most happy, when you really are happy—not excited, not just thrilled, but deeply happy. This requires a little bit of self-analysis. What is it that makes you happy? Stay with it, no matter what people tell you. This is what I call "following your bliss."

MOYERS: But how does mythology tell you about what makes you happy?

CAMPBELL: It won't tell you what makes you happy, but it will tell you what happens when you begin to follow your happiness, what the obstacles are that you're going to run into.

For example, there's a motif in American Indian stories that I call "the refusal of suitors." There's a young girl, beautiful, charming, and the young men invite her to marriage. "No, no, no," she says, "there's nobody around good enough for me." So a serpent comes, or, if it's a boy who won't have anything to do with girls, the serpent queen of a great lake might come. As soon as you have refused the suitors, you have elevated yourself out of the local field and put yourself in the field of higher power, higher danger. The question is, are you going to be able to handle it?

Another American Indian motif involves a mother and two little boys. The mother says, "You can play around the houses, but don't go north." So they go north. There's the adventurer.

MOYERS: And the point?

CAMPBELL: With the refusal of suitors, of the passing over a boundary, the adventure begins. You get into a field that's unprotected, novel. You can't have creativity unless you leave behind the bounded, the fixed, all the rules.

Now, there's an Iroquois story that illustrates the motif of the rejection of suitors. A girl lived with her mother in a wigwam on the edge of a village. She was a very beautiful girl but extremely proud and would not accept any of the boys. The mother was terribly annoyed with her.

One day they're out collecting wood quite a long way from the village and, while they are out, an ominous darkness comes down over them. Now, this wasn't the dark of night descending. When you have a darkness of this kind, there's a magician at work somewhere behind it. So the mother says, "Let's gather some bark and make a little wigwam for ourselves and collect wood for a fire, and we'll just spend the night here."

So they do exactly that and prepare a little supper, and the mother falls asleep. Suddenly the girl looks up, and there is a magnificent young man standing there before her with a wampum sash, glorious black feathers—a very handsome fellow. He says, "I've come to marry you, and I'll await your reply."

And she says, "I have to consult with my mother."

She does so, the mother accepts the young man, and he gives the mother the wampum belt to prove he's serious about the proposal. Then he says to the girl, "Tonight I would like you to come to my camp." And so she leaves with him. Mere human beings weren't good enough for this young lady, and so now she has something really special.

MOYERS: If she hadn't said no to the first suitors who came through the routine social convention—

CAMPBELL: —she wouldn't be having this adventure. Now the adventure is strange and marvelous. She accompanies the man to his village, and they enter his lodge. They spend two nights and days together, and on the third day he says to her, "I'm going off today to hunt." So he leaves. But after he has closed the flap of the entrance, she hears a strange sound outside. She spends the day in the hut alone and, when evening comes, she hears the strange sound again. The entrance flap is flung open, and in slides a prodigious serpent with tongue darting. He puts his head on her lap and says to her, "Now search my head for lice." She finds all sorts of horrible things there, and when she has killed them all, he withdraws his head, slides out of the lodge, and in a moment, after the door flap has closed, it opens again, and in comes her same beautiful young man. "Were you afraid of me when I came in that way just now?" he asks.

"No," she replies, "I wasn't afraid at all."

So the next day he goes off to hunt again, and presently she steps out of the lodge to gather firewood. The first thing she sees is an enormous serpent basking on the rocks—and then another, and another. She begins to feel very strange, homesick and discouraged, and returns to the lodge.

That evening, the serpent again comes sliding in, again departs and returns as a man. The third day when he has gone, the young woman decides she's going to try to get out of this place. She leaves the lodge and is in the woods alone, standing, thinking, when she hears a voice. She turns, and there's a little old man, who says, "Darling, you are in trouble. The man you've married is one of seven brothers. They are all great magicians and, like many people of this kind, their hearts are not in their bodies. Go back into the lodge, and in a bag that is hidden under the bed of the one to whom you are married, you will find a collection of seven hearts." This is a standard worldwide shamanic motif. The heart is not in the body, so the magician can't be killed. You have to find and destroy the heart.

She returns to the lodge, finds the bag full of hearts, and is running out with it when a voice calls to her, "Stop, stop." This is the voice, of course, of the magician. But she continues to run. And the voice calls after, "You may think you can get away from me, but you never will."

Just at that point, she is beginning to faint, when she hears again the voice of the little old man. "I'll help you," it says and, to her surprise, he's pulling her out of the water. She hadn't known that she was in water. That is to say, that with her marriage she had moved out of the rational, conscious sphere into the field of compulsions of the unconscious. That's always what's represented in such adventures under water. The character has slipped out of the realm of controlled action into that of transpersonal compulsions and events. Now, maybe these can be handled, maybe they can't.

What happens next in this story is that when the old man has pulled her out of the water, she finds herself in the midst of a company of old men standing along the shore, all looking exactly like her rescuer. They are the Thunderers, powers of the upper air. That is, she is still in the transcendent realm into which she brought herself by her refusal of suitors; only now, having torn herself away from the negative aspect of the powers, she has come into possession of the positive.

There is a lot more to this Iroquois tale, of how this young woman, now in the service of the higher powers, enabled them to destroy the negative powers of the abyss, and how, after that, she was conducted back, through a rainstorm, to the lodge of her mother.

MOYERS: Would you tell this to your students as an illustration of how, if they follow their bliss, if they take chances with their lives, if they do what they want to, the adventure is its own reward?

CAMPBELL: The adventure is its own reward—but it's necessarily dangerous, having both negative and positive possibilities, all of them beyond control. We are following our own way, not our daddy's or our mother's way. So we are beyond protection in a field of higher powers than we know. One has to have some sense of what the conflict possibilities will be in this field, and here a few good archetypal stories like this may help us to know what to expect. If we have been impudent and altogether ineligible for the role into which we have cast ourselves, it is going to be a demon marriage and a real mess. However, even here there may be heard a rescuing voice, to convert the adventure into a glory beyond anything ever imagined.

MOYERS: It's easier to stay home, stay in the womb, not take the journey.

CAMPBELL: Yes, but then life can dry up because you're not off on your own adventure. On the other hand, I have had an opposite, and to me quite surprising, experience in meeting and coming to know someone whose whole youth was controlled and directed by others, from first to last. My friend is a Tibetan who as a child was recognized as being the reincarnation of an abbot who had been reincarnating since about the seventeenth century. He was taken into a monastery at the age of about four and, from that moment, never was asked what he would like to do, but in all things followed to the letter the rules and instruction of his masters. His entire life was planned for him according to the ritual requirements of Tibetan Buddhist monastery life. Every stage in his spiritual development was celebrated with a ceremony. His personal life was translated into an archetypal journey so that, although on the surface he would seem to be enjoying no personal existence whatsoever, he was actually living on a very deep spiritual level an archetypal life like that of a divinity.

In 1959, this life ended. The Chinese Communist military station in Lhasa bombed the summer palace of the Dalai Lama and a season of massacres began. There were monasteries around Lhasa of as many as six thousand monks—all were destroyed, and their monks and abbots were killed and tortured. Many fled, together with hundreds of other refugees, across the almost impassable Himalayas to India. It is a terrible story—largely untold.

Finally all these shattered people arrived in India, which can hardly take care of its own population, and among the refugees were the Dalai Lama himself and a number of the leading officers and abbots of the great monasteries now destroyed. And they all agreed, Buddhist Tibet is finished. My friend and the other young monks who had managed to escape were advised, therefore, to regard their vows now as of the past, and to feel free to choose, either to continue somehow as monks, or to give up the monastic life and try to find a way to reshape their lives to the requirements and possibilities of the modern secular man.

My friend chose the latter way, not realizing, of course, what this would mean in the way of frustration, poverty, and suffering. He has had a really difficult time, but he has survived it with the will and composure of a saint. Nothing fazes him. I've known and worked with him now for over a decade, and in all this time I haven't heard one word, either of recrimination against the Chinese or of complaint about the treatment he has received here in the West. Nor from the Dalai Lama himself will you ever hear a word of resentment or condemnation. These men and all their friends have been the victims of a terrific upheaval, of terrific violence, and yet they have no hatred. I have learned

what religion is from these men. Here is true religion, alive—
today.

MOYERS: Love thine enemies.

CAMPBELL: Love thine enemies because they are the instruments of your destiny.

MOYERS: What do myths tell us about a God who lets two
sons in one family die in a relatively short period of time, and
who continues to visit on that family one ordeal after another?
I remember the story of the young Buddha, who saw the decrepit
old man and said, "Shame on birth because to everyone who is
born, old age will come." What does mythology say about suffering?

CAMPBELL: Since you bring up the Buddha, let's talk about
that example. The story of the Buddha's childhood is that he
was born as a prince and that, at the time of his birth, a prophet
told his father that the infant would grow up to be either a world
ruler or a world teacher. The good king was interested in his
own profession, and the last thing he wanted was that his son
should become a teacher of any kind. So he arranged to have
the child brought up in an especially beautiful palace where he
should experience nothing the least bit ugly or unpleasant that
might turn his mind to serious thoughts. Beautiful young women
played music and took care of the child. And there were beautiful
gardens, lotus ponds, and all.

But then one day the young prince said to his chariot driver,
his closest friend, "I'd like to go out and see what life is like in
the town." His father, on hearing this, tried to make everything
nice so that his son, the young prince, should see nothing of the
pain and misery of life in this world. The gods, however, saw to
it that the father's program for his son should be frustrated.

So, as the royal chariot was rolling along through the town,
which had been swept clean, with everything ugly kept out of
sight, one of the gods assumed the form of a decrepit old man
and was standing there, within view. "What's that?" the young

prince asked his charioteer, and the reply he received was, "That's an old man. That's age."

"Are all men then to grow old?" asked the prince.

"Ah, yes," the charioteer replied.

"Then shame on life," said the traumatized young prince, and he begged, sick at heart, to be driven home.

On a second trip, he saw a sick man, thin and weak and tottering, and again, on learning the meaning of this sight, his heart failed him, and the chariot returned to the palace.

On the third trip, the prince saw a corpse followed by mourners. "That," said the charioteer, "is death."

"Turn back," said the prince, "that I may somehow find deliverance from these destroyers of life—old age, sickness, and death."

Just one trip more—and what he sees this time is a mendicant monk; "What sort of man is that?" he asks.

"That is a holy man," the driver replies, "one who has abandoned the goods of this world and lives without desire or fear." Whereupon the young prince, on returning to his palace, resolved to leave his father's house and to seek a way of release from life's sorrows.

MOYERS: Do most myths say that suffering is an intrinsic part of life, and that there's no way around it?

CAMPBELL: I can't think of any that say that if you're going to live, you won't suffer. Myths tell us how to confront and bear and interpret suffering, but they do not say that in life there can or should be no suffering.

When the Buddha declares there is escape from sorrow, the escape is Nirvana, which is not a place, like heaven, but a psychological state of mind in which you are released from desire and fear.

MOYERS: And your life becomes—

CAMPBELL: —harmonious, centered, and affirmative.

MOYERS: Even with suffering?

CAMPBELL: Exactly. The Buddhists speak of the bodhisattva —the one who knows immortality, yet voluntarily enters into the field of the fragmentation of time and participates willingly and joyfully in the sorrows of the world. And this means not only experiencing sorrows oneself but participating with compassion in the sorrows of others. Compassion is the awakening of the heart from bestial self-interest to humanity. The word "compassion" means literally "suffering with."

MOYERS: But you don't mean compassion condones suffering, do you?

CAMPBELL: Of course compassion condones suffering in that it recognizes, yes, suffering is life.

MOYERS: That life is lived with suffering—

CAMPBELL: —with the suffering—but you're not going to get rid of it. Who, when or where, has ever been quit of the suffering of life in this world?

I had an illuminating experience from a woman who had been in severe physical pain for years, from an affliction that had stricken her in her youth. She had been raised a believing Christian and so thought this had been God's punishment of her for something she had done or not done at that time. She was in spiritual as well as physical pain. I told her that if she wanted release, she should affirm and not deny her suffering was her life, and that through it she had become the noble creature that she now was. And while I was saying all this, I was thinking, "Who am I to talk like this to a person in real pain, when I've never had anything more than a toothache?" But in this conversation, in affirming her suffering as the shaper and teacher of her life, she experienced a conversion—right there. I have kept in touch with her since—that was years and years ago—and she is indeed a transformed woman.

MOYERS: There was a moment of illumination?

CAMPBELL: Right there—I saw it happen.

MOYERS: Was it something you said mythologically?

CAMPBELL: Yes, although it's a little hard to explain. I gave her the belief that she was herself the cause of her suffering, that she had somehow brought it about. There is an important idea in Nietzsche, of *Amor fati*, the "love of your fate," which is in fact your life. As he says, if you say no to a single factor in your life, you have unraveled the whole thing. Furthermore, the more challenging or threatening the situation or context to be assimilated and affirmed, the greater the stature of the person who can achieve it. The demon that you can swallow gives you its power, and the greater life's pain, the greater life's reply.

My friend had thought, "God did this to me." I told her, "No, you did it to yourself. The God is within you. You yourself are your creator. If you find that place in yourself from which you brought this thing about, you will be able to live with it and affirm it, perhaps even enjoy it, as your life."

MOYERS: The only alternative would be not to live.

CAMPBELL: "All life is suffering," said the Buddha, and Joyce has a line—"Is life worth leaving?"

MOYERS: But what about the young person who says, "I didn't choose to be born—my mother and father made the choice for me."

CAMPBELL: Freud tells us to blame our parents for all the shortcomings of our life, and Marx tells us to blame the upper class of our society. But the only one to blame is oneself. That's the helpful thing about the Indian idea of karma. Your life is the fruit of your own doing. You have no one to blame but yourself.

MOYERS: But what about chance? A drunken driver turns the corner and hits you. That isn't your fault. You haven't done that to yourself.

CAMPBELL: From that point of view, is there anything in your life that did not occur as by chance? This is a matter of being able to accept chance. The ultimate backing of life is chance— the chance that your parents met, for example! Chance, or what might seem to be chance, is the means through which life is realized. The problem is not to blame or explain but to handle the life that arises. Another war has been declared somewhere, and you are drafted into an army, and there go five or six years of your life with a whole new set of chance events. The best advice is to take it all *as if* it had been of your intention—with that, you evoke the participation of your will.

MOYERS: In all of these journeys of mythology, there's a place everyone wishes to find. The Buddhists talk of Nirvana, and Jesus talks of peace, of the mansion with many rooms. Is that typical of the hero's journey—that there's a place to find?

CAMPBELL: The place to find is within yourself. I learned a little about this in athletics. The athlete who is in top form has a quiet place within himself, and it's around this, somehow, that his action occurs. If he's all out there in the action field, he will not be performing properly. My wife is a dancer, and she tells me that this is true in dance as well. There's a center of quietness within, which has to be known and held. If you lose that center, you are in tension and begin to fall apart.

The Buddhist Nirvana is a center of peace of this kind. Buddhism is a psychological religion. It starts with the psychological problem of suffering: all life is sorrowful; there is, however, an escape from sorrow; the escape is Nirvana—which is a state of mind or consciousness, not a place somewhere, like heaven. It is right here, in the midst of the turmoil of life. It is the state you find when you are no longer driven to live by compelling desires, fears, and social commitments, when you have found your center of freedom and can act by choice out of that. Voluntary action out of this center is the action of the bodhisattvas—joyful participation in the sorrows of the world. You are not grabbed, because you have released yourself from the grabbers of fear, lust, and duties. These are the rulers of the world.

There is an instructive Tibetan Buddhist painting in which the so-called Wheel of Becoming is represented. In monasteries, this painting would not appear inside the cloister but on the outer wall. What is shown is the mind's image of the world when still caught in the grip of the fear of the Lord Death. Six realms of being are represented as spokes of the ever revolving wheel: one is of animal life, another of human life, another of the gods in heaven, and a fourth of the souls being punished in hell. A fifth realm is of the belligerent demons, antigods, or Titans. And the sixth, finally, is of the hungry ghosts, the souls of those in whose love for others there was attachment, clinging, and expectation. The hungry ghosts have enormous, ravenous bellies and pinpoint mouths. However, in the midst of each of these realms there is a Buddha, signifying the possibility of release and illumination.

In the hub of the wheel are three symbolic beasts—a pig, a cock, and a serpent. These are the powers that keep the wheel revolving—ignorance, desire, and malice. And then, finally, the rim of the wheel represents the bounding horizon of anyone's consciousness who is moved by the triad of powers of the hub and held in the grip of the fear of death. In the center, surrounding the hub and what are known as the "three poisons," are souls descending in darkness and others ascending to illumination.

MOYERS: What is the illumination?

CAMPBELL: The illumination is the recognition of the radiance of one eternity through all things, whether in the vision of time these things are judged as good or as evil. To come to this, you must release yourself completely from desiring the goods of this world and fearing their loss. "Judge not that you be not judged," we read in the words of Jesus. "If the doors of perception were cleansed," wrote Blake, "man would see everything as it is, infinite."

MOYERS: That's a tough trip.

CAMPBELL: That's a *heavenly* trip.

MOYERS: But is this really just for saints and monks?

CAMPBELL: No, I think it's also for artists. The real artist is the one who has learned to recognize and to render what Joyce has called the "radiance" of all things, as an epiphany or showing forth of their truth.

MOYERS: But doesn't this leave all the rest of us ordinary mortals back on shore?

CAMPBELL: I don't think there is any such thing as an ordinary mortal. Everybody has his own possibility of rapture in the experience of life. All he has to do is recognize it and then cultivate it and get going with it. I always feel uncomfortable when people speak about ordinary mortals because I've never met an ordinary man, woman, or child.

MOYERS: But is art the only way one can achieve this illumination?

CAMPBELL: Art and religion are the two recommended ways. I don't think you get it through sheer academic philosophy, which gets all tangled up in concepts. But just living with one's heart open to others in compassion is a way wide open to all.

MOYERS: So the experience of illumination is available to anyone, not just saints or artists. But if it is potentially in every one of us, deep in that unlocked memory box, how do you unlock it?

CAMPBELL: You unlock it by getting somebody to help you unlock it. Do you have a dear friend or good teacher? It may come from an actual human being, or from an experience like an automobile accident, or from an illuminating book. In my own life, mostly it comes from books, though I have had a long series of magnificent teachers.

MOYERS: When I read your work, I think, "Moyers, what mythology has done for you is to place you on a branch of a very ancient tree. You're part of a society of the living and dead that came long before you were here and will be here long after you are gone. It nourished you and protected you, and you have to nourish it and protect it in return."

CAMPBELL: Well, it's been a wonderful support for life, I can tell you. It's been tremendous what this kind of resource pouring into my life has done.

MOYERS: But people ask, isn't a myth a lie?

CAMPBELL: No, mythology is not a lie, mythology is poetry, it is metaphorical. It has been well said that mythology is the penultimate truth—penultimate because the ultimate cannot be put into words. It is beyond words, beyond images, beyond that bounding rim of the Buddhist Wheel of Becoming. Mythology pitches the mind beyond that rim, to what can be known but not told. So this is the penultimate truth.

It's important to live life with the experience, and therefore the knowledge, of its mystery and of your own mystery. This gives life a new radiance, a new harmony, a new splendor. Thinking in mythological terms helps to put you in accord with the inevitables of this vale of tears. You learn to recognize the positive values in what appear to be the negative moments and aspects of your life. The big question is whether you are going to be able to say a hearty yes to your adventure.

MOYERS: The adventure of the hero?

CAMPBELL: Yes, the adventure of the hero—the adventure of being alive.

VI

THE GIFT OF
THE GODDESS

Myths of the Great Goddess teach compassion for all living beings. There you come to appreciate the real sanctity of the earth itself, because it is the body of the Goddess.

MOYERS: The Lord's Prayer begins, "Our Father which art in Heaven . . ." Could it have begun "Our Mother"?

CAMPBELL: This is a symbolic image. All of the references of religious and mythological images are to planes of consciousness, or fields of experience that are potential in human spirit. And these images evoke attitudes and experiences that are appropriate to a meditation on the mystery of the source of your own being.

There have been systems of religion where the mother is the prime parent, the source. The mother is really a more immediate parent than the father because one is born from the mother, and the first experience of any infant is the mother. I have frequently thought that mythology is a sublimation of the mother image. We talk of Mother Earth. And in Egypt you have the Mother Heavens, the Goddess Nut, who is represented as the whole heavenly sphere.

MOYERS: I was seized in Egypt upon first seeing the figure of Nut in the ceiling of one of those temples.

CAMPBELL: Yes, I know the temple.

MOYERS: It's overwhelming in both its ability to evoke awe and in its sensual character.

CAMPBELL: Yes. The idea of the Goddess is related to the fact that you're born from your mother, and your father may be unknown to you, or the father may have died. Frequently, in the epics, when the hero is born, his father has died, or his father is in some other place, and then the hero has to go in quest of his father.

In the story of the incarnation of Jesus, the father of Jesus was the father in heaven, at least in terms of the symbology. When Jesus goes to the cross, he is on the way to the father, leaving the mother behind. And the cross, which is symbolic of the earth, is the mother symbol. So on the cross, Jesus leaves his body on the mother, from whom he has acquired his body, and he goes to the father, who is the ultimate transcendent mystery source.

MOYERS: What impact has this father quest had on us down through the centuries?

CAMPBELL: It's a major theme in myth. There's a little motif that occurs in many narratives related to a hero's life, where the boy says, "Mother, who is my father?" She will say, "Well, your father is in such and such a place," and then he goes on the father quest.

In the *Odyssey*, Odysseus' son Telemachus is a tiny babe when Odysseus goes off to the Trojan War. The war lasts for ten years, and then, on his journey home, Odysseus is lost for ten more years in the mysterious world of the mythological Mediterranean. Athena comes to Telemachus, who is now twenty years old, and says, "Go find your father." He doesn't know where his father is. He goes to Nestor and asks, "Where do you think my father would be?" And Nestor says, "Well, go ask Proteus." He's on the father quest.

MOYERS: In *Star Wars*, Luke Skywalker says to his companions, "I wish I had known my father." There's something powerful in the image of the father quest. But why no mother quest?

CAMPBELL: Well, the mother's right there. You're born from your mother, and she's the one who nurses you and instructs you and brings you up to the age when you must find your father.

Now, the finding of the father has to do with finding your own character and destiny. There's a notion that the character is inherited from the father, and the body and very often the mind from the mother. But it's your character that is the mystery, and your character is your destiny. So it is the discovery of your destiny that is symbolized by the father quest.

MOYERS: So when you find your father, you find yourself?

CAMPBELL: We have the word in English, "at-one-ment" with the father. You remember the story of Jesus lost in Jerusalem when he's a little boy about twelve years old. His parents hunt for him, and when they find him in the temple, in conversation with the doctors of the law, they ask, "Why did you abandon us this way? Why did you give us this fear and anxiety?" And he says, "Didn't you know I had to be about my father's business?" He's twelve years old—that's the age of the adolescent initiations, finding who you are.

MOYERS: But what happened along the way to this reverence that in primitive societies was directed toward the Goddess figure, the Great Goddess, the mother earth—what happened to that?

CAMPBELL: Well, that was associated primarily with agriculture and the agricultural societies. It has to do with earth. The human woman gives birth just as the earth gives birth to the plants. She gives nourishment, as the plants do. So woman magic and earth magic are the same. They are related. And the personification of the energy that gives birth to forms and nourishes forms is properly female. It is in the agricultural world of ancient Mesopotamia, the Egyptian Nile, and in the earlier planting-culture systems that the Goddess is the dominant mythic form.

We have found hundreds of early European Neolithic figurines of the Goddess, but hardly anything there of the male figure at all. The bull and certain other animals, such as the boar and the goat, may appear as symbolic of the male power, but the Goddess was the only visualized divinity at that time.

And when you have a Goddess as the creator, it's her own body that is the universe. She is identical with the universe. That's the sense of that Goddess Nut figure that you saw in the Egyptian temple. She is the whole sphere of the life-enclosing heavens.

MOYERS: There is one scene of the Goddess swallowing the sun. Remember?

CAMPBELL: The idea is that she swallows the sun in the west and gives birth to the sun in the east, and it passes through her body at night.

MOYERS: So it would be natural for people trying to explain the wonders of the universe to look to the female figure as the explanation of what they see in their own lives.

CAMPBELL: Not only that, but when you move to a philosophical point of view, as in the Goddess religions of India— where the Goddess symbology is dominant to this day—the female represents *maya*. The female represents what in Kantian terminology we call the *forms of sensibility*. She is time and space itself, and the mystery beyond her is beyond all pairs of opposites. So it isn't male and it isn't female. It neither is nor is not. But *everything* is within her, so that the gods are her children. Everything you can think of, everything you can see, is a production of the Goddess.

I once saw a marvelous scientific movie about protoplasm. It was a revelation to me. It is in movement all the time, flowing. Sometimes it seems to be flowing this way and that, and then it shapes things. It has a potentiality for bringing things into shape. I saw this movie in northern California, and as I drove down the coast to Big Sur, all the way, all I could see was protoplasm in the form of grass being eaten by protoplasm in the form of cows; protoplasm in the form of birds diving for protoplasm in the form of fish. You just got this wonderful sense of the abyss from which all has come. But each form has its own intentions, its own possibilities, and that's where meaning comes. Not in the protoplasm itself.

MOYERS: We are right back, then, to the Indians, who believe that the informing life and energy of all things is the earth. You quote those lines from the Upanishads: "Thou art the dark blue bird, and the green parrot with red eyes. Thou hast the lightning as thy child. Thou art the season and the seas. Having no beginning, thou dost abide with immanence, whereof all things are born." That is this idea, isn't it—that we and the earth are the same?

But wasn't it inevitable that this idea would die under the weight of scientific discoveries? We know now that plants don't grow out of the bodies of dead people, they grow according to the laws of seed, and soil, and sun. Didn't Newton kill myth?

CAMPBELL: Oh, I think myth is coming back. There's a young scientist today who's using the term "morphogenetic field," the field that produces forms. That's who the Goddess is, the field that produces forms.

MOYERS: What's the significance for us?

CAMPBELL: Well, it means to find what is the source of your own life, and what is the relationship of your body, your physical form, to this energy that animates it. The body without the energy isn't alive, is it? So you distinguish in your own life that which is of the body and that which is of energy and consciousness.

In India, the most common ultimate symbol is of the phallus, or lingam, as they call it, of the generating god penetrating the vagina, or the yoni, as they call it, of the Goddess. In contemplating this symbol, you are contemplating the generating moment itself of all life. The entire mystery of the generation of life is symbolically contemplated in that sign.

You see, the sexual mystery in India, and in most of the world, is a holy mystery. It is the mystery of the generation of life. The act of generating a child is a cosmic act and is to be understood as holy. And so the symbol that most immediately represents this mystery of the pouring of the energy of life into the field of time is the lingam and the yoni, the male and female powers in creative conjunction.

MOYERS: What would it have meant to us if somewhere along the way we had begun to pray to "Our Mother" instead of "Our Father"? What psychological difference would it have made?

CAMPBELL: It certainly has made a psychological difference in the character of our culture. For example, the basic birth of Western civilization occurred in the great river valleys—the Nile, the Tigris-Euphrates, the Indus, and later the Ganges. That was the world of the Goddess. The name of the river Ganges (Gangā) is the name of a goddess, for example.

And then there came the invasions. Now, these started seriously in the fourth millennium B.C. and became more and more devastating. They came in from the north and from the south and wiped out cities overnight. Just read the story in the Book of Genesis of the part played by Jacob's tribe in the fall of the city of Shechem. Overnight, the city is wiped out by these herding people who have suddenly appeared. The Semite invaders were herders of goats and sheep, the Indo-Europeans of cattle. Both were formerly hunters, and so the cultures are essentially animal-oriented. When you have hunters, you have killers. And when you have herders, you have killers, because they're always in movement, nomadic, coming into conflict with other people and conquering the areas into which they move. And these invasions bring in warrior gods, thunderbolt hurlers, like Zeus, or Yahweh.

MOYERS: The sword and death instead of the phallus and fertility?

CAMPBELL: That's right, and they are equated.

MOYERS: There's a story you tell about the overthrow of the mother goddess Tiamat.

CAMPBELL: I guess that could be taken as the key archetypal event here.

MOYERS: You called it a critical moment in history.

CAMPBELL: Yes. The Semitic people were invading the world of the Mother Goddess systems, and so the male-oriented mythologies became dominant, and the Mother Goddess becomes, well—sort of Grandmother Goddess, way, way back.

It was in the time of the rise of the city of Babylon. And each of these early cities had its own protective god or goddess. The characteristic of an imperialistic people is to try to have its own local god dubbed big boy of the whole universe, you see. No other divinity counts. And the way to bring this about is by annihilating the god or goddess who was there before. Well, the one that was here before the Babylonian god Marduk was the All-Mother Goddess. So the story begins with a great council of the male gods up in the sky, each god a star, and they have heard that the Grandma is coming, old Tiamat, the Abyss, the inexhaustible Source. She arrives in the form of a great fish or dragon—and what god will have the courage to go against Grandma and do her in? And the one who has the courage is, of course, the god of our present great city. He's the big one.

So when Tiamat opens her mouth, the young god Marduk of Babylon sends winds into her throat and belly that blow her to pieces, and he then dismembers her and fashions the earth and heavens out of the parts of her body. This motif of dismembering a primordial being and turning its body into the universe appears in many mythologies in many forms. In India it comes up with the figure of Purusha, the reflection of whose body is the universe.

Now, the mother goddess in old mother-goddess mythologies was herself already the universe, so the great creative deed of Marduk was a supererogatory act. There was no need for him to cut her up and make the universe out of her, because she was already the universe. But the male-oriented myth takes over, and *he* becomes—apparently—the creator.

MOYERS: And the interest turned from the Goddess to her son, this young political upstart who—

CAMPBELL: Well, the interest turned to the interest specifically of the male governors of the city of Babylon.

MOYERS: So the matriarchal society began to give way to a—

CAMPBELL: Oh, by that time—1750 B.C. or so—it was finished.

MOYERS: There are women today who say that the spirit of the Goddess has been in exile for five thousand years, since the—

CAMPBELL: You can't put it that far back, five thousand years. She was a very potent figure in Hellenistic times in the Mediterranean, and she came back with the Virgin in the Roman Catholic tradition. You don't have a tradition with the Goddess celebrated any more beautifully and marvelously than in the twelfth- and thirteenth-century French cathedrals, every one of which is called Notre Dame.

MOYERS: Yes, but all of those motifs and themes were controlled by males—priests, bishops—who excluded women, so whatever the form might have meant to the believer, for the purpose of power the image was in the hands of the dominant male figure.

CAMPBELL: You can put an accent on it that way, but I think it's a little too strong because there were the great female saints. Hildegarde of Bingen—she was a match for Innocent III. And Eleanor of Aquitaine—I don't think there is anybody in the

Middle Ages who has the stature to match hers. One now can look back and quarrel with the whole situation, but the situation of women was not that bad by any means.

MOYERS: No, but none of those saints would ever become pope.

CAMPBELL: Becoming pope, that's not much of a job, really. That's a business position. None of the popes could ever have become the mother of Christ. There are different roles to play. It was the male's job to protect the women.

MOYERS: That's where the paternalistic idea grew.

CAMPBELL: Women are booty, they are goods. With the fall of a city, every woman in the city would be raped.

MOYERS: There's this ethical contradiction mentioned in your book, quoting Exodus: "Thou shalt not kill, thou shalt not covet thy neighbor's wife—except abroad. Then you should put all males to the sword, and the women you shall take as booty to yourself." That's right out of the Old Testament.

CAMPBELL: Deuteronomy. Those are fierce passages.

MOYERS: And what do they say to you about women?

CAMPBELL: They say more about Deuteronomy than about women. The Hebrews were absolutely ruthless with respect to their neighbors. But this passage is an extreme statement of something that is inherent in most sociologically oriented mythologies. That is to say, love and compassion are reserved for the in-group, and aggression and abuse are projected outward on others. Compassion is to be reserved for members of your own group. The out-group is to be treated in a way described there in Deuteronomy.

Now, today there is no out-group anymore on the planet. And the problem of a modern religion is to have such compassion work for the whole of humanity. But then what happens to the aggression? This is a problem that the world is going to have to face—because aggression is a natural instinct just as much as, and more immediate than, compassion, and it is always going to be there. It's a biological fact. Of course, in biblical times, when the Hebrews came in, they really wiped out the Goddess. The term for the Canaanite goddess that's used in the Old Testament is "the Abomination." Apparently, throughout the period represented in the Book of Kings, for example, there was a back and forth between the two cults. Many of the Hebrew kings were condemned in the Old Testament for having worshiped on the mountaintops. Those mountains were symbols of the Goddess. And there was a very strong accent against the Goddess in the Hebrew, which you do not find in the Indo-European mythologies. Here you have Zeus *marrying* the Goddess, and then the two play together. So it's an extreme case that we have in the Bible, and our own Western subjugation of the female is a function of biblical thinking.

MOYERS: Because when you substitute the male for the female, you get a different psychology, a different cultural bias. And it's permissible in your culture to do what your gods do, so you just—

CAMPBELL: That's exactly it. I would see three situations here. First, the early one of the Goddess, when the male is hardly a significant divinity. Then the reverse, when the male takes over her role. And finally, then, the classical stage, where the two are in interaction—as they are also, for example, in India.

MOYERS: Where does that arise?

CAMPBELL: It comes from the attitude of the Indo-Europeans, who did not completely devaluate the female principle.

MOYERS: What about the virgin birth? Suddenly, the Goddess reappears in the form of the chaste and pure vessel chosen for God's action.

CAMPBELL: In the history of Western religions, this is an

extremely interesting development. In the Old Testament, you have a God who creates a world without a goddess. Then when you come to Proverbs, there she is, Sophia, the Goddess of Wisdom, who says, "When He created the world, I was there, and I was His greatest joy." But in the Hebrew tradition the idea of a *son* of God is repulsive, it is not considered at all. The Messiah as the son of God is not actually God's son. He is one who in his character and dignity is worthy to be *likened* to the son of God. I'm sure there's no idea of a virgin birth in that tradition. The virgin birth comes into Christianity by way of the Greek tradition. When you read the four gospels, for example, the only one in which the virgin birth appears is the Gospel According to Luke, and Luke was a Greek.

MOYERS: And in the Greek tradition there were images, legends, myths of virgin births?

CAMPBELL: Oh, yes—Leda and the swan, Persephone and the serpent, and this one and that one and the other one. The virgin birth is represented throughout.

MOYERS: This was not a new idea, then, in Bethlehem. But what is the meaning of the virgin birth?

CAMPBELL: I think the best way to answer that is to talk about a system they have in India that describes stages of spiritual development. In India, there is a system of seven psychological centers up the spine. They represent psychological planes of concern and consciousness and action. The first is at the rectum, representing alimentation, the basic, life-sustaining function. The serpent well represents this compulsion—as a kind of traveling esophagus going along just eating, eating, eating. None of us would be here if we weren't forever eating. What you eat is always something that just a moment before was alive. This is the sacramental mystery of food and eating, which doesn't often come to our minds when we sit ourselves down to eat. If we say grace before meals, we thank this figure out of the Bible for our food. But in earlier mythologies, when people would sit down to eat, they would thank the animal they were about to consume for having given of itself as a willing sacrifice.

There's a wonderful saying in one of the Upanishads: "Oh wonderful, oh wonderful, oh wonderful, I am food, I am food, I am food! I am an eater of food, I am an eater of food, I am an eater of food." We don't think that way today about ourselves. But holding on to yourself and not letting yourself become food is the primary life-denying negative act. You're stopping the flow! And a yielding to the flow is the great mystery experience that goes with thanking an animal that is about to be eaten for having given of itself. You, too, will be given in time.

MOYERS: I'm nature, nature is me.

CAMPBELL: Yes. Now, the second psychological center is symbolized in the Indian order of spiritual development by the sex organs, which is to say the urge to procreation. A third center is at the level of the navel, and here is the center of the will to power, to mastery and achievement, or, in its negative aspect, to the conquering, mastering, smashing, and trashing of others. This is the third, or aggressive, function. And as we are given to recognize in the symbolism of the Indian psychological system, the first function, alimentation, is of an animal instinct; the second, procreation, is of an animal instinct; and the third, mastery and conquest, is also of an animal instinct—and these three centers are located symbolically in the pelvic basin.

The next, or fourth, center is at the level of the heart; and this is of the opening to compassion. Here you move out of the field of animal action into a field that is properly human and spiritual.

And for each of these four centers there is envisioned a symbolic form. At the base, for example, the first one, the symbol is the lingam and yoni, the male and female organs in conjunction. And at the heart center, there is *again* the lingam and yoni, that is to say, male and female organs in conjunction, but here they are represented in gold as symbolic of the virgin birth, that is to say, it is the birth of spiritual man out of the animal man.

MOYERS: And it happens—

CAMPBELL: It happens when you awaken at the level of the heart to compassion, com-passion, shared suffering: experienced participation in the suffering of another person. That's the beginning of humanity. And the meditations of religion properly are on that level, the heart level.

MOYERS: You say that's the beginning of humanity. But in these stories, that's the moment when gods are born. The virgin birth—it's a god who emerges.

CAMPBELL: And do you know who that god is? It's *you*. All of these symbols in mythology refer to you. You can get stuck out *there*, and think it's all out *there*. So you're thinking about Jesus with all the sentiments relevant to how he suffered—out there. But that suffering is what ought to be going on in you. Have you been spiritually reborn? Have you died to your animal nature and come to life as a human incarnation of compassion?

MOYERS: Why is it significant that this is of a virgin?

CAMPBELL: The begetter is of the spirit. This is a spiritual birth. The virgin conceived of the word through the ear.

MOYERS: The word came like a shaft of light.

CAMPBELL: Yes. And the Buddha, with the same meaning, is said to have been born from his mother's side from the level of the heart chakra.

MOYERS: Heart Chakra meaning . . . ?

CAMPBELL: Oh, the heart chakra is the symbolic center associated with the heart. The chakra means "circle" or "sphere."

MOYERS: So the Buddha comes out—

CAMPBELL: —the Buddha is born from his mother's side. That's a symbolic birth. He wasn't physically born from his mother's side, but symbolically.

MOYERS: But the Christ came the way you and I did.

CAMPBELL: Yes, but of a virgin. And then, according to Roman Catholic doctrine, her virginity was restored. So nothing happened physically, you might say. What is symbolically referred to is not Jesus' physical birth but his spiritual significance. That's what the virgin birth represents. Heroes and demigods are born that way as beings motivated by compassion and not mastery, sexuality, or self-preservation.

This is the sense of the second birth, when you begin to live out of the heart center. The lower three centers are not to be refuted but transcended, when they become subject to and servant to the heart.

MOYERS: If we go back into antiquity, do we find images of the Madonna as the mother of the savior child?

CAMPBELL: The antique model for the Madonna, actually, is Isis with Horus at her breast.

MOYERS: Isis?

CAMPBELL: It's a complicated story. Indeed all of these get to be pretty complicated. But Isis and her husband Osiris were twins, born of the Goddess Nut. And their younger relatives were Seth and Nephthys, who were also twins born from Nut. One night, Osiris slept with Nephthys, thinking she was Isis—a kind of inattention to details, you might say. From that night's event, Anubis was born, Osiris' oldest son, but by the wrong wife. Seth, her husband, took this badly and planned to kill his older brother, Osiris. Secretly he took Osiris' measurements and had a beautiful sarcophagus made that would exactly fit him. And then, one evening, when there was a lively party in progress among the gods, Seth came in with his sarcophagus and declared that anyone whom it perfectly fitted could have it as a gift for his tomb.

Everyone at the party tried, and of course when Osiris got in, the sarcophagus fitted him perfectly. Immediately seventy-two accomplices came rushing out, and they clapped the lid on, strapped it together, and threw it into the Nile. So what we have here is the death of a god. And whenever you have the death of such a god as this, you may next expect a resurrection.

The death of Osiris was symbolically associated with the annual rising and flooding of the river Nile, by which the soil of Egypt was annually fertilized. It was as though the rotting of the body of Osiris fertilized and vitalized the land.

Osiris went floating down the Nile and was washed ashore on a beach in Syria. A beautiful tree with a wonderful aroma grew up and incorporated the sarcophagus in its trunk. The local king had just had a son born to him and happened at the time to be about to build a palace. And because the aroma of that tree was so wonderful, he had it cut down and brought in to become the central pillar in the main room of the palace.

Meanwhile the poor goddess Isis, whose husband had been thrown into the Nile, started off on a search for his body. This theme of the search for the God who is the spouse of the soul is a prime mythological theme of the period: of the Goddess who goes in quest of her lost spouse or lover and, through loyalty and a descent into the realm of death, becomes his redeemer.

Isis comes in time to the palace and there learns of the aromatic column in the royal palace. She suspects this may have something to do with Osiris, and she gets a job as nurse to the newborn child. Well, she lets the child nurse from her finger—after all, she's a goddess, and there's a limit to the degree of stooping to conquer. But she loves the little boy and decides to give him immortality by placing him in the fireplace to burn his mortal body away. As a goddess, she could prevent the fire from killing him, you understand. And every evening, while the child is in the fire, she transforms herself into a swallow and goes flying mournfully around the column in which her husband is enclosed.

One evening the child's mother comes into the room while this little scene is in progress, sees her infant in the fireplace, lets out a scream, which breaks the spell, and the child has to be rescued from incineration. The swallow, meanwhile, has turned back into the gorgeous nurse and goddess, who explains the situation and says to the queen, "By the way, it's my husband there in that column, and I'd be grateful if you would just let me take him home." So the king, who has appeared on the scene, says, "Why, yes! Certainly." He has the column removed, turns it over to Isis, and the beautiful sarcophagus containing Osiris is placed on a royal barge.

On the way back to the Nile Delta, Isis removes the lid of the coffin, lies upon her dead husband, and conceives. This is a motif that appears in the ancient mythologies all the time under many symbolic forms—*out of death comes life*. When the barge has landed, the Goddess gives birth in the papyrus swamp to her child, Horus; and it was the figure of this divine mother with her child conceived of God that became the model for the Madonna.

MOYERS: And the swallow became, did it not, the dove?

CAMPBELL: Well, the dove, the bird in flight, is a pretty nearly universal symbol of the spirit, as in Christianity, of the Holy Ghost—

MOYERS: —associated with the sacred mother?

CAMPBELL: With the mother as conceiving of the spirit, yes. But one more little detail here. The jealous younger brother, Seth, meanwhile, has usurped the throne of Osiris. However, properly to represent the throne, he should marry Isis. In Egyptian iconography, Isis represents the throne. The Pharaoh sits on the throne, which is Isis, as a child on its mother's lap. And so, when you stand before the cathedral of Chartres, you will see over one of the portals of the western front an image of the Madonna as the throne upon which the child Jesus sits and blesses the world as its emperor. That is precisely the image that has come down to us from most ancient Egypt. The early fathers and the early artists took over these images intentionally.

MOYERS: The Christian fathers took the image of Isis?

CAMPBELL: Definitely. They say so themselves. Read the text where it is declared that "those forms which were merely mythological forms in the past are now actual and incarnate in our Savior." The mythologies here referred to were of the dead and resurrected god: Attis, Adonis, Gilgamesh, Osiris, one after the other. The death and resurrection of the god is everywhere associated with the moon, which dies and is resurrected every month. It is for two nights, or three days dark, and we have Christ for two nights, or three days in the tomb.

No one knows what the actual date of the birth of Jesus might have been, but it has been put on what used to be the date of the winter solstice, December 25, when the nights begin to be shorter and the days longer. That is the moment of the rebirth of light. That was exactly the date of the birth of the Persian God of light, Mithra, Sol, the Sun.

MOYERS: What does this say to you?

CAMPBELL: It says to me that there's an idea of death to the past and birth to the future in our lives and our thinking: death to the animal nature and birth to the spiritual. These symbols are talking about this one way or another.

MOYERS: So Isis is able to say, "I am she that is the natural mother of all things. Mistress and governess of all the elements. Chief of the powers divine, queen of all that are in hell, but principal of all them that dwell in heaven. Manifested alone and under one form of all the gods and goddesses."

CAMPBELL: That is a very late statement of this whole theme. That comes in Apuleius' *Golden Ass*, second century A.D. *The Golden Ass* is one of the first novels, by the way. Its leading character, its hero, has been by lust and magic converted into an ass, and he has to undergo an ordeal of painful and humiliating adventures until his redemption comes through the grace of the Goddess Isis. She appears with a rose in her hand (symbolic of divine love, not lust), and when as an ass he eats this rose, he is converted back into a man. But he is now more than a man, he is an illuminated man, a saint. He has experienced the second virgin birth, you see. So from mere animal-like carnality, one may pass through a spiritual death and become reborn. The second birth is of an exalted, spiritually informed incarnation.

And the Goddess is the one who brings this about. The second birth is through a spiritual mother. Notre Dame de Paris, Notre Dame de Chartres—our Mother Church. We are reborn spiritually by entering and leaving a church.

MOYERS: There's a power there unique to the feminine principle.

CAMPBELL: In this novel it has been put that way, but it's not necessarily unique to her. You can have rebirth through the male also. But using this system of symbols, the woman becomes the regenerator.

MOYERS: So when the Council of Ephesus met in the year 431 after the death of Christ, and proclaimed Mary to be the Mother of God, it wasn't the first time?

CAMPBELL: No, in fact that argument had been going on in the Church for some time. But the place where this decision was made, at Ephesus, happened at that time to be the greatest temple city in the Roman Empire of the Goddess Artemis, or Diana. And there is a story that when the council was in session, arguing this point, the people of Ephesus formed picket lines and shouted in praise of Mary, "The Goddess, the Goddess, of course she's the Goddess."

Well, what you have then in the Catholic tradition is a coming together of the patriarchal, monotheistic Hebrew idea of the Messiah as one who is to unite the spiritual and temporal powers, and the Hellenistic, classical idea of the Savior as the dead and resurrected son of the Great Goddess by a virgin birth. There were plenty of such saviors reborn.

In the Near East, the god who descended into the field of time was originally a goddess. Jesus took over what is really the God-dess' role in coming down in compassion. But when the Virgin acquiesces in being the vessel of the incarnation, she has herself already affected the redemption. It has become more and more apparent that the Virgin is equivalent in her suffering to the suffering of her son. In the Catholic Church now I think she is called the "co-savior."

MOYERS: What does all of this say about the reunion of the male and female? For a long while in primitive societies, the female is the dominant mythological image. Then along comes this masculine, aggressive, warlike image, and soon we're back to the female playing a role in creation and recreation. Does it say something about the basic yearning of men and women for each other?

CAMPBELL: Yes, but I think of it rather in historical terms. It is a very interesting thing to see that this Mother Goddess was the queen right across to the Indus Valley in India. From the Aegean to the Indus, she is the dominant figure. Then you have the Indo-Europeans coming down from the north, into Persia, India, Greece, Italy, and you have a male-oriented mythology coming in, all along the line. In India it's the Vedas, in Greece it's the Homeric tradition, and then about five hundred years later, the Goddess begins coming back. There is actually an Upanishad from about the seventh century B.C.—which is just about the time she is coming back to force in the Aegean as well—where the Vedic gods are together, and they see a strange sort of amorphous thing down the way, a kind of smoky fog, and they ask, "What's that?" None of them knows what it could be. So one of them suggests, "I'll go find out what that is." And he goes over to this smoky thing and says, "I'm Agni, the Lord of Fire; I can burn anything. Who are you?" And out of the fog there comes flying a piece of straw, which falls on the ground, and a voice says, "Let's see you burn that." Agni finds that he can't ignite it. So he goes back to the other gods and says, "This surely is strange!" "Well, then," says the Lord of Wind, "let me try." So over he goes, and the same sort of thing takes place. "I'm Vayu, Lord of the Wind, I can blow anything around." Again a straw is thrown. "Let's see you blow that." And he can't. So he, too, returns. Then Indra, the greatest of the Vedic gods, approaches, but as he draws near, the apparition vanishes, and where it had been, a woman appears, a beautiful, mysterious woman, who instructs the gods, revealing to them the mystery of the ground of their own being. "That is the ultimate mystery of all being," she tells them, "from which you boys yourselves have received your powers. And It can turn your powers off or on, as It wills." The Indian name for that Being of all beings is *brahman*, which is a neuter noun, neither male nor female. And the Indian name for the woman is Maya-Shakti-Devi, "Goddess Giver of Life and Mother of Forms." And there in that Upanishad she appears as the teacher of the Vedic gods themselves concerning the ultimate ground and source of their own powers and being.

MOYERS: It's the female wisdom.

CAMPBELL: It's the female as the giver of forms. She is the one who gave life to the forms and she knows where they came from. It is from that which is beyond male and female. It is from that which is beyond being and nonbeing. It both is and is not. It neither is nor is not. It is beyond all categories of thought and the mind.

MOYERS: There is that wonderful saying in the New Testament, "In Jesus there is no male or female." In the ultimate sense of things, there is neither.

CAMPBELL: It would have to be. If Jesus represents the source of our being, we are all, as it were, thoughts in the mind of Jesus. He is the word that has become flesh in us, too.

MOYERS: You and I possess characteristics that are both male and female?

CAMPBELL: The body does. I don't know anything about the actual dating of all this, but sometime in the fetal period it becomes apparent that this child is going to be male, and this one is going to be female. Meanwhile, it's a body with the potentialities for either inflection.

MOYERS: So through life we are honoring or suppressing one or the other.

CAMPBELL: And in that yin/yang figure from China, in the dark fish, or whatever you want to call it, there is the light spot. And in the light one, there's a dark spot. That's how they can relate. You couldn't relate at all to something in which you did not somehow participate. That's why the idea of God as the Absolute Other is a ridiculous idea. There could be no relationship to the Absolute Other.

MOYERS: In this spiritual transformation that you're talking about, won't the changes depend on those feminine characteristics such as nurturing, creativity, and collaboration instead of competition? Isn't this at the heart of the feminine principle we're discussing?

CAMPBELL: Well, the mother loves all her children—the stupid ones, the bright ones, the naughty ones, the good ones. It doesn't matter what their particular character is. So the feminine represents, in a way, the inclusive love for progeny. The father is more disciplinarian. He's associated much more with the social order and the social character. This is actually the way it works in societies. The mother gives birth to his nature, and the father gives birth to his social character, you might say, how he is to function.

So moving back toward nature will certainly bring forth the mother principle again. How it will relate to the patriarchal principle I do not know, because the organization of the planet is going to be an enormous operation, and that's the male function, so that you can't predict what the new thing is going to be. But certainly nature is coming back.

MOYERS: So when we say, "Save the earth," we're talking about saving ourselves.

CAMPBELL: Yes. All this hope for something happening in society has to wait for something in the human psyche, a whole new way of experiencing a society. And the crucial question here, as I see it, is simply: With what society, what social group, do you identify yourself? Is it going to be with all the people of the planet, or is it going to be with your own particular in-group? This is the question, essentially, that was in the minds of the founders of our nation when the people of the thirteen states began thinking of themselves as of one nation, yet without losing consideration for the special interests of each of the several states. Why can't something of that kind take place in the world right now?

MOYERS: A question arises in discussing all this—the male-female principle, the virgin birth, the spiritual power that gives us the second birth. The wise people of all times have said that we can live the good life if we learn to live spiritually. But how does one learn to live spiritually if one is of the flesh? Paul said, "The desires of the flesh are against the spirit and the desires of the spirit are against the flesh." How do we learn to live spiritually?

CAMPBELL: In ancient times, that was the business of the teacher. He was to give you the clues to a spiritual life. That is what the priest was for. Also, that was what ritual was for. A ritual can be defined as an *enactment* of a myth. By participating in a ritual, you are actually experiencing a mythological life. And it's out of that participation that one can learn to live spiritually.

MOYERS: The stories of mythology actually point the way to the spiritual life?

CAMPBELL: Yes, you've got to have a clue. You've got to have a road map of some kind, and these are all around us. But they are not all the same. Some speak only of the interests of this in-group or of that, this tribal god or that. Others, and especially those that are given as revelations of the Great Goddess, mother of the universe and of us all, teach compassion for all living beings. There also you come to appreciate the real sanctity of the earth itself, because it is the body of the Goddess. When Yahweh creates, he creates man of the earth and breathes life into the formed body. He's not himself there present in that form. But the Goddess is within as well as without. Your body is of her body. There is in these mythologies a recognition of that kind of universal identity.

MOYERS: That's why I'm not so sure the future of the race and the salvation of the journey is in space. I think it might be right here on earth, in the body, in the womb of our being.

CAMPBELL: Well, it certainly is. When you go out into space, what you're carrying is your body, and if that hasn't been trans-formed, space won't transform you. But thinking about space may help you to realize something. There's a two-page spread in a world atlas which shows our galaxy within many galaxies, and within our galaxy the solar system. And here you get a sense of the magnitude of this space that we're now finding out about. What those pages opened to me was the vision of a universe of unimaginable magnitude and inconceivable violence. Billions upon billions of roaring thermonuclear furnaces scattering from each other. Each thermonuclear furnace a star, and our sun among them. Many of them actually blowing themselves to pieces, littering the outermost reaches of space with dust and gas out of which new stars with circling planets are being born right now. And then from still more remote distances beyond all these there come murmurs, microwaves that are echoes of the greatest cataclysmic explosion of all, namely the big bang of creation, which, according to some reckonings, may have occurred some eighteen billion years ago.

That's where we are, kiddo, and to realize that, you realize how really important you are, you know—one little microbit in that great magnitude. And then must come the experience that you and that are in some sense one, and you partake of all of that.

MOYERS: And it begins here.

CAMPBELL: It begins here.

VII
TALES OF LOVE
AND MARRIAGE

So through the eyes love attains the heart:
For the eyes are the scouts of the heart,
And the eyes go reconnoitering
For what it would please the heart to possess.
And when they are in full accord
And firm, all three, in the one resolve,
At that time, perfect love is born
From what the eyes have made welcome to the heart.
Not otherwise can love either be born or have commencement
Than by this birth and commencement moved by inclination.

By the grace and by command
Of these three, and from their pleasure,
Love is born, who its fair hope
Goes comforting her friends.
For as all true lovers
Know, love is perfect kindness,
Which is born—there is no doubt—from the heart and eyes.
The eyes make it blossom; the heart matures it:
Love, which is the fruit of their very seed.

—GUIRAUT DE BORNEILH (ca. 1138–1200?)

MOYERS: Love is such a vast subject that—well, if I came to you and said, "Let's talk about love," where would you begin?

CAMPBELL: I'd begin with the troubadours in the twelfth century.

MOYERS: And who were they?

CAMPBELL: The troubadours were the nobility of Provence
and then later other parts of France and Europe. In Germany
they're known as the Minnesingers, the singers of love. *Minne*
is the medieval German word for love.

MOYERS: Were they the poets of their age?

CAMPBELL: They were poets of a certain character, yes. The
period for the troubadours is the twelfth century. The whole
troubadour tradition was extinguished in Provence in the so-
called Albigensian Crusade of 1209, which was launched by Pope
Innocent III, and which is regarded as one of the most monstrous
crusades in the history of Europe.

The troubadours became associated with the Manichean heresy of the Albigensians that was rampant at that time—though
the Albigensian movement was really a protest against the cor-
ruption of the medieval clergy. So the troubadours and their
transformation of the idea of love got mixed up in religious life
in a very complicated way.

MOYERS: The transformation of love? What do you mean?

CAMPBELL: The troubadours were very much interested in the
psychology of love. And they're the first ones in the West who
really thought of love the way we do now—as a person-to-person
relationship.

MOYERS: What had it been before that?

CAMPBELL: Before that, love was simply Eros, the god who
excites you to sexual desire. This is not the experience of falling
in love the way the troubadours understood it. Eros is much more
impersonal than falling in love. You see, people didn't know
about Amor. Amor is something personal that the troubadours
recognized. Eros and Agape are *impersonal* loves.

MOYERS: Explain.

CAMPBELL: Eros is a biological urge. It's the zeal of the organs for each other. The personal factor doesn't matter.

MOYERS: And Agape?

CAMPBELL: Agape is love thy neighbor as thyself—spiritual love. It doesn't matter who the neighbor is.

MOYERS: Now, this is not passion in the sense that Eros mandates it, this is compassion, I would think.

CAMPBELL: Yes, it is compassion. It is a heart opening. But it is not individuated as Amor is.

MOYERS: Agape is a religious impulse.

CAMPBELL: Yes. But Amor could become a religious impulse, too. The troubadours recognized Amor as the highest spiritual experience.

You see, the experience of Eros is a kind of seizure. In India, the god of love is a big, vigorous youth with a bow and a quiver of arrows. The names of the arrows are "Death-bringing Agony" and "Open Up" and so forth. Really, he just drives this thing into you so that it's a total physiological, psychological explosion.

Then the other love, Agape, is a love of the neighbor as thyself. Again, it doesn't matter who the person is. It is your neighbor, and you must have that kind of love.

But with Amor we have a purely personal ideal. The kind of seizure that comes from the meeting of the eyes, as they say in the troubadour tradition, is a person-to-person experience.

MOYERS: There's a poem in one of your books about this meeting of the eyes: "So through the eyes love attains the heart. . . ."

CAMPBELL: That's completely contrary to everything the Church stood for. It's a personal, individual experience, and I think it's the essential thing that's great about the West and that makes it different from all other traditions I know.

MOYERS: So the courage to love became the courage to affirm one's own experience against tradition—the tradition of the Church. Why was that important in the evolution of the West?

CAMPBELL: It was important in that it gave the West this accent on the individual, that one should have faith in his experience and not simply mouth terms handed down to him by others. It stresses the validity of the individual's experience of what humanity is, what life is, what values are, against the monolithic system. The monolithic system is a machine system: every machine works like every other machine that's come out of the same shop.

MOYERS: What did you mean when you wrote that the beginning of romantic love in the West was "libido over credo"?

CAMPBELL: Well, the credo says "I believe," and I believe not only in the laws, but I believe that these laws were instituted by God, and there's no arguing with God. These laws are a heavy weight on me, and disobeying these is sin and has to do with my eternal character.

MOYERS: That's the credo?

CAMPBELL: That's the credo. You believe, and then you go to confession, and you run down through the list of sins, and you count yourself against those, and instead of going into the priest and saying, "Bless me, father, for I have been great this week," you meditate on the sins, and in meditating on the sins, then you really become a sinner in your life. It's a condemnation, actually, of the will to life, that's what the credo is.

MOYERS: And libido?

CAMPBELL: The libido is the impulse to life. It comes from the heart.

MOYERS: And the heart is—

CAMPBELL: —the heart is the organ of opening up to somebody else. That's the human quality as opposed to the animal qualities, which have to do with self-interest.

MOYERS: So you're talking about romantic love as opposed to lust, or passion, or a general religious sentiment?

CAMPBELL: Yes. You know, the usual marriage in traditional cultures was arranged for by the families. It wasn't a person-to-person decision at all. In India to this day, you have columns in the newspapers of advertisements for wives that are put in by marriage brokers. I remember, in one family that I knew there, the daughter was going to marry. She had never seen the young man she was going to marry, and she would ask her brothers, "Is he tall? Is he dark? Is he light? What?"

In the Middle Ages, that was the kind of marriage that was sanctified by the Church. And so the troubadour idea of real person-to-person Amor was very dangerous.

MOYERS: Because it was heresy?

CAMPBELL: Not only heresy, it was adultery, what might be called spiritual adultery. Since the marriages were all arranged by society, the love that came from the meeting of the eyes was of a higher spiritual value.

For example, in the Tristan romance, Isolde is engaged to marry King Mark. They have never seen each other. Tristan is sent to fetch Isolde to Mark. Isolde's mother prepares a love potion, so that the two who are to be married will have real love for each other. And this love potion is put in the charge of the nurse, who is to go with Isolde. The love potion is left unguarded, and Tristan and Isolde think it's wine, and they drink it. They're overtaken with love. But they had already been in love, they just didn't know it. The love potion just touched it off. One remembers that kind of experience from one's own youth.

The problem from the troubadour point of view is that King Mark and Isolde, who are to be married, are not really qualified for love. They have never even seen each other. The true marriage is the marriage that springs from the recognition of identity in the other, and the physical union is simply the sacrament in which that is confirmed. It doesn't start the other way around, with the physical interest that then becomes spiritualized. It starts from the spiritual impact of love—Amor.

MOYERS: Christ spoke of "the adulterer at heart," the violation of the union that takes place spiritually, in the mind and heart.

CAMPBELL: And every marriage was such a violation when it was arranged by the society and not by the heart. That's the sense of courtly love in the Middle Ages. It is in direct contradiction to the way of the Church. The word AMOR spelt backwards is ROMA, the Roman Catholic Church, which was justifying marriages that were simply political and social in their character. And so came this movement validating individual choice, what I call following your bliss.

But there's danger, too, of course. In the Tristan romance, when the young couple has drunk their love potion and Isolde's nurse realizes what has happened, she goes to Tristan and says, "You have drunk your death." And Tristan says, "By my death, do you mean this pain of love?"—because that was one of the main points, that one should feel the sickness of love. There's no possible fulfillment in this world of that identity one is experiencing. Tristan says, "If by my death, you mean this agony of love, that is my life. If by my death, you mean the punishment that we are to suffer if discovered, I accept that. And if by my death, you mean eternal punishment in the fires of hell, I accept that, too." Now, that's big stuff.

MOYERS: Especially for medieval Catholics, who believed in a literal hell. So what's the significance of what Tristan was saying?

CAMPBELL: What he was saying is that his love is bigger even than death and pain, than anything. This is the affirmation of the pain of life in a big way.

MOYERS: And he would choose this pain of love now even though it might mean everlasting pain and damnation in hell.

CAMPBELL: Any life career that you choose in following your bliss should be chosen with that sense—that nobody can frighten me off from this thing. And no matter what happens, this is the validation of my life and action.

MOYERS: And in choosing love, too?

CAMPBELL: In choosing love, too.

MOYERS: You wrote once that the point about hell, as about heaven, is that, when you're there, you're in your proper place, which is finally where you want to be.

CAMPBELL: That was Bernard Shaw's idea, and really Dante's idea, also. The punishment in hell is that you have for eternity that which you thought you wanted on earth.

MOYERS: Tristan wanted his love, he wanted his bliss, and he was willing to suffer for it.

CAMPBELL: Yes. But then William Blake says in his wonderful series of aphorisms *The Marriage of Heaven and Hell*, "As I was walking among the fires of hell . . . which to angels look like torment"—that is to say, for the people who are there, who are not angels, it's not the fire of pain, it's the fire of delight.

MOYERS: I remember in Dante's *Inferno*, as Dante is looking on the great lovers of history in hell, he sees Helen, and he sees Cleopatra, and he sees Tristan. What's the significance of that?

CAMPBELL: Dante is taking the Church's attitude that this is hell, and that they're suffering there. Remember, he sees the two young lovers from the Italy of his day, Paolo and Francesca. Francesca had a love affair with Paolo, the brother of her husband. And Dante, like a social scientist, says, "Darling, how did this happen? What brought this about?" And then come the most famous lines in Dante. Francesca says that Paolo and she were sitting under a tree in the garden reading the story of Lancelot and Guinevere. "And when we read of their first kiss,

we looked at each other and read no more in the book that day."
And that was the beginning of their fall.

That this wonderful experience should be condemned as a sin
is the thing the troubadour just says no to. Love is the meaning
of life—it is the high point of life.

MOYERS: Is that what Wagner meant in his great opera on
Tristan and Isolde, when he said, "In this world let me have my
world, to be damned with it or to be saved"?

CAMPBELL: Yes, that's exactly what Tristan said.

MOYERS: Meaning, I want my love, I want my life.

CAMPBELL: This is my life, yes. And I'm willing to take any
kind of pain for it.

MOYERS: And this took a courage, didn't it?

CAMPBELL: *Doesn't* it? Even to think of it.

MOYERS: "*Doesn't* it"—you put it in the present tense.

CAMPBELL: Yes.

MOYERS: Even now?

CAMPBELL: Yes.

MOYERS: You have said that the point of all these pioneers in
love is that they decided to be the author and means of their
own self-fulfillment, that the realization of love is to be nature's
noblest work, and that they were going to take their wisdom
from their own experience and not from dogma, politics, or any
current concepts of social good. And is this the beginning of the
romantic idea of the Western individual taking matters into his
or her own hands?

CAMPBELL: Absolutely. You can see examples in Oriental stories of this kind of thing, but it did not become a social system.
It has now become the ideal of love in the Western world.

MOYERS: Love from one's own experience, taking one's own experience as the source of wisdom?

CAMPBELL: Yes, that's the individual. The best part of the Western tradition has included a recognition of and respect for the individual as a living entity. The function of the society is to cultivate the individual. It is not the function of the individual to support society.

MOYERS: But what happens to institutions—to universities, to corporations, to churches, to the political institutions of our society—if we all just run off and follow our love? Isn't there a tension in this? Individual versus society? There has to be some legitimate point beyond which individual intuition, the individual libido, the individual desire, the individual love, the individual impulse to do what you want to do must be restrained— otherwise, you'd have tumult and anarchy, and no institution could survive. Are you really saying that we should follow our bliss, follow our love, wherever it leads?

CAMPBELL: Well, you've got to use your head. They say, you know, a narrow path is a very dangerous path— the razor's edge.

MOYERS: So the head and the heart should not be at war?

CAMPBELL: No, they should not. They should be in cooperation. The head should be present, and the heart should listen to it now and then.

MOYERS: Are there times when the heart is in the lead?

CAMPBELL: That would be the desirable situation most of the time. The five main virtues of the medieval knight might be brought in here. One is temperance, another is courage, another is love, another is loyalty, and another is courtesy. Courtesy is respect for the decorum of the society in which you are living.

MOYERS: So love doesn't go riding alone, love is attended by—

CAMPBELL: It is one of a number of functions. One way to go crazy is to have one function dominate the whole system and not serve the order. And the medieval idea, in spite of the fact that these people were in protest against the ecclesiastical authorities, was respect for the society in which they were participating. Everything was done according to rules. When two knights fought, they did not violate the rules of combat although they were engaged in *mortal* combat. This courtesy has to be held in mind.

MOYERS: Were there rules of law? Rules of love? Were there restraints on adultery, for example? If your eyes met someone who was not your wife or husband, what was to be your response in the medieval era?

CAMPBELL: Well, that was the beginning of the courtly love relationship. There were game rules there, and they played it according to the rules. They had their own system of rules. They were not those of the Church, but they were rules for playing the game harmoniously and with the results that were intended. Anything you do involves a system of rules that state how a thing is to be done and done well. It has been said that art is the making of things well. And the conduct of a love affair—well, you could be a clumsy lout in this, but how much nicer to have the knowledge of certain rules that enable the expression to become more eloquent and gratifying.

MOYERS: So the age of chivalry was growing up as the age of romantic love was reaching out.

CAMPBELL: I'd say these were the same thing. It was a very strange period because it was terribly brutal. There was no central law. Everyone was on his own, and, of course, there were great violations of everything. But within this brutality, there was a civilizing force, which the women really represented because they were the ones who established the rules for this game. And the men had to play it according to the requirements of the women.

MOYERS: How did it happen that the women had the dominant influence?

CAMPBELL: Because, if you want to make love to a woman, she's already got the drop on you. The technical term for the woman's granting of herself was "merci." The woman grants her "merci." Now, that might consist in her permission to kiss her on the back of the neck once every Whitsuntide, you know, something like that—or it might be a full giving in love. That would depend upon her estimation of the character of the candidate.

MOYERS: So there were rules to determine the testing?

CAMPBELL: Yes. There was an essential requirement—that one must have a gentle heart, that is, a heart capable of love, not simply of lust. The woman would be testing to find whether the candidate for her love had a gentle heart, whether he was capable of love.

We have to remember also that these ladies were all of the nobility, and the nobility in that time were pretty sophisticated and competent people, both in their brutality and in their tenderness. Today I don't know what one would do to test the temperament to see if he had a gentle heart, or whether that would be an ideal that anyone would even want—a gentle heart.

MOYERS: What does the idea of the gentle heart suggest to you?

CAMPBELL: One that is capable of—well, the key word for me is compassion.

MOYERS: Which means?

CAMPBELL: Suffering with. "Passion" is "suffering," and "com-" is "with." The German word really gives it in a clearer way: mitleid, "with" (mit) "sorrow or suffering" (leid). The essential idea was to test this man to make sure that he would suffer things for love, and that this was not just lust.

MOYERS: Joe, that may have emerged in the troubadour period, but it was still alive and well in the early 1950s in East Texas.

CAMPBELL: That's the force of this position. It originated in twelfth-century Provence, and you've got it now in twentieth-century Texas.

MOYERS: It's been shattered of late, I have to tell you that. I mean, I'm not sure that it's as much of a test as it used to be. I was grateful for the test—I think. I'm not sure. . . .

CAMPBELL: The tests that were given then involved, for example, sending a chap out to guard a bridge. The traffic in the Middle Ages was somewhat encumbered by these youths guarding bridges. But also the tests included going into battle. A woman who was too ruthless in asking her lover to risk real death before she would acquiesce in anything was considered *sauvage* or "savage." Also, the woman who gave herself without the testing was "savage." There was a very nice psychological estimation game going on here.

MOYERS: The troubadours weren't aiming, were they, to dissolve marriages or the world, nor was their aim carnal intercourse, lust, or even the quenching of the soul of God. You write, "Rather, they celebrated life directly in the experience of love as a refining, sublimating force, opening the heart to the sad bittersweet melody of being through love, one's own anguish and one's own joy." They weren't trying to destroy things, were they?

CAMPBELL: No, you see, that motive of power was not what was in them. It was the motive of personal experience and sublimation. It's quite different. There was no direct attack on the Church. The idea was to sublimate life into a spiritual plane of experiences.

MOYERS: Love is right in front of me. Amor is the path directly before me, the eyes—

CAMPBELL: —the meeting of the eyes, that idea. "So through the eyes love attains the heart: / For the eyes are the scouts of the heart."

MOYERS: What was it that the troubadours learned about the psyche? We've heard about the psyche—Eros loved Psyche—and we're told in our day that you must understand your psyche. What did the troubadours discover about the human psyche?

CAMPBELL: What they discovered was a certain individual aspect of it that cannot be talked about in purely general terms. The individual experience, the individual commitment to experience, the individual believing in his experience and living it—that is the main point here.

MOYERS: So love is not love in general, it is love for *that* woman?

CAMPBELL: For that one woman. That's right.

MOYERS: Why do you think we fall in love with one person and not another?

CAMPBELL: Well, I wouldn't be one to say. It's a very mysterious thing, that electric thing that happens, and then the agony that can follow. The troubadours celebrate the agony of the love, the sickness the doctors cannot cure, the wounds that can be healed only by the weapon that delivered the wound.

MOYERS: Meaning?

CAMPBELL: The wound is the wound of my passion and the agony of my love for this creature. The only one who can heal me is the one who delivered the blow. That's a motif that appears in symbolic form in many medieval stories of the lance that delivers a wound. It is only when that lance can touch the wound again that the wound can be healed.

MOYERS: Wasn't there something of this idea in the legend of the Holy Grail?

CAMPBELL: In the monastic version of the story, the Grail is associated with Christ's passion. The Grail is the chalice of the Last Supper and the chalice that received Christ's blood when he was taken from the cross.

MOYERS: What does the Grail represent then?

CAMPBELL: There's a very interesting statement about the origin of the Grail. One early writer says that the Grail was brought from heaven by the neutral angels. You see, during the war in heaven between God and Satan, between good and evil, some angelic hosts sided with Satan and some with God. The Grail was brought down through the middle by the neutral angels. It represents that spiritual path that is between pairs of opposites, between fear and desire, between good and evil.

The theme of the Grail romance is that the land, the country, the whole territory of concern has been laid waste. It is called a wasteland. And what is the nature of the wasteland? It is a land where everybody is living an inauthentic life, doing as other people do, doing as you're told, with no courage for your own life. That is the wasteland. And that is what T. S. Eliot meant in his poem *The Waste Land*.

In a wasteland the surface does not represent the actuality of what it is supposed to be representing, and people are living inauthentic lives. "I've never done a thing I wanted to in all my life. I've done as I was told." You know?

MOYERS: And the Grail becomes?

CAMPBELL: The Grail becomes the—what can we call it?— that which is attained and realized by people who have lived their own lives. The Grail represents the fulfillment of the highest spiritual potentialities of the human consciousness.

The Grail King, for example, was a lovely young man, but he had not *earned* the position of Grail King. He rode forth from his castle with the war cry "Amor!" Well, that's proper for youth, but it doesn't belong to the guardianship of the Grail. And as he's riding forth, a Muslim, a pagan knight, comes out of the woods. They both level their lances at each other, and they drive at each other. The lance of the Grail King kills the pagan, but the pagan's lance castrates the Grail King.

What that means is that the Christian separation of matter and spirit, of the dynamism of life and the realm of the spirit, of natural grace and supernatural grace, has really castrated nature. And the European mind, the European life, has been, as it were, emasculated by this separation. The true spirituality, which would have come from the union of matter and spirit, has been killed. And then what did the pagan represent? He was a person from the suburbs of Eden. He was regarded as a nature man, and on the head of his lance was written the word "Grail." That is to say, nature intends the Grail. Spiritual life is the bouquet, the perfume, the flowering and fulfillment of a human life, not a supernatural virtue imposed upon it.

And so the impulses of nature are what give authenticity to life, not the rules coming from a supernatural authority—that's the sense of the Grail.

MOYERS: Is this what Thomas Mann meant when he talked about mankind being the noblest work because it joins nature and spirit?

CAMPBELL: Yes.

MOYERS: Nature and spirit are yearning for each other to meet in this experience. And the Grail that these romantic legends were searching for is the union once again of what has been divided, the peace that comes from joining.

CAMPBELL: The Grail becomes symbolic of an authentic life that is lived in terms of its own volition, in terms of its own impulse system, that carries itself between the pairs of opposites of good and evil, light and dark. One writer of the Grail legend starts his long epic with a short poem saying, "Every act has both good and evil results." Every act in life yields pairs of opposites in its results. The best we can do is lean toward the light, toward the harmonious relationships that come from compassion with suffering, from understanding the other person. This is what the Grail is about. And this is what comes out in the romance.

In the Grail legend young Perceval has been brought up in the country by a mother who refused the courts and wanted her son to know nothing about the court rules. Perceval's life is lived in terms of the dynamic of his own impulse system until he becomes more mature. Then he is offered a lovely young girl in marriage by her father, who has trained him to be a knight. And Perceval says, "No, I must earn a wife, not be given a wife." And that's the beginning of Europe.

MOYERS: The beginning of Europe?

CAMPBELL: Yes—the individual Europe, the Grail Europe.

Now, when Perceval comes to the Grail castle, he meets the Grail King, who is brought in on a litter, wounded, kept alive simply by the presence of the Grail. Perceval's compassion moves him to ask, "What ails you, Uncle?" But he doesn't ask the question because he has been taught by his instructor that a knight doesn't ask unnecessary questions. So he obeys the rule, and the adventure fails.

And then it takes him five years of ordeals and embarrassments and all kinds of things to get back to that castle and ask the question that heals the king and heals society. The question is an expression, not of the rules of the society, but of compassion, the natural opening of the human heart to another human being. That's the Grail.

MOYERS: And it is a kind of love that—

CAMPBELL: Well, it is spontaneous compassion, a suffering with.

MOYERS: What was it Jung said—that the soul cannot exist in peace until it finds its other, and the other is always a you? Is that what the romantic—

CAMPBELL: Yes, exactly, romance. That's romance. That's what myth is all about.

MOYERS: Not a sentimental kind of romance?

CAMPBELL: No, sentiment is an echo of violence. It's not really a vital expression.

MOYERS: What do you think all of this says about romantic love? About our individual selves?

MOYERS: It says that we're in two worlds. We're in our own world, and we're in the world that has been given us outside, and the problem is to achieve a harmonious relationship between the two. I come into this society, so I've got to live in terms of this society. It's ridiculous not to live in terms of this society because, unless I do, I'm not living. But I mustn't allow this society to dictate to me how I should live. One has to build up one's own system that may violate the expectations of the society, and sometimes society doesn't accept that. But the task of life is to live within the field provided by the society that is really supporting you.

A point comes up—for instance, a war, where the young men have to register for the draft. This involves an enormous decision. How far are you going to go in acceding to what the society is asking of you—to kill other people whom you don't know? For what? For whom? All that kind of thing.

MOYERS: That's what I meant a minute ago when I said society couldn't exist if every heart were vagrant, every eye were wandering.

CAMPBELL: Yes, that's certainly so. But there are some societies that shouldn't exist, you know.

MOYERS: Sooner or later they—

CAMPBELL: —crack up.

MOYERS: The troubadours cracked up that old world.

CAMPBELL: I don't think it was they, really, who cracked it up.

MOYERS: It was love.

CAMPBELL: It was—well, it was much the same thing. Luther was, in a way, a troubadour of Christ. He had his own idea of what it meant to be a priest. And that smashed up the medieval Church, really. It never recovered.

You know, it's very interesting to think of the history of Christianity. During the first five centuries, there were lots of Christianities, lots of ways of being Christian. And then, in the period of Theodosius in the fourth century, the only religion allowed in the Roman Empire was the Christian religion, and the only form of Christianity allowed in the Roman Empire was the Christianity of Byzantium's throne. The vandalism involved in the destruction of the pagan temples of antiquity is hardly matched in world history.

MOYERS: Destroyed by the organized Church?

CAMPBELL: By the organized Church. And why couldn't Christians live with another religion? What was the matter with them?

MOYERS: What do you think?

CAMPBELL: It's power, it's power. I think the power impulse is the fundamental impulse in European history. And it got into our religious traditions.

One of the very interesting things about the Grail legends is that they occur about five hundred years after Christianity has been imposed upon Europe. They represent a coming together of two traditions.

Around the end of the twelfth century, the Abbot Joachim of Floris wrote of the three ages of the spirit. After the Fall in the Garden, he said, God had to compensate for the disaster and reintroduce the spiritual principle into history. He chose a race to become the vehicle of this communication, and that is the age of the Father and of Israel. And then this race, having been prepared as a priestly race, competent to become the vessel of the Incarnation, produces the Son. Thus, the second age is of the Son and the Church, when not a single race but the whole of humanity is to receive the message of the spiritual will of God.

The third age, which this philosopher in around 1260 said was now about to begin, is the age of the Holy Spirit, who speaks directly to the individual. Anyone who incarnates or brings into his life the message of the Word is equivalent to Jesus—that's the sense of this third age. Just as Israel has been rendered archaic by the institution of the Church, so the Church is rendered archaic by the individual experience.

That began a whole movement of hermits going into the forests to receive the experience. The saint who is regarded as the first representative of this was St. Francis of Assisi, who represented the equivalent of Christ, and who was himself a manifestation in the physical world of the Holy Spirit.

Now, that is what lay behind the quest of the Grail. Galahad on his quest was equivalent to Christ. He was introduced to Arthur's court in flaming red armor, on the Feast of Pentecost, which is the feast of the descent of the Holy Ghost upon the apostles in the form of fire. Each of us can be a Galahad, you know. That's a Gnostic position with respect to the message of Christianity. The Gnostic documents, buried in the desert during the time of Theodosius, express this idea.

In the Gnostic Gospel According to Thomas, for example, Jesus says, "He who drinks from my mouth will become as I am and I shall be he." That is the idea in those romances of the Grail.

MOYERS: You've said that what happened in the twelfth and thirteenth centuries was one of the most important mutations of human feeling and spiritual consciousness, that a new way of experiencing love came into expression.

CAMPBELL: Yes.

MOYERS: And it was in opposition to the ecclesiastical despotism over the heart that required people, particularly young girls, to marry whomever the Church or their parents wanted them to marry. What had this done to the passion of the heart?

CAMPBELL: Well, to say a word for the other first—one has to recognize that in domestic life there grows up a love relationship between the husband and wife even when they're put together in an arranged marriage. In other words, in arranged marriages of this kind, there is a lot of love. There's family love, a rich love life on that level. But you don't get this other thing, of the seizure that comes in recognizing your soul's counterpart in the other person. And that's what the troubadours stood for, and that has become the ideal in our lives today.

But marriage is marriage, you know. Marriage is not a love affair. A love affair is a totally different thing. A marriage is a commitment to that which you are. That person is literally your other half. And you and the other are one. A love affair isn't that. That is a relationship for pleasure, and when it gets to be unpleasurable, it's off. But a marriage is a life commitment, and a life commitment means the prime concern of your life. If marriage is not the prime concern, you're not married.

MOYERS: Does romance in marriage last?

CAMPBELL: In some marriages, it does. In others, it doesn't. But the problem, you see, the big word in this troubadour tradition, is "loyalty."

MOYERS: What do you mean by loyalty?

CAMPBELL: Not cheating, not defecting—through whatever trials or suffering, you remain true.

MOYERS: The Puritans called marriage "the little church within the Church." In marriage, every day you love, and every day you forgive. It is an ongoing sacrament—love and forgiveness.

CAMPBELL: Well, the real word, I think, is "ordeal," in its proper sense. That is the submission of the individual to something superior to itself. The real life of a marriage or of a true love affair is in the relationship, which is where you are, too. You understand what I mean?

MOYERS: No, I'm not clear on that.

CAMPBELL: Like the yin/yang symbol, you see. Here I am, and here she is, and here we are. Now when I have to make a sacrifice, I'm not sacrificing to her, I'm sacrificing to the relationship. Resentment against the other one is wrongly placed. Life is in the relationship, that's where your life now is. That's what a marriage is—whereas, in a love affair, you have two lives in a more or less successful relationship to each other for a certain length of time, as long as it seems agreeable.

MOYERS: In the sacred marriage, what God has joined together is one and cannot be sundered by man.

CAMPBELL: It was one to begin with, and the marriage restates that unity symbolically.

MOYERS: It was one to begin with?

CAMPBELL: Marriage is the symbolic recognition of our identity—two aspects of the same being.

MOYERS: You know the curious old legend of the blind prophet Tiresias?

CAMPBELL: Yes, that's a grand story. Tiresias was walking through the forest one day when he saw two copulating serpents. And he placed his staff between them and was transformed into a woman, and lived as a woman for a number of years. Then again, Tiresias the woman was walking through the forest when she saw two copulating serpents and placed her staff between them and was turned back into a man.

Well, one fine day on Capitol Hill, the Hill of Zeus—

MOYERS: Mount Olympus?

CAMPBELL: —Mount Olympus, yes—Zeus and his wife were

arguing as to who enjoyed sexual intercourse the more, the male or the female. And of course nobody there could decide because they were only on one side of the net, you might say. Then someone said, "Let's ask Tiresias."

So they go to Tiresias, and they ask him the question, and he says, "Why, the woman, nine times more than the man." Well, for some reason that I don't really understand, Hera, the wife of Zeus, took this badly and struck him blind. And Zeus, feeling a certain responsibility, gave Tiresias the gift of prophecy within his blindness. There's a good point there—when your eyes are closed to distracting phenomena, you're in your intuition, and you may come in touch with the morphology, the basic form of things.

MOYERS: Well, what's the point—that Tiresias, having been transformed into a man and then a woman by the serpents, had knowledge of both the female and the male experience and knew more than either the god or the goddess knew alone?

CAMPBELL: That's correct. Furthermore, he represented symbolically the fact of the unity of the two. And when Odysseus was sent to the underworld by Circe, his true initiation came when he met Tiresias and realized the unity of male and female.

MOYERS: I've often thought that if you could get in touch with your feminine side, or, if you're a woman, your masculine side, you would know what the gods know and maybe beyond what the gods know.

CAMPBELL: That's the information that one gets from being married. That's the way you get in touch with your feminine side.

MOYERS: But what happens to this self-discovery in love when you meet someone else, and you suddenly feel, "I know that person," or "I want to know that person"?

CAMPBELL: That's very mysterious. It's almost as though the

future life that you're going to have with that person has already told you, This is the one whom you will have that life with.

MOYERS: Is that something coming from within our inventory of memories that we don't understand and don't recognize? Reaching out and being touched by that person in a way—

CAMPBELL: It's almost as though you were reacting to the future. It's talking to you from what is to be. This has to do with the mystery of time and the transcendence of time. But I think we're touching a very deep mystery here.

MOYERS: Do you in your own life just leave it there as a mystery? Or do you think that one can successfully have a marriage and a relationship other than the marriage?

CAMPBELL: Technically, one could say, "Why, yes, of course."

MOYERS: But it seems that whatever one gives to the love affair is barred from the marriage relationship and diminishes the loyalty to the relationship.

CAMPBELL: I think one has to work out these things oneself. There could be a love seizure after you have a commitment to marriage, and it could be such a seizure that not responding to it might—what can I say?—dull the whole experience of the vitality of love.

MOYERS: I think that's the core of the question. If the eyes scout for the heart and bring back that which the heart passionately desires, is the heart only going to desire once?

CAMPBELL: Love does not immunize the person to other relationships, let me just say that. But whether one could have a full-fledged love affair, I mean a real full-fledged love affair, and at the same time be loyal to the marriage—well, I don't think that could happen now.

MOYERS: Because?

CAMPBELL: It would break off. But loyalty doesn't forbid you to have an affectionate, even a loving relationship to another person of the opposite sex. The way in which the knightly romances describe the tenderness of the relationships to other women, of one who is being loyal to his own love, is very graceful and sensitive.

MOYERS: The troubadours would sing to their ladies even if there was very little hope of furthering a relationship with them.

CAMPBELL: Yes.

MOYERS: Now, does mythology say anything about whether it is better to have loved and lost?

CAMPBELL: Mythology in a general way doesn't really deal with the problem of personal, individual love. One marries the one that one is allowed to marry, you know. If you belong to that clan, then you can marry that one but not that one, and so forth.

MOYERS: Then what does love have to do with morality?

CAMPBELL: Violates it.

MOYERS: Violates it?

CAMPBELL: Yes. Insofar as love expresses itself, it is not expressing itself in terms of the socially approved manners of life. That's why it is all so secret. Love has nothing to do with social order. It is a higher spiritual experience than that of socially organized marriage.

MOYERS: When we say God is love, does that have anything to do with romantic love? Does mythology ever link romantic love and God?

CAMPBELL: That's what it did do. Love was a divine visitation, and that's why it was superior to marriage. That was the trou-

badour idea. If God is love, well then, love is God. Meister
Eckhart said, "Love knows no pain." And that's exactly what
Tristan meant when he said, "I'm willing to accept the pains of
hell for my love."

MOYERS: But you've been saying that love involves suffering.

CAMPBELL: That is the other idea. Tristan was experiencing
love—Meister Eckhart was talking about it. The pain of love is
not the other kind of pain, it is the pain of life. Where your
pain is, there is your life, you might say.

MOYERS: There's that passage in Corinthians where Paul says,
"Love beareth all things, endureth all things."

CAMPBELL: That's the same thing.

MOYERS: And yet one of my favorite myths is the story from
Persia that Satan was condemned to hell because he loved God
so much.

CAMPBELL: Yes, that's a basic Muslim idea about Satan being
God's greatest lover. There are a number of ways of thinking
about Satan, but this is based on the question, Why was Satan
thrown into hell? The standard story is that, when God created
the angels, he told them to bow to none but himself. Then he
created man, whom he regarded as a higher form than the angels,
and he asked the angels to serve man. And Satan would not
bow to man.

Now, this is interpreted in the Christian tradition, as I recall
from my boyhood instruction, as being the egotism of Satan. He
would not bow to man. But in the Persian story, he could not
bow to man because of his love for God—he could bow only to
God. God had changed his signals, do you see? But Satan had
so committed himself to the first set of signals that he could not
violate those, and in his—I don't know if Satan has a heart or
not—but in his mind, he could not bow to anyone but God,
whom he loved. And then God says, "Get out of my sight."

Now, the worst of the pains of hell, insofar as hell has been described, is the absence of the Beloved, which is God. So how does Satan sustain the situation in hell? By the memory of the echo of God's voice, when God said, "Go to hell." That is a great sign of love.

MOYERS: Well, it's certainly true in life that the greatest hell one can know is to be separated from the one you love. That's why I've liked the Persian myth. Satan is God's lover—

CAMPBELL: —and he is separated from God, and that's the real pain of Satan.

MOYERS: There's another story from Persia about the first two parents.

CAMPBELL: That's a great one, yes. They were really one in the beginning and grew as a kind of plant. But then they separated and became two, and begat children. And they loved the children so much that they ate them up. God thought, "Well, this can't go on." So he reduced parental love by something like ninety-nine and nine-tenths percent, so parents wouldn't eat up their children.

MOYERS: What was that myth—

CAMPBELL: I've heard people say, "This is such a delicious little thing, I could eat it up."

MOYERS: The power of love?

CAMPBELL: The power of love.

MOYERS: So intense it had to be reduced.

CAMPBELL: Yes. I saw a picture once of a mouth wide open swallowing more, and a heart was in it. That's the kind of love that eats you up. That's the kind of love that mothers have to learn to reduce.

MOYERS: Lord, teach me when to let go.

CAMPBELL: Yes. There were in India little rituals to help

mothers let go, particularly of their sons. The guru, the chaplain of the family, would come and ask the mother to give him that which she most prized. And it might be some very valuable jewel or something. And then there were these exercises, where the mother would be learning to give up that which she most prized. And then, finally, she would have to give up her son.

MOYERS: So joy and pain are in love.

CAMPBELL: Yes. Love is the burning point of life, and since all life is sorrowful, so is love. The stronger the love, the more the pain.

MOYERS: But love bears all things.

CAMPBELL: Love itself is a pain, you might say—the pain of being truly alive.

VIII

MASKS
OF ETERNITY

The images of myth are reflections of the spiritual potentialities of every one of us. Through contemplating these, we evoke their powers in our own lives.

MOYERS: As you've moved among various world views, dipping in and out of cultures, civilizations, and religions, have you found something in common in every culture that creates the need for God?

CAMPBELL: Anyone who has had an experience of mystery knows that there is a dimension of the universe that is not that which is available to his senses. There is a pertinent saying in one of the Upanishads: "When before the beauty of a sunset or of a mountain you pause and exclaim, 'Ah,' you are participating in divinity." Such a moment of participation involves a realization of the wonder and sheer beauty of existence. People living in the world of nature experience such moments every day. They live in the recognition of something there that is much greater than the human dimension. Man's tendency, however, is to personify such experiences, to anthropomorphize natural forces.

Our way of thinking in the West sees God as the final source or cause of the energies and wonder of the universe. But in most

Oriental thinking, and in primal thinking, also, the gods are rather manifestations and purveyors of an energy that is finally impersonal. They are not its source. The god is the vehicle of its energy. And the force or quality of the energy that is involved or represented determines the character and function of the god. There are gods of violence, there are gods of compassion, there are gods that unite the two worlds of the unseen and the seen, and there are gods that are simply the protectors of kings or nations in their war campaigns. These are all personifications of the energies in play. But the ultimate source of the energies remains a mystery.

MOYERS: Doesn't this make fate a kind of anarchy, a continuing war among principalities?

CAMPBELL: Yes, as it is in life itself. Even in our minds—when it comes to making a decision, there will be a war. In acting in relationship to other people, for example, there may be four or five possibilities. The influence of the dominant divinity in my mind will be what determines my decision. If my guiding divinity is brutal, my decision will be brutal, as well.

MOYERS: What does that do to faith? You are a man of faith, of wonder, and—

CAMPBELL: No, I don't have to have faith, I have experience.

MOYERS: What kind of experience?

CAMPBELL: I have experience of the wonder of life. I have experience of love. I have experience of hatred, malice, and wanting to punch this guy in the jaw. From the point of view of symbolic imaging, those are different forces operating in my mind. One may think of them—wonder, love, hatred—as inspired by different divinities.

When I was a little boy being brought up as a Roman Catholic, I was told I had a guardian angel on my right side and a tempting devil on my left, and that the decisions I made in life would depend on whether the devil or the angel had the greater influence upon me. As a boy, I concretized these thoughts, and I think my teachers did, too. We thought there was really an angel there, and that the angel was a fact, and that the devil was also a fact. But instead of regarding them as facts, I can now think of them as metaphors for the impulses that move and guide me.

MOYERS: Where do these energies come from?

CAMPBELL: From your own life, from the energies of your own body. The different organs in the body, including your head, are in conflict with each other.

MOYERS: And your life comes from where?

CAMPBELL: From the ultimate energy that is the life of the universe. And then do you say, "Well, there must be somebody generating that energy"? Why do you have to say that? Why can't the ultimate mystery be impersonal?

MOYERS: Can men and women live with an impersonality?

CAMPBELL: Yes, they do all over the place. Just go east of Suez. You know there is this tendency in the West to anthropomorphize and accent the humanity of the gods, the personifications: Yahweh, for example, as either a god of wrath, of justice and punishment, or as a favoring god who is the support of your life, as we read, for example, in the Psalms. But in the East, the gods are much more elemental, much less human and much more like the powers of nature.

MOYERS: When someone says, "Imagine God," the child in our culture will say, "An old man in a long white robe with a beard."

CAMPBELL: In our culture, yes. It's our fashion to think of God in masculine form, but many traditions think of divine power principally in female form.

MOYERS: The idea is that you cannot imagine what you cannot personify. Do you think it's possible to center the mind on what Plato called "thoughts immortal and divine"?

CAMPBELL: Of course. That's what a meditation is. Meditation means constantly thinking on a certain theme. It can be on any level. I don't make a big split in my thinking between the physical and the spiritual. For example, meditation on money is a perfectly good meditation. And bringing up a family is a very important meditation. But there is an alone meditation, when you go into the cathedral, for example.

MOYERS: So prayer is actually a meditation.

CAMPBELL: Prayer is relating to and meditating on a mystery.

MOYERS: Calling a power from within.

CAMPBELL: There is a form of meditation you are taught in Roman Catholicism where you recite the rosary, the same prayer, over and over and over again. That pulls the mind in. In Sanskrit, this practice is called *japa*, "repetition of the holy name." It blocks other interests out and allows you to concentrate on one thing, and then, depending on your own powers of imagination, to experience the profundity of this mystery.

MOYERS: How does one have a profound experience?

CAMPBELL: By having a profound sense of the mystery.

MOYERS: But if God is the god we have only imagined, how can we stand in awe of our own creation?

CAMPBELL: How can we be terrified by a dream? You have to break past your image of God to get through to the connoted illumination. The psychologist Jung has a relevant saying: "Religion is a defense against the experience of God."

The mystery has been reduced to a set of concepts and ideas, and emphasizing these concepts and ideas can short-circuit the transcendent, connoted experience. An intense experience of mystery is what one has to regard as the ultimate religious experience.

MOYERS: There are many Christians who believe that, to find

out who Jesus is, you have to go past the Christian faith, past the Christian doctrine, past the Christian Church—

CAMPBELL: You have to go past the imagined image of Jesus. Such an image of one's god becomes a final obstruction, one's ultimate barrier. You hold on to your own ideology, your own little manner of thinking, and when a larger experience of God approaches, an experience greater than you are prepared to receive, you take flight from it by clinging to the image in your mind. This is known as preserving your faith.

You know the idea of the ascent of the spirit through the different centers or archetypal stages of experience. One begins with the elementary animal experiences of hunger and greed, and then of sexual zeal, and on to physical mastery of one kind or another. These are all empowering stages of experience. But then, when the center of the heart is touched, and a sense of compassion awakened with another person or creature, and you realize that you and that other are in some sense creatures of the one life in being, a whole new stage of life in the spirit opens out. This opening of the heart to the world is what is symbolized mythologically as the virgin birth. It signifies the birth of a spiritual life in what was formerly an elementary human animal living for the merely physical aims of health, progeny, power, and a little fun.

But now we come to something else. For to experience this sense of compassion, accord, or even identity with another, or with some ego-transcending principle that has become lodged in your mind as a good to be revered and served, is the beginning, once and for all, of the properly religious way of life and experience; and this may then lead to a life-consuming quest for a full experience of that one Being of beings of which all temporal forms are the reflections.

Now, this ultimate ground of all being can be experienced in two senses, one as with form and the other as without and beyond form. When you experience your god as with form, there is your envisioning mind, and there is the god. There is a subject, and there is an object. But the ultimate mystical goal is to be united with one's god. With that, duality is transcended and forms disappear. There is nobody there, no god, no you. Your mind, going past all concepts, has dissolved in identification with the ground of your own being, because that to which the metaphorical image of your god refers is the ultimate mystery of your own being, which is the mystery of the being of the world as well. And so this is it.

MOYERS: Of course the heart of the Christian faith is that God was in Christ, that these elemental forces you're talking about embodied themselves in a human being who reconciled mankind to God.

CAMPBELL: Yes, and the basic Gnostic and Buddhist idea is that that is true of you and me as well. Jesus was a historical person who realized in himself that he and what he called the Father were one, and he lived out of that knowledge of the Christhood of his nature.

I remember, I was once giving a lecture in which I spoke about living out of the sense of the Christ in you, and a priest in the audience (as I was later told) turned to the woman beside him and whispered, "That's blasphemy."

MOYERS: What did you mean by Christ in you?

CAMPBELL: What I meant was that you must live not in terms of your own ego system, your own desires, but in terms of what you might call the sense of mankind—the Christ—in you. There is a Hindu saying, "None but a god can worship a god." You have to identify yourself in some measure with whatever spiritual principle your god represents to you in order to worship him properly and live according to his word.

MOYERS: In discussing the god within, the Christ within, the illumination or the awakening that comes within, isn't there a danger of becoming narcissistic, of an obsession with self that leads to a distorted view of oneself and the world?

CAMPBELL: That can happen, of course. That's a kind of short-circuiting of the current. But the whole aim is to go past oneself, past one's concept of oneself, to that of which one is but an imperfect manifestation. When you come out of a meditation, for example, you are supposed to end by yielding all the benefits, whatever they may be, to the world, to all living beings, not holding them to yourself.

You see, there are two ways of thinking "I am God." If you think, "I here, in my physical presence and in my temporal character, am God," then you are mad and have short-circuited the experience. You are God, not in your ego, but in your deepest being, where you are at one with the nondual transcendent.

MOYERS: Somewhere you say that we can become savior figures to those in our circle—our children, our wives, our loved ones, our neighbors—but never the Savior. You say we can be mother and father but never the Mother and the Father. That's a recognition of limitation, isn't it?

CAMPBELL: Yes, it is.

MOYERS: What do you think about the Savior Jesus?

CAMPBELL: We just don't know very much about Jesus. All we know are four contradictory texts that purport to tell us what he said and did.

MOYERS: Written many years after he lived.

CAMPBELL: Yes, but in spite of this, I think we may know approximately what Jesus said. I think the sayings of Jesus are probably pretty close to the originals. The main teaching of Christ, for example, is, Love your enemies.

MOYERS: How do you love your enemy without condoning what the enemy does, without accepting his aggression?

CAMPBELL: I'll tell you how to do that: do not pluck the mote from your enemy's eyes, but pluck the beam from your own. No one is in a position to disqualify his enemy's way of life.

MOYERS: Do you think Jesus today would be a Christian?

CAMPBELL: Not the kind of Christian we know. Perhaps some of the monks and nuns who are really in touch with high spiritual mysteries would be of the sort that Jesus was.

MOYERS: So Jesus might not have belonged to the Church militant?

CAMPBELL: There's nothing militant about Jesus. I don't read anything like that in any of the gospels. Peter drew his sword and cut off the servant's ear, and Jesus said, "Put back thy sword, Peter." But Peter has had his sword out and at work ever since.

I've lived through the twentieth century, and I know what I was told as a boy about a people who weren't yet and never had been our enemies. In order to represent them as potential enemies, and to justify our attack upon them, a campaign of hatred, misrepresentation, and denigration was launched, of which the echoes ring to this day.

MOYERS: And yet we're told God is love. You once took the saying of Jesus, "Love your enemies and pray for those who persecute you, so that you may be sons of your Father who is in heaven; for he makes the sun to rise on the evil and the good, and sends rain on the just and the unjust"—you once took this to be the highest, the noblest, the boldest of the Christian teachings. Do you still feel that way?

CAMPBELL: I think of compassion as the fundamental religious experience and, unless that is there, you have nothing.

MOYERS: I'll tell you what the most gripping scripture in the Christian New Testament is for me: "I believe. Help thou my unbelief." I believe in this ultimate reality, that I can and do experience it. But I don't have answers to my questions. I believe in the question, Is there a God?

CAMPBELL: A couple of years ago, I had a very amusing experience. I was in the New York Athletic Club swimming pool, where I was introduced to a priest who was a professor at one of our Catholic universities. So after I had had my swim, I came and sat in a lounging chair in what we call the "horizontal athlete" position, and the priest, who was beside me, asked, "Now, Mr. Campbell, are you a priest?"

I answered, "No, Father."

He asked, "Are you a Catholic?"

I answered, "I was, Father."

Then he asked—and I think it interesting that he phrased the question in this way—"Do you believe in a personal god?"

"No, Father," I said.

And he replied, "Well, I suppose there is no way to prove by logic the existence of a personal god."

"If there were, Father," said I, "what then would be the value of faith?"

"Well, Mr. Campbell," said the priest quickly, "it's nice to have met you." And he was off. I felt I had executed a jujitsu throw.

But that was an illuminating conversation to me. The fact that a Catholic father had asked, "Do you believe in a personal god?" meant to me that he also recognized the possibility of an impersonal god, namely, a transcendent ground or energy in itself. The idea of Buddha consciousness is of an immanent, luminous consciousness that informs all things and all lives. We unthinkingly live by fragments of that consciousness, fragments of that energy. But the religious way of life is to live not in terms of the self-interested intentions of this particular body at this particular time but in terms of the insight of that larger consciousness.

There is an important passage in the recently discovered Gnostic Gospel According to St. Thomas: " 'When will the kingdom come?' Christ's disciples ask." In Mark 13, I think it is, we read that the end of the world is about to come. That is to say, a mythological image—that of the end of the world—is there taken as predicting an actual, physical, historical fact to be. But in Thomas' version, Jesus replies: "The kingdom of the Father will not come by expectation. The kingdom of the Father is spread upon the earth and men do not see it"—so I look at you now in that sense, and the radiance of the presence of the divine is known to me through you.

MOYERS: Through me?

CAMPBELL: You, sure. When Jesus says, "He who drinks from my mouth will become as I am and I shall be he," he's talking from the point of view of that being of beings, which we call the Christ, who is the being of all of us. Anyone who lives in relation to that is as Christ. Anyone who brings into his life the message of the Word is equivalent to Jesus, that's the sense of that.

MOYERS: So that's what you mean when you say, "I am radiating God to you."

CAMPBELL: You are, yes.

MOYERS: And you to me?

CAMPBELL: And I am speaking this seriously.

MOYERS: I take it seriously. I do sense that there is divinity in the other.

CAMPBELL: Not only that, but what you represent in this conversation and what you're trying to bring out is a realization of these spiritual principles. So you are the vehicle. You are radiant of the spirit.

MOYERS: Is this true for everyone?

CAMPBELL: It is true for everyone who has reached in his life the level of the heart.

MOYERS: You really believe there is a geography of the psyche?

CAMPBELL: This is metaphorical language, but you can say that some people are living on the level of the sex organs, and that's all they're living for. That's the meaning of life. This is

Freud's philosophy, is it not? Then you come to the Adlerian philosophy of the will to power, that all of life is centered on obstructions and overcoming the obstructions. Well, sure, that's a perfectly good life, and those are forms of divinity also. But they are on the animal level. Then there comes another kind of life, which involves giving oneself to others one way or another. This is the one that's symbolized in the opening of the heart.

MOYERS: What is the source of that life?

CAMPBELL: It must be a recognition of your life in the other, of the one life in the two of us. God is an image for that one life. We ask ourselves where this one life comes from, and people who think everything has to have been made by somebody will think, "Well, God made it." So God's the source of all this.

MOYERS: Well then, what is religion?

CAMPBELL: The word "religion" means *religio*, linking back. If we say it is the one life in both of us, then my separate life has been linked to the one life, *religio*, linked back. This has become symbolized in the images of religion, which represent that connecting link.

MOYERS: Jung, the famous psychologist, says that one of the most powerful religious symbols is the circle. He says that the circle is one of the great primordial images of mankind and that, in considering the symbol of the circle, we are analyzing the self. What do you make of that?

CAMPBELL: The whole world is a circle. All of these circular images reflect the psyche, so there may be some relationship between these architectural designs and the actual structuring of our spiritual functions.

When a magician wants to work magic, he puts a circle around himself, and it is within this bounded circle, this hermetically sealed-off area, that powers can be brought into play that are lost outside the circle.

MOYERS: I remember reading about an Indian chief who said, "When we pitch camp, we pitch a camp in a circle. When the eagle builds a nest, the nest is in a circle. When we look at the horizon, the horizon is in a circle." Circles were very important to some Indians, weren't they?

CAMPBELL: Yes. But they're also in much that we've inherited from Sumerian mythology. We've inherited the circle with the four cardinal points and three hundred and sixty degrees. The official Sumerian year was three hundred and sixty days with five holy days that don't count, which are outside of time and in which they had ceremonies relating their society to the heavens. Now we're losing this sense of the circle in relation to time, because we have digital time, where you just have time buzzing by. Out of the digital you get the sense of the flow of time. At Penn Station in New York, there's a clock with the hours, the minutes, the seconds, the tenths of seconds, and the hundredths of seconds. When you see the hundredths of a second buzzing by, you realize how time is running through you.

The circle, on the other hand, represents totality. Everything within the circle is one thing, which is encircled, enframed. That would be the spatial aspect. But the temporal aspect of the circle is that you leave, go somewhere, and always come back. God is the alpha and the omega, the source and the end. The circle suggests immediately a completed totality, whether in time or in space.

MOYERS: No beginning, no end.

CAMPBELL: Round and round and round. Take the year, for example. When November rolls around, we have Thanksgiving again. Then December comes, and we have Christmas again. Not only does the month roll around again, but also the moon cycle, the day cycle. We're reminded of this when we look at our watches and see the cycle of time. It's the same hour, but another day.

MOYERS: China used to call itself the Kingdom of the Center, and the Aztecs had a similar saying about their own culture. I suppose every culture using the circle as the cosmological order puts itself at the center. Why do you suppose the circle became so universally symbolic?

CAMPBELL: Because it's experienced all the time—in the day, in the year, in leaving home to go on your adventure—hunting or whatever it may be—and coming back home. Then there is a deeper experience, too, the mystery of the womb and the tomb. When people are buried, it's for rebirth. That's the origin of the burial idea. You put someone back into the womb of mother earth for rebirth. Very early images of the Goddess show her as a mother receiving the soul back again.

MOYERS: When I read your works—*The Masks of God*, or *The Way of the Animal Powers*, or *The Mythic Image*—I often come across images of the circle, whether it's in magical designs or in architecture, both ancient and modern; whether it's in the dome-shaped temples of India or the Paleolithic rock engravings of Rhodesia or the calendar stones of the Aztecs or the ancient Chinese bronze shields or the visions of the Old Testament prophet Ezekiel, who talks about the wheel in the sky. I keep coming across this image. And this ring, my wedding ring, is a circle, too. What does that symbolize?

CAMPBELL: That depends on how you understand marriage. The word "sym-bol" itself means two things put together. One person has one half, the other the other half, and then they come together. Recognition comes from putting the ring together, the completed circle. This is my marriage, this is the merging of my individual life in a larger life that is of two, where the two are one. The ring indicates that we are in one circle together.

MOYERS: When a new pope is installed, he takes the fisherman's ring—another circle.

CAMPBELL: That particular ring is symbolic of Jesus calling

the apostles, who were fishermen. He said, "I will make you fishers of men." This is an old motif that is earlier than Christianity. Orpheus is called "The Fisher," who fishes men, who are living as fish in the water, out up into the light. It's an old idea of the metamorphosis of the fish into man. The fish nature is the crudest animal nature of our character, and the religious line is intended to pull you up out of that.

MOYERS: A new king or new queen of England is given the coronation ring.

CAMPBELL: Yes, because there's another aspect of the ring— it is a bondage. As king, you are bound to a principle. You are living not simply your own way. You have been marked. In initiation rites, when people are sacrified and tattooed, they are bonded to another and to the society.

MOYERS: Jung speaks of the circle as a mandala.

CAMPBELL: "Mandala" is the Sanskrit word for "circle," but a circle that is coordinated or symbolically designed so that it has the meaning of a cosmic order. When composing mandalas, you are trying to coordinate your personal circle with the universal circle. In a very elaborate Buddhist mandala, for example, you have the deity in the center as the power source, the illumination source. The peripheral images would be manifestations or aspects of the deity's radiance.

In working out a mandala for yourself, you draw a circle and then think of the different impulse systems and value systems in your life. Then you compose them and try to find out where your center is. Making a mandala is a discipline for pulling all those scattered aspects of your life together, for finding a center and ordering yourself to it. You try to coordinate your circle with the universal circle.

MOYERS: To be at the center?

CAMPBELL: At the center, yes. For instance, among the Navaho Indians, healing ceremonies are conducted through sand paintings, which are mostly mandalas on the ground. The person who is to be treated moves into the mandala as a way of moving into a mythological context that he will be identifying with—he identifies himself with the symbolized power. This idea of sand painting with mandalas, and their use for meditation purposes, appears also in Tibet. Tibetan monks practice sand painting, drawing cosmic images to represent the forces of the spiritual powers that operate in our lives.

MOYERS: There is some effort, apparently, to try to center one's life with the center of the universe—

CAMPBELL: —by way of mythological imagery, yes. The image helps you to identify with the symbolized force. You can't very well expect a person to identify with an undifferentiated something or other. But when you give it qualities that point toward certain realizations, the person can follow.

MOYERS: There is one theory that the Holy Grail represented the center of perfect harmony, the search for perfection, for totality and unity.

CAMPBELL: There are a number of sources for the Holy Grail. One is that there is a cauldron of plenty in the mansion of the god of the sea, down in the depths of the unconscious. It is out of the depths of the unconscious that the energies of life come to us. This cauldron is the inexhaustible source, the center, the bubbling spring from which all life proceeds.

MOYERS: Do you think that is the unconscious?

CAMPBELL: Not only the unconscious but also the vale of the world. Things are coming to life around you all the time. There is a life pouring into the world, and it pours from an inexhaustible source.

MOYERS: Now, what do you make of that—that in very different cultures, separated by time and space, the same imagery emerges?

CAMPBELL: This speaks for certain powers in the psyche that

are common to all mankind. Otherwise you couldn't have such detailed correspondences.

MOYERS: So if you find that many different cultures tell the story of creation, or the story of a virgin birth, or the story of a savior who comes and dies and is resurrected, they are saying something about what is inside us, and our need to understand.

CAMPBELL: That's right. The images of myth are reflections of the spiritual potentialities of every one of us. Through contemplating these we evoke their powers in our own lives.

MOYERS: So when a scripture talks about man being made in God's image, it's talking about certain qualities that every human being possesses, no matter what that person's religion or culture or geography or heritage?

CAMPBELL: God would be the ultimate elementary idea of man.

MOYERS: The primal need.

CAMPBELL: And we are all made in the image of God. That is the ultimate archetype of man.

MOYERS: Eliot speaks about the still point of the turning world, where motion and stasis are together, the hub where the movement of time and the stillness of eternity are together.

CAMPBELL: That's the inexhaustible center that is represented by the Grail. When life comes into being, it is neither afraid nor desiring, it is just becoming. Then it gets into being, and it begins to be afraid and desiring. When you can get rid of fear and desire and just get back to where you're becoming, you've hit the spot. Goethe says godhead is effective in the living and not in the dead, in the becoming and the changing, not in what has already become and set fast. So reason is concerned, he states, with striving toward the divine through the becoming and the changing, while intelligence makes use of the set fast, what is knowable, known, and so to be used for the shaping of a life.

But the goal of your quest for knowledge of yourself is to be found at that burning point in yourself, that becoming thing in yourself, which is innocent of the goods and evils of the world as already become, and therefore desireless and fearless. That is the con- dition of a warrior going into battle with perfect courage. That is life in movement. That is the essence of the mysticism of war as well as of a plant growing. I think of grass—you know, every two weeks a chap comes out with a lawnmower and cuts it down. Suppose the grass were to say, "Well, for Pete's sake, what's the use if you keep getting cut down this way?" Instead, it keeps on growing. That's the sense of the energy of the center. That's the meaning of the image of the Grail, of the inexhaustible fountain, of the source. The source doesn't care what happens once it gives into being. It's the giving and coming into being that counts, and that's the becoming life point in you. That's what all these myths are concerned to tell you.

In the study of comparative mythology, we compare the images in one system with the images in another, and both become illuminated because one will accent and give clear expression to one aspect of the meaning, and another to another. They clarify each other.

When I started teaching comparative mythology, I was afraid I might destroy my students' religious beliefs, but what I found was just the opposite. Religious traditions, which didn't mean very much to them, but which were the ones their parents had given them, suddenly became illuminated in a new way when we compared them with other traditions, where similar images had been given a more inward or spiritual interpretation.

I had Christian students, Jewish students, Buddhist students, a couple of Zoroastrian students—they all had this experience. There's no danger in interpreting the symbols of a religious system and calling them metaphors instead of facts. What that does is to turn them into messages for your own inward experience and life. The system suddenly becomes a personal experience.

MOYERS: I feel stronger in my own faith knowing that others

experienced the same yearnings and were seeking for similar images to try to express an experience beyond the costume of ordinary human language.

CAMPBELL: This is why clowns and clown religions are helpful. Germanic and Celtic myths are full of clown figures, really grotesque deities. This makes the point, I am not the ultimate image, I am transparent to something. Look through me, through my funny form.

MOYERS: There's a wonderful story in some African tradition of the god who's walking down the road wearing a hat that is colored red on one side and blue on the other side. When the farmers in the field go into the village in the evening, they say, "Did you see that god with the blue hat?" And the others say, "No, no, he had a red hat on." And they get into a fight.

CAMPBELL: Yes, that's the Nigerian trickster god, Edshu. He makes it even worse by first walking in one direction and then turning around and turning his hat around, too, so that again it will be red or blue. Then when these two chaps get into a fight and are brought before the king for judgment, this trickster god appears, and he says, "It's my fault, I did it, and I meant to do it. Spreading strife is my greatest joy."

MOYERS: There's a truth in that.

CAMPBELL: There sure is. Heraclitus said strife is the creator of all great things. Something like that may be implicit in this symbolic trickster idea. In our tradition, the serpent in the Garden did the job. Just when everything was fixed and fine, he threw an apple into the picture.

No matter what the system of thought you may have, it can't possibly include boundless life. When you think everything is just that way, the trickster arrives, and it all blows, and you get change and becoming again.

MOYERS: I notice when you tell these stories, Joe, you tell

them with humor. You always seem to enjoy them, even when they're about odd and cruel things.

CAMPBELL: A key difference between mythology and our Judeo-Christian religion is that the imagery of mythology is rendered with humor. You realize that the image is symbolic of something. You're at a distance from it. But in our religion, everything is prosaic, and very, very serious. You can't fool around with Yahweh.

MOYERS: How do you explain what the psychologist Maslow called "peak experiences" and what James Joyce called "epiphanies"?

CAMPBELL: Well, they are not quite the same. The peak experience refers to actual moments of your life when you experience your relationship to the harmony of being. My own peak experiences, the ones that I knew were peak experiences after I had them, all came in athletics.

MOYERS: Which was the Everest of your experience?

CAMPBELL: When I was running at Columbia, I ran a couple of races that were just beautiful. During the second race, I knew I was going to win even though there was no reason for me to know this, because I was touched off as anchor in the relay with the leading runner thirty yards ahead of me. But I just knew, and it was my peak experience. Nobody could beat me that day. That's being in full form and really knowing it. I don't think I have ever done anything in my life as competently as I ran those two races—it was the experience of really being at my full and doing a perfect job.

MOYERS: Not all peak experiences are physical.

CAMPBELL: No, there are other kinds of peak experiences. But those were the ones that come to my mind when I think about peak experiences.

MOYERS: What about James Joyce's epiphanies?

CAMPBELL: Now, that's something else. Joyce's formula for the aesthetic experience is that it does not move you to want to possess the object. A work of art that moves you to possess the object depicted, he calls pornography. Nor does the aesthetic experience move you to criticize and reject the object—such art he calls didactic, or social criticism in art. The aesthetic experience is a simple beholding of the object. Joyce says that you put a frame around it and see it first as one thing, and that, in seeing it as one thing, you then become aware of the relationship of part to part, each part to the whole, and the whole to each of its parts. This is the essential, aesthetic factor—rhythm, the harmonious rhythm of relationships. And when a fortunate rhythm has been struck by the artist, you experience a radiance. You are held in aesthetic arrest. That is the epiphany. And that is what might in religious terms be thought of as the all-informing Christ principle coming through.

MOYERS: The face of the saint beholding God?

CAMPBELL: It doesn't matter who it is. You could take someone whom you might think of as a monster. The aesthetic experience transcends ethics and didactics.

MOYERS: That's where I would disagree with you. It seems to me that in order to experience the epiphany, the object you behold but do not want to possess must be beautiful in some way. And a moment ago, when you talked about your peak experience, running, you said it was beautiful. "Beautiful" is an aesthetic word. Beauty is the harmony.

CAMPBELL: Yes.

MOYERS: And yet you said it's also in Joyce's epiphanies, and that concerns art and the aesthetic.

CAMPBELL: Yes.

MOYERS: It seems to me they are the same if they're both beautiful. How can you behold a monster and have an epiphany?

CAMPBELL: There's another emotion associated with art, which is not of the beautiful but of the sublime. What we call monsters can be experienced as sublime. They represent powers too vast for the normal forms of life to contain them. An immense expanse of space is sublime. The Buddhists know how to achieve this effect in situating their temples, which are often up on high hills. For example, some of the temple gardens in Japan are designed so that you will first be experiencing close-in, intimate arrangements. Meanwhile, you're climbing, until suddenly you break past a screen and an expanse of horizon opens out, and somehow, with this diminishment of your own ego, your consciousness expands to an experience of the sublime.

Another mode of the sublime is of prodigious energy, force, and power. I've known a number of people who were in Central Europe during the Anglo-American saturation bombings of their cities—and several have described this inhuman experience as not only terrible but in a measure sublime.

MOYERS: I once interviewed a veteran of the Second World War. I talked to him about his experience at the Battle of the Bulge, in that bitter winter when the surprise German assault was about to succeed. I said, "As you look back on it, what was it?" And he said, "It was sublime."

CAMPBELL: And so the monster comes through as a kind of god.

MOYERS: And by the monster you mean—

CAMPBELL: By a monster I mean some horrendous presence or apparition that explodes all of your standards for harmony, order, and ethical conduct. For example, Vishnu at the end of the world appears as a monster. There he is, destroying the universe, first with fire and then with a torrential flood that drowns out the fire and everything else. Nothing is left but ash. The whole universe with all its life and lives has been utterly wiped out. That's God in the role of destroyer. Such experiences go past ethical or aesthetic judgments. Ethics is wiped out. Whereas in our religions, with their accent on the human, there is also an accent on the ethical—God is qualified as good. No, no! God is horrific. Any god who can invent hell is no candidate for the Salvation Army. The end of the world, think of it! But there is a Muslim saying about the Angel of Death: "When the Angel of Death approaches, he is terrible. When he reaches you, it is bliss."

In Buddhist systems, more especially those of Tibet, the meditation Buddhas appear in two aspects, one peaceful and the other wrathful. If you are clinging fiercely to your ego and its little temporal world of sorrows and joys, hanging on for dear life, it will be the wrathful aspect of the deity that appears. It will seem terrifying. But the moment your ego yields and gives up, that same meditation Buddha is experienced as a bestower of bliss.

MOYERS: Jesus did talk of bringing a sword, and I don't believe he meant to use it against your fellow. He meant it in terms of opening the ego—I come to cut you free from the binding ego of your own self.

CAMPBELL: This is what is known in Sanskrit as *viveka*, "discrimination." There is a very important Buddha figure who is shown holding a flaming sword high over his head—and so what is that sword for? It is the sword of discrimination, separating the merely temporal from the eternal. It is the sword distinguishing that which is enduring from that which is merely passing. The tick-tick-tick of time shuts out eternity. We live in this field of time. But what is reflected in this field is an eternal principle made manifest.

MOYERS: The experience of the eternal.

CAMPBELL: The experience of what you are.

MOYERS: Yes, but whatever eternity is, it is here right now.

CAMPBELL: And nowhere else. Or everywhere else. If you don't experience it here and now, you're not going to get it in heaven. Heaven is not eternal, it's just everlasting.

MOYERS: I don't follow that.

CAMPBELL: Heaven and hell are described as forever. Heaven is of unending time. It is not eternal. Eternal is beyond time. The concept of time shuts out eternity. It is over the ground of that deep experience of eternity that all of these temporal pains and troubles come and go. There is a Buddhist ideal of participating willingly and joyfully in the passing sorrows of the world. Wherever there is time, there is sorrow. But this experience of sorrow moves over a sense of enduring being, which is our own true life.

MOYERS: There's some image of Shiva, the god Shiva, surrounded by circles of flame, rings of fire.

CAMPBELL: That's the radiance of the god's dance. Shiva's dance is the universe. In his hair is a skull and a new moon, death and rebirth at the same moment, the moment of becoming. In one hand he has a little drum that goes tick-tick-tick. That is the drum of time, the tick of time which shuts out the knowledge of eternity. We are enclosed in time. But in Shiva's opposite hand there is a flame which burns away the veil of time and opens our minds to eternity.

Shiva is a very ancient deity, perhaps the most ancient worshiped in the world today. There are images from 2000 or 2500 B.C., little stamp seals showing figures that clearly suggest Shiva.

In some of his manifestations he is a really horrendous god, representing the terrific aspects of the nature of being. He is the archetypal yogi, canceling the illusion of life, but he is also the creator of life, its generator, as well as illuminator.

MOYERS: Myths deal with metaphysics. But religion also deals with ethics, good and evil, and how I am to relate to you, and how I should behave toward you and toward my wife and toward my fellow man under God. What is the place and role of ethics in mythology?

CAMPBELL: We spoke of the metaphysical experience in which you realize that you and the other are one. Ethics is a way of teaching you how to live as though you were one with the other. You don't have to have the experience because the doctrine of the religion gives you molds of actions that imply a compassionate relationship with the other. It offers an incentive for doing this by teaching you that simply acting in your own self-interest is sin. That is identification with your body.

MOYERS: Love they neighbor as thyself because thy neighbor is thyself.

CAMPBELL: That is what you have learned when you have done so.

MOYERS: Why do you think so many people have a deep yearning to live forever?

CAMPBELL: That's something I don't understand.

MOYERS: Does it come out of the fear of hell and the desirable alternative?

CAMPBELL: That's good standard Christian doctrine—that at the end of the world there will be a general judgment and those who have acted virtuously will be sent to heaven, and those who have acted in an evil way, to hell.
This is a theme that goes back to Egypt. Osiris is the god who died and was resurrected and in his eternal aspect will sit as judge of the dead. Mummification was to prepare the person to face the god. But an interesting thing in Egypt is that the person going to the god is to recognize his identity with the god. In the Christian tradition, that's not allowed. So if you're saying that the alternative is hell or heaven, well, give me heaven forever. But when you realize that heaven is a beholding of the beatific image of God—that would be a timeless moment. Time explodes,

so again, eternity is not something everlasting. You can have it right here, now, in your experience of your earthly relationships.

I've lost a lot of friends, as well as my parents. A realization has come to me very, very keenly, however, that I haven't lost them. That moment when I was with them has an everlasting quality about it that is now still with me. What it gave me then is still with me, and there's a kind of intimation of immortality in that.

There is a story of the Buddha, who encountered a woman who had just lost her son, and she was in great grief. The Buddha said, "I suggest that you just ask around to meet somebody who has not lost a treasured child or husband or relative or friend." Understanding the relationship of mortality to something in you that is transcendent of mortality is a difficult task.

MOYERS: Myths are full of the desire for immortality, are they not?

CAMPBELL: Yes. But when immortality is misunderstood as being an everlasting body, it turns into a clown act, really. On the other hand, when immortality is understood to be identification with that which is of eternity in your own life now, it's something else again.

MOYERS: You've said that the whole question of life revolves around being versus becoming.

CAMPBELL: Yes. Becoming is always fractional. And being is total.

MOYERS: What do you mean?

CAMPBELL: Well, let's say you are going to become fully human. In the first few years you are a child, and that is only a fraction of the human being. In a few more years you are in adolescence, and that is certainly a fraction of the human being. In maturity you are still fractional—you are not a child, but you are not old yet. There is an image in the Upanishads of the original, concentrated energy which was the big bang of creation that set forth the world, consigning all things to the fragmentation of time. But to see through the fragments of time to the full power of original being—that is a function of art.

MOYERS: Beauty is an expression of that rapture of being alive.

CAMPBELL: Every moment should be such an experience.

MOYERS: And what we are going to become tomorrow is not important as compared to this experience.

CAMPBELL: This is the great moment, Bill. What we are trying to do in a certain way is to get the being of our subject rendered through the partial way we have of expressing it.

MOYERS: But if we can't describe God, if our language is not adequate, how is it that we build these buildings that are sublime? How do we create these works of art that reflect what artists think of God? How do we do this?

CAMPBELL: Well, that's what art reflects—what artists think of God, what people experience of God. But the ultimate, unqualified mystery is beyond human experience.

MOYERS: So whatever it is we experience we have to express in language that is just not up to the occasion.

CAMPBELL: That's it. That's what poetry is for. Poetry is a language that has to be penetrated. Poetry involves a precise choice of words that will have implications and suggestions that go past the words themselves. Then you experience the radiance, the epiphany. The epiphany is the showing through of the essence.

MOYERS: So the experience of God is beyond description, but we feel compelled to try to describe it?

CAMPBELL: That's right. Schopenhauer, in his splendid essay called "On an Apparent Intention in the Fate of the Individual," points out that when you reach an advanced age and look back over your lifetime, it can seem to have had a consistent order and plan, as though composed by some novelist. Events that when they occurred had seemed accidental and of little moment turn out to have been indispensable factors in the composition of a consistent plot. So who composed that plot? Schopenhauer suggests that just as your dreams are composed by an aspect of yourself of which your consciousness is unaware, so, too, your whole life is composed by the will within you. And just as people whom you will have met apparently by mere chance became leading agents in the structuring of your life, so, too, will you have served unknowingly as an agent, giving meaning to the lives of others. The whole thing gears together like one big symphony, with everything unconsciously structuring everything else. And Schopenhauer concludes that it is as though our lives were the features of the one great dream of a single dreamer in which all the dream characters dream, too; so that everything links to everything else, moved by the one will to life which is the universal will in nature.

It's a magnificent idea—an idea that appears in India in the mythic image of the Net of Indra, which is a net of gems, where at every crossing of one thread over another there is a gem reflecting all the other reflective gems. Everything arises in mutual relation to everything else, so you can't blame anybody for anything. It is even as though there were a single intention behind it all, which always makes some kind of sense, though none of us knows what the sense might be, or has lived the life that he quite intended.

MOYERS: And yet we all have lived a life that had a purpose. Do you believe that?

CAMPBELL: I don't believe life has a purpose. Life is a lot of protoplasm with an urge to reproduce and continue in being.

MOYERS: Not true—not true.

CAMPBELL: Wait a minute. Just sheer life cannot be said to have a purpose, because look at all the different purposes it has all over the place. But each incarnation, you might say, has a potentiality, and the mission of life is to live that potentiality. How do you do it? My answer is, "Follow your bliss." There's something inside you that knows when you're in the center, that knows when you're on the beam or off the beam. And if you get off the beam to earn money, you've lost your life. And if you stay in the center and don't get any money, you still have your bliss.

MOYERS: I like the idea that it is not the destination that counts, it's the journey.

CAMPBELL: Yes. As Karlfried Graf Dürckheim says, "When you're on a journey, and the end keeps getting further and further away, then you realize that the real end is the journey."

The Navaho have that wonderful image of what they call the pollen path. Pollen is the life source. The pollen path is the path to the center. The Navaho say, "Oh, beauty before me, beauty behind me, beauty to the right of me, beauty to the left of me, beauty above me, beauty below me, I'm on the pollen path."

MOYERS: Eden was not. Eden will be.

CAMPBELL: Eden *is*. "The kingdom of the Father is spread upon the earth, and men do not see it."

MOYERS: Eden *is*—in this world of pain and suffering and death and violence?

CAMPBELL: That is the way it feels, but this is it, this is Eden. When you see the kingdom spread upon the earth, the old way of living in the world is annihilated. That is the end of the world. The end of the world is not an event to come, it is an event of psychological transformation, of visionary transformation. You see not the world of solid things but a world of radiance.

MOYERS: I interpreted that powerful and mysterious statement, "The word was made flesh," as this eternal principle finding itself in the human journey, in our experience.

CAMPBELL: And you can find the word in yourself, too.

MOYERS: Where do you find it if you don't find it in yourself?

CAMPBELL: It's been said that poetry consists of letting the word be heard beyond words. And Goethe says, "All things are metaphors." Everything that's transitory is but a metaphorical reference. That's what we all are.

MOYERS: But how does one worship a metaphor, love a metaphor, die for a metaphor?

CAMPBELL: That's what people are doing all over the place —dying for metaphors. But when you really realize the sound, "AUM," the sound of the mystery of the word everywhere, then you don't have to go out and die for anything because it's right there all around. Just sit still and see it and experience it and know it. That's a peak experience.

MOYERS: Explain AUM.

CAMPBELL: "AUM" is a word that represents to our ears that sound of the energy of the universe of which all things are manifestations. You start in the back of the mouth "ahh," and then "oo," you fill the mouth, and "mm" closes the mouth. When you pronounce this properly, all vowel sounds are included in the pronunciation. AUM. Consonants are here regarded simply as interruptions of the essential vowel sound. All words are thus fragments of AUM, just as all images are fragments of the Form of forms. AUM is a symbolic sound that puts you in touch with that resounding being that is the universe. If you heard some of the recordings of Tibetan monks chanting AUM, you would know what the word means, all right. That's the AUM of being in the world. To be in touch with that and to get the sense of that is the peak experience of all.

A-U-M. The birth, the coming into being, and the dissolution that cycles back. AUM is called the "four-element syllable." A-U-M—and what is the fourth element? The silence out of which AUM arises, and back into which it goes, and which underlies it. My life is the A-U-M, but there is a silence underlying it, too. That is what we would call the immortal. This is the mortal and that's the immortal, and there wouldn't be the mortal if there weren't the immortal. One must discriminate between the mortal aspect and the immortal aspect of one's own existence. In the experience of my mother and father who are gone, of whom I was born, I have come to understand that there is more than what was our temporal relationship. Of course there were certain moments in that relationship when an emphatic demonstration of what the relationship was would be brought to my realization. I clearly remember some of those. They stand out as moments of epiphany, of revelation, of the radiance.

MOYERS: The meaning is essentially wordless.

CAMPBELL: Yes. Words are always qualifications and limitations.

MOYERS: And yet, Joe, all we puny human beings are left with is this miserable language, beautiful though it is, that falls short of trying to describe—

CAMPBELL: That's right, and that's why it is a peak experience to break past all that, every now and then, and to realize, "Oh . . . ah. . . ."

INDEX

Bill Moyers would like to thank the following people
for making the television series possible:

EXECUTIVE PRODUCERS: Joan Konner, Alvin H. Perlmutter
SERIES PRODUCER: Catherine Targe
ASSOCIATE PRODUCER: Vera Aronow
SERIES CONSULTANT: Betty Sue Flowers
RESEARCHERS: Lynn Novick, Elizabeth Fischer, Ilisa Barbash
PRODUCTION ASSISTANTS: John Farinet, John Moyers
PRODUCTION EXECUTIVE: Douglas P. Sinsel
VIDEOTAPE EDITORS: Leonard Feinstein, Girish Bhargava

Taped at the Library of Lucasfilm Ltd., Skywalker Ranch, San
Rafael, California, and The American Museum of Natural
History, New York City.

Produced with the cooperation of Alfred van der Marck Editions.

A production of
Apostrophe S Productions, Inc., in association with
Alvin H. Perlmutter, Inc., and
Public Affairs Television, Inc.

The broadcasts of *Moyers: Joseph Campbell and the Power of Myth*
were made possible by grants from the Corporation for Public
Broadcasting, public television stations, and the John D. and
Catherine T. MacArthur Foundation.

Joseph Campbell (1904–87) began his career in 1934 as an instructor at Sarah Lawrence College, where he taught for almost forty years, and where the Joseph Campbell Chair in Comparative Mythology was established in his honor. He is the author of numerous books, including the bestselling *The Hero with a Thousand Faces*.

Bill Moyers is an acclaimed journalist, widely respected for his work both at CBS News and at PBS. One of his primary efforts has been to bring to television outstanding thinkers of our time, most recently in the immensely popular and highly celebrated PBS series and bestselling book *A World of Ideas*. His conversations with Joseph Campbell were one of the highlights of television programming in the 1980s.

Betty Sue Flowers teaches poetry and myth at the University of Texas at Austin. She is the author and coauthor of several books, including *Browning and the Modern Tradition*, *Four Shields of Power*, and *Daughters and Fathers*.